The Shelleys and the Brownings
Textual Re-Imaginings and
the Question of Influence

ENGLISH ASSOCIATION STUDIES, 9

English Association Monographs: English at the Interface

Established in 1906, The English Association is the oldest established association in the UK for all those interested in English at all levels, from primary to higher education. Its aim is to further knowledge, understanding and enjoyment of the English language and its literatures and to foster good practice in its teaching and learning at all levels. In 2006, the English Association launched a new series – *English Association Monographs*, which is now published by Liverpool University Press.

English Association Monographs invites submissions that explore or represent English Studies at the interface with other languages, cultures, professions and disciplines from the medieval period to the present day. It also welcomes submissions that reflect on or contribute to interdisciplinary conversations, or which are the product of thinking across disciplines or across sectors, or which explore the intersections between English Studies, Digital Humanities, and the new technologies of any period. The General Editors and the Editorial Board will work with authors to produce books that are written clearly and eloquently, and represent the best and most exciting new work in English Language and Literature.

RIEKO SUZUKI

The Shelleys and the Brownings

Textual Re-Imaginings and the Question of Influence

LIVERPOOL UNIVERSITY PRESS
THE ENGLISH ASSOCIATION

First published 2022 by
Liverpool University Press
4 Cambridge Street
Liverpool
L69 7ZU

British Library Cataloguing-in-Publication data
A British Library CIP record is available

ISBN 978-1-800-85647-9

Typeset by Carnegie Book Production, Lancaster
Printed and bound by CPI Group (UK) Ltd, Croydon CR0 4YY

Contents

In Memoriam
June and Doug Strickland

Acknowledgements

This book would not have been possible without the research leave and research grant provided by the School of Law, Waseda University, for which I am truly grateful. Equally, my research in New York would not have materialised had it not been for the Center for European and Mediterranean Studies at New York University who kindly sponsored me as a Visiting Scholar there for a year and a half. My thanks go to Larry Wolff, Mikhala Stein Kotlyar and Anastasia Skoybedo. Not only was my time in New York fruitful and enjoyable thanks to them, I have come to feel quite at home at NYU. John Maynard of the English Department at NYU has made my research on the Shelleys and the Brownings extra special for sharing with me his expertise and his office, for which I am thankful.

I have benefitted from many libraries in the US, UK and Japan. My thanks go to Elmer Holmes Bobst Library and Fales Library & Special Collections, NYU; Armstrong Browning Library, Balyor University; New York Public Library, The Carl H. Pforzheimer Collection of Shelley and His Circle and Henry W. and Albert A. Berg Collection of English and American Literature; Firestone Library, Rare Books and Special Collections, Princeton University; Clapp Library, Special Collections, Wellesley College; The Joseph Regenstein Library and Special Collections, The University of Chicago; The British Library, London; Waseda University and Keio University Libraries, Tokyo, Japan.

My fellowship at Armstrong Browning Library over two different periods has resulted in the original essays, 'Shelley's *The Cenci* and Browning's *The Ring and the Book*', and 'Shelley's "The Triumph of Life" and Browning's *Fifine at the Fair*', published in the *Humanities* and *Keats-Shelley Review*, the developed versions of which have become Chapters 4 and 5 respectively. Various members of staff at

ABL have been extremely helpful during my fellowship there. My thanks go to Jennifer Borderud, Rita Patteson, Cyndie Burgess, Melvin Schutz and Christi Klempnauer.

I first presented what became Chapter 1 at the Victorian Media Conference held in Richmond, Virginia in the US, in 2012; Chapter 2 at BARS/NASSR Conference in Bologna, Italy, in 2008; Chapter 6 Section 2 at The Wordsworth Summer Conference held in Rydal, Enlgand, in 2013.

Many conversations with various people over the course of time have made possible my scholarly work on the Shelleys and the Brownings. My thanks go to Jack Donovan, Mike Rossington, John Woolford, Danny Karlin, Joe Phelan, Jim Chandler, Nora Crook, Nick Roe, Daivd Latane, J. B. Bullen, Michael O'Neill, Marjorie Stone, Alice Chapman, Rich Calichman, Sharon Ruston, Jerome de Groot, Akiko Murata, Naoko Yuge, Kiyoshi Nishiyama, Kazuo Oikawa, Yorimichi Kasahara, Saeko Yoshikawa, Itsuki Kitani and Lawrence Masakazu Yoneta. Needless to say, friends and colleagues' moral support was indispensable in persevering with my research and maintaining my sanity while writing the book. My thanks go to colleagues at the School of Law, and especially English Professors, Gaye Rowley and Tetsu Motoyama, and Law Professors, Yoshiki Kurumisawa, Yasunobu Wakabayashi and Satomi Tayama. I have been especially gifted with many friends and mentors who have given me much support and encouragement over the years: Hannah Osbourne, Itsuko Kamoto, Diane Cook, Elise Langan, Harry Harootunian, Peter Johnson, Hal Momma, Toshi Takamiya, Noriyuki Harada, Sterre van der Hell, Jerome Young, Derek Yakiwchuk, Tricia Okada, Geraldo Faria, Flora Zabeli, Holly Strickland, Samantha Fujisaka, Kai Fujisaka, Shannon Kirk, Richard Mohrfeld, Jan Mohrfeld, Kate Johnson, Chris Mohrfeld, John Cunningham, Carolyn Cunningham, Laura Barrett, Kevin Barrett and Cathy Cunningham. During the last stages of the writing, my father, Akira Suzuki, was especially helpful and encouraging.

My thanks go to Hugh Osbourne who meticulously went through my monograph and edited it with much insight and precision. This was possible due to the financial aid provided by Waseda Research Portal and International Office.

I am thankful to the committee members of the board for Liverpool University Press. The Series Editors, Claire Jowett and Jennifer Richards, were warmly encouraging in the initial stages of the book, for which I am truly grateful. The peer reviewers for the book have provided me with many areas for improvement. Christabel Scaife of Liverpool University Press and Sarah Warren and the Production Editors have been extremely helpful.

I would like to thank all the unnamed individuals whose input has made a difference and also made possible my writing of the book.

Finally, I dedicate the book to my host parents in the US who never failed to encourage and support me over the past decades since I first went to live with them as a sophomore in high school.

Notes on the Texts

All quotations from the texts and letters of the Shelleys and the Brownings are from the following editions unless specified otherwise. References to them will appear in abbreviated forms.

Browning, Elizabeth Barrett. *The Works of Elizabeth Barrett Browning*. General editor, Sandra Donaldson. 5 volumes. London: Pickering & Chatto, 2010. [*Works of EBB*]

Browning, Robert. *The Poems of Browning*. Edited by John Woolford, Daniel Karlin and J. P. Phelan. Harlow: Longman, 1991–. [*Poems of Browning*]
—. *The Brownings' Correspondence*. Edited by Philip Kelley, Ronald Hudson and Scott Lewis. Winfield, KS: Wedgestone Press, 1984–. [*Brownings' Correspondence*]

Shelley, Mary. *The Letters of Mary Wollstonecraft Shelley*. Edited by Betty T. Bennett. Baltimore: Johns Hopkins University Press, 1980. [*Letters of MWS*]
—. *The Novels and Selected Works of Mary Shelley*. General editor, Nora Crook with Pamela Clemit. 8 volumes. London: William Picker, 1996. [*N&SW of Mary Shelley*]

Shelley, Percy Bysshe. *The Letters of Percy Bysshe Shelley*. Edited by Frederick L. Jones. Oxford: Oxford University Press, 1964. [*Letters of PBS*]
—. *The Poems of Shelley*. Volume 1. Edited by Geoffrey Matthews and Kelvin Everest. London: Longman, 1989. [*Poems of Shelley* 1]

—. *The Poems of Shelley*. Volume 2. Edited by Kelvin Everest and Geoffrey Matthews with contributing editors, Jack Donovan, Ralph Pite and Michael Rossington. Harlow: Pearson, 2000. [*Poems of Shelley 2*]

—. *The Poems of Shelley*. Volume 3. Edited by Jack Donovan, Cian Duffy, Kelvin Everest and Michael Rossington. Harlow: Pearson, 2011. [*Poems of Shelley 3*]

—. *The Poems of Shelley*. Volume 4. Edited by Michael Rossington, Jack Donovan and Kelvin Everest. Abingdon: Routledge, 2014. [*Poems of Shelley 4*]

Introduction

This book brings together two eminent literary couples: the Shelleys and the Brownings. Each of the couples' love affairs has achieved an almost mythical status in English literary history, and each has spawned a wealth of biographical material telling and re-telling their respective stories. Moreover, the perceived influence of the earlier couple on the later one lends a pleasing symmetry to the biography of each when considered in tandem. For instance, the Shelleys eloped to continental Europe, whereas the Brownings secretly got married in England and fled together to Florence. In addition, the two couples self-consciously fashioned their romances by seeking to model them on a precedent. Mary's confession of her love and proposal to Shelley at St Pancras Churchyard, where her mother was buried, was a gesture that was deliberately intended to evoke the romance that had brought her parents, William Godwin and Mary Wollstonecraft, together, whilst the Brownings' elopement to Italy was, among other things, a deliberate emulation of the Shelleys themselves. In addition to the biographical fascination that each couple has long attracted when treated together *as* a couple, there has been a concomitant critical fascination deriving from the fact that each also worked together, reading and writing together whilst providing commentaries on each other's writings. *Frankenstein* is probably the most famous example of Shelley's participation in Mary Shelley's literary output, whilst the Brownings developed a shared language through their courtship correspondence.[1]

---

1 The dialogic nature of their literary relationships has also attracted much commentary: a controversy over the part Shelley played in the composition

The present book aims to amalgamate the biographical and the literary, not by trying, in that well-worn way, to track down biographical references and inspirations in selected literary texts, but by offering creative interpretations of the two that work together to 'effect' across time and space. By this, I mean (to borrow Julie A. Carlson's term) to privilege the 'psycho-historical situation of any particular reader' over 'the intentionality of an author'.[2] To this end, I take on board the methodology put forward, and deployed, by Carlson in her *England's First Family of Writers*, which 'employs critical strategies that affirm in these writers [Mary Wollstonecraft, William Godwin and Mary Shelley] the inseparability of biography and fiction, living and writing'. Carlson deploys 'a reading of a family of writers whose writings seek to defamiliarise what has counted as family in order to clear space for new species and manners of being'.[3] My aim is to do something similar for the Shelleys and Brownings: each coupling has further interpretive implications that exceed the confines of that coupling. Carlson promotes what she terms 'reading for tendency' as 'the most promising aspect of their life/writings for literary-cultural study'.[4] By 'tendency' (a word first used by Godwin), she means the 'actual effect it is calculated to produce upon the reader and [that] cannot be completely ascertained but by the experiment'.[5] This recalls Shelley's imaginary engagement with a future readership (as a corrective measure to his less-than-happy engagement with his contemporary readership) on the basis of the idea that poets are privileged to travel across time and space:

of *Frankenstein* dominated the critical scene of the 1970s and the 1980s. See James Rieger's Introduction to *Frankenstein, or The Modern Prometheus: The 1818 Text* (Chicago: University of Chicago Press, 1974); E. B. Murray's 'Shelley's Contribution to Mary's Frankenstein', *Keats-Shelley Memorial Bulletin* 29 (1978): 50–68; Anne K. Mellor, *Mary Shelley: Her Life, Her Fiction, Her Monsters* (New York: Routledge, 1988), pp. 58–69. Daniel Karlin's *Robert Browning and Elizabeth Barrett: The Courtship Correspondence 1845–1846* (Oxford: Oxford University Press, 1989) enables us to see the dialogic force at work in the letters addressed to each other by the Brownings.

2 Julie A. Carlson, *England's First Family of Writers: Mary Wollstonecraft, William Godwin, Mary Shelley* (Baltimore: Johns Hopkins University Press, 2007), p. 19.

3 Carlson, *England's First Family*, p. 13.

4 Carlson, *England's First Family*, p. 20.

5 These are Godwin's words as quoted by Carlson, *England's First Family*, p. 19.

The poetry of Dante may be considered as the Bridge thrown over the stream of Time which unites the modern and ancient World. The distorted notions of invisible things which Dante and his rival Milton have idealized are merely the mask and mantle in which these great poets walk through eternity enveloped and disguised.[6]

Although both Dante and Milton can be defined by their historical specificity (i.e. 'the mask and mantle'), their poetry is nonetheless capable of reaching out to a future audience (i.e. 'walk through eternity'), a notion that comes close to what Carlson teases out for Godwin, Wollstonecraft and Shelley:

By identifying text and author in their effects, not as each other's cause, it decouples the two and propels both into uncertain histories of reading. It produces analyses that are deeply contexualized but not historically specific; the intertextual and transferential dimensions of texts not only call and respond to each other across time but also locate their hope in measuring the space between them.[7]

Shifting the emphasis to their 'effects', text and author have a way of reconstituting themselves in the minds of the reader and writer. That is to say, rather than seeking meaning in the causal relationship between text and author, which is inevitably a source-hunting exercise, readers can liberate the texts from their historical specificity by re-imagining the texts and authors and creating new relationships of meaning.

Read this way, Anna Mercer's recent book on the Shelleys enables a fuller understanding of the couple that not only serves as a corrective measure to the previously held notion of their relationship between 1818 and 1822 (as being one of near-breakdown), but also reminds us of the ways in which that relationship actually remained collaborative, with all the ramifications—creative, editorial and complementary—that this entails.[8] In addition to *Frankenstein*, as

6 *A Defence of Poetry*, in *Poems and Prose*, ed. Timothy Webb (London: J. M. Dent, 1995), p. 267.

7 Carlson, *England's First Family*, p. 20.

8 Anna Mercer, *The Collaborative Literary Relationship of Percy Bysshe Shelley and Mary Wollstonecraft Shelley* (London: Routledge, 2020).

an exemplary case in point Mary Shelley's editing of Shelley's poems (and at times 'versioning' of texts) after his death in 1822 stands out as her paramount contribution to their collaborative relationship. Mercer, however, reminds us that there was more. 'A History of a Six Weeks' Tour' (1814) illustrates their partnership in terms of life and writing and, in some ways, lays the foundation of their future collaboration, which was sustained throughout their lives, if somewhat problematic at times. For example, Mercer reads Shelley's *The Cenci* and Mary Shelley's *Matilda* (both written mostly in 1819) side by side to show how the latter was a response to the former (the subject matter of which they both took great interest in). 'Julian and Maddalo', which had previously been read as providing evidence of Shelley's emotional strain and alienation from Mary Shelley, is re-addressed with a different interpretation.[9] More importantly, Mercer speculates on the possibility of Mary Shelley's intervention in establishing the text of Shelley's *The Mask of Anarchy*. Even if her contribution cannot be discussed at the same level as Shelley's input into *Frankenstein*, it still lends itself to the argument that Mary Shelley's collaborative effort went beyond that of an amanuensis.[10] Whilst Mercer goes on to examine Mary Shelley's editing (of Shelley's poems) and her own output as a novelist (and even as a poet) in her post-Shelley years, suffice it to say that Shelley's presence—in her personal memory and inscribed in her texts—remained much of the source of her creativity.

Mercer's project should be seen as part of a general focus in recent years on the nature and effect of literary 'communities' that fostered creative activity in individual writers. In other words, writers are no longer seen to be operating in isolation but rather working within networks of friends, lovers and sometimes enemies.[11] All

---

9 Mercer, *Collaborative Literary Relationship*, p. 108.

10 Mercer, *Collaborative Literary Relationship*, pp. 104–07.

11 Good examples of studies on the importance of literary coteries are Jeffrey Cox's book *Poetry and Politics in the Cockney School: Keats, Shelley, Hunt and Their Circle* (Cambridge: Cambridge University Press, 2004), Alison Chapman's *Networking the Nation: British and American Women's Poetry and Italy 1840–1870* (Oxford: Oxford University Press, 2015) and Tim Fulford's *Romantic Poetry and Literary Coteries: The Dialect of the Tribe* (New York: Palgrave Macmillan, 2015). Chapman devotes a full chapter to Elizabeth Barrett's *Casa Guidi Windows* (a poem I shall be examining in Chapter Six), which, she insists, should be understood in the context of the

of these critical works manifest, despite their nuanced differences, the understanding that writers did not work in isolation and were aided in their creativity by the networks that surrounded them and of which they were a constituent part. It is in light of such recent scholarship that this book examines the intertextualising of the four writers under consideration by casting them as their own—as it were—micro-community. Plainly, this is fictional, but it takes the Brownings' imaginary participation in the creation of the Shelleys' literary productions as its basis. In addition to the oft-cited influence that Shelley exerted over the young Browning, there is, I contend, a case to be made for Mary Shelley's influence on the later poet. Browning is tapping into and responding to the dialogic relationship of the Shelleys' writings. In that sense, it is a participation by Browning in a coterie of his imagination. And whilst Elizabeth Barrett[12] stands somewhat independently from this tightly knit group of writers, her marriage to, and thereby her close literary relationship with, Browning encouraged her to join this imaginary coterie.

Before proceeding any further, it is perhaps necessary to gloss these terms—'influence' and 'intertextuality'—to explain how each relates to my overall argument. 'Influence', as a critical conception, was mainly developed by Harold Bloom, if somewhat problematically, to denote the relationship between male poets of the Western canon. As his *Anxiety of Influence* argues,[13] the latecomer tries to wrestle with his precursor so that he will be able to overcome the precursor's influence by establishing his originality of voice. This takes the form of 'misreading', in which he commits to distancing himself and moving away from the precursor. This idea has been applied to a number of poets, including Browning. Therefore, it is almost inevitable that one has to talk about 'influence' in Browning studies. What 'influence' argues for is the psychological participation

Anglo-American Florentine community of female writers, all collaborating to express their political views. Another example that cuts across literary periods is *Literary Couplings: Writing Couples, Collaborations, and the Construction of Authorship*, ed. Marjorie Stone and Judith Thompson (Madison: University of Wisconsin Press, 2006).

12 For the sake of clarity, I refer to the poet throughout this book as Elizabeth Barrett.

13 See Harold Bloom, *The Anxiety of Influence: A Theory of Poetry* (New York: Oxford University Press, 1973).

of the author in negotiating his way towards literary originality; therefore, the existence of the author as agent of such an engagement is fundamental to this very idea. On the other hand, there have been other theoretical developments that have refuted the importance of the author, as in the case of Roland Barthes's 'The Death of the Author'.[14] Julia Kristeva formulated this strand of argument, which focuses on 'intertextuality', rather than relationships among authors.[15] In short, once a text is written, it becomes an independent entity for readers to make sense of without having to consider the authorial presence. A text takes on a life of its own and comes to signify in its various intertextual as well as social and cultural relations. What the critic must then do is to unravel such signification inscribed within the linguistic and social code. The two camps are fundamentally at odds with each other regarding their treatment of the text. For Bloom, it is the outcome of the psychological battle of the author with his predecessor, whilst for the poststructuralists, the text is the sole object of critical attention, denuded of any authorial intention. Both feminism and postcolonialism have then levelled criticism at both camps, challenging Bloomian 'influence' by arguing that Bloom's selection of poets is too limited and that it should be more inclusive of women and other non-canonical writers.[16] They have also challenged notions of 'intertextuality' by problematising the effacing of the author, the agent, which consequently leads to the silent acceptance of the status quo.[17]

For the discussion of Browning's texts, Shelleyan influence is something we cannot avoid completely, as we know for a fact that Browning had a vested interest in Shelley and that he wanted to emulate Shelley. Also, when discussing Mary Shelley, I shall argue that Mary Shelley's influence on Browning is marked as Shelley's.

14 See 'The Death of the Author', in *Image-Music-Text*, trans. Stephen Heath (London: Fontana, 1977), pp. 142–49.

15 See 'The Bounded Text', in *Desire in Language: A Semiotic Approach to Literature and Art*, ed. Leon S. Roudiez, trans. Thomas Gora et al. (New York: Columbia University Press, 1980), p. 36.

16 For a feminist approach to delegitimising the male canon, see Griselda Pollock, *Differing the Canon: Feminist Desire and the Writing of Art Histories* (New York and London: Routledge, 1999).

17 See Nancy K. Miller, *Subject to Change: Reading Feminist Writing* (New York: Columbia University Press, 1988) as an example of a gynocritical approach that argues that it is important whether texts are written by men or women.

Elizabeth Barrett presents a slightly different case. It is paradoxically easier to read her early poems as comprising a kind of 'intertext' with Shelley's writings precisely because she was not self-consciously 'influenced' by him; he was merely one among a variety of Romantic writers who formed part of her reading material. Having said that, I argue that her later poem *Casa Guidi Windows* should be read as an instance of a text deliberately written to utilise Shelleyan poetics. Thus, the theoretical underpinning of my discussion will shift, depending on which text the focus is on.

As I have intimated above, Harold Bloom's celebrated idea of the 'anxiety of influence', as applied to the works of Browning in relation to Shelley, has dominated how critical discourse has sought to understand these two poets. Indeed, Browning serves as a textbook example of a Bloomian poet struggling to overcome his predecessor, Shelley. This critical trope, to emphasise 'the relations between poets as cases akin to what Freud called the family romance',[18] has served its purpose. Unlike the previous 'source study', what Bloom sought with his 'poetic influence' was 'an analysis of misprision or revisionism [...] conducted through examination of tropes, imagery or psychological defenses'.[19] It is in light of such revisionism that Browning's poems came to be read and interpreted.[20] Bloom's critical engagements with Browning's texts in relation to Shelley have been predominantly with 'Childe Roland to the Dark Tower Came' (1855) and 'Thamuris Marching' (1875), as a virtual appendix to the former poem.[21] According to Bloom, 'Roland's negative moment' is 'self-knowledge yielding its power to a doomed love of others, in the recognition that those others, like Shelley, had more grandly surrendered knowledge and its powers to love, however illusory';

18 Bloom, *Anxiety of Influence*, p. 8.
19 Bloom, *A Map of Misreading* (Oxford: Oxford University Press, 1975), p. 116.
20 John Woolford's *Browning the Revisionary* (Basingstoke: Macmillan, 1988), Chapter 1 is another analogous instance of this reading.
21 Bloom worked out his ideas through a series of book chapters. See 'Browning's *Childe Roland*: All Things Deformed and Broken', in *Ringers in the Tower* (Chicago: University of Chicago Press, 1971), pp. 157–67; 'Testing the Map: Browning's *Childe Roland*', in *Map of Misreading*, pp. 106–22; 'Browning: Good Moments and Ruined Quests', in *Poetry and Repression* (New Haven: Yale University Press, 1976), pp. 175–204; 'Shelley's Heir: Browning and Yeats', in *The Anatomy of Influence: Literature as a Way of Life* (New Haven: Yale University Press, 2011), pp. 172–93.

put differently, 'Childe Roland dies, if he dies, in the magnificence of a belatedness that can accept itself as such'.[22] If 'Childe Roland' denotes 'a negative triumph of the Sublime made Grotesque', then, in 'Thamuris Marching', 'the joyous struggle is joined overtly, and the repressed [namely Shelley] partly returns, to be repressed again into the true Sublime'.[23] It is the long-sustained psychological drama that binds the two poems and gives a distinct nature to the relationship between Shelley and Browning.

Other critics have tended to focus on Browning's early texts, such as *Pauline* (1833) and *Paracelsus* (1835), thereby largely overlooking his later poems, the underlying rationale being that Browning's emulation of, followed by his divergence from, Shelleyan lyricism paved the way for the poetic innovation that would become Browning's dramatic monologue.[24] *Pauline* is an obvious example of Shelley's influence on Browning as he addresses him at the beginning of Book I: 'thou, spirit, come not near / Now—nor this time desert thy cloudy place / To scare me, thus employed, with that pure face!' (i 60–62). Despite his dismissal of Shelley at the outset, his presence is reinstated in the following lines: as Browning laments the loss of Shelley's life—'Thou art gone from us (l. 152)—as Shelley's poetry continues to inspire him—'But thou art still for me' (ll. 162, 168)—and, finally, as Browning affirms Shelley's immortality—'that one so pure as thou / Could never die' (ll. 208–09). It is not only Browning's references to Shelley in the poem that indicate Shelley's ongoing influence, but also his poetic style and content that have been noted as being emulative of Shelleyan lyricism and introspection. J. S. Mill

---

22 Bloom, *Map of Misreading*, p. 122.

23 See Bloom's *Poetry and Repression*, pp. 201–04 (204). Bloom mentions 'Thamuris Marching' again in a similar context in *Anatomy of Influence*, p. 177.

24 Whilst it is impossible to mention all the works that refer to Shelley's influence on the young Browning and his early works, those that deal with it at some length include Frederick Pottle, *Shelley and Browning: A Myth and Some Facts* (1923; Hamden, CT: Anchor Books, 1965); Sylvia Norman, *Flight of the Skylark: The Development of Shelley's Reputation* (London: Marx Reinhardt, 1954), pp. 83–106; Thomas J. Collins, 'Shelley and God in Browning's *Pauline*: Unresolved Problems', *Victorian Poetry* 3 (1965): 151–60; Paul Cundiff, *Robert Browning: A Shelley Promethean* (St Petersburg, FL: Valkyrie Press, 1977); Herbert F. Tucker, *Browning's Beginnings: The Art of Disclosure* (Minneapolis: University of Minnesota Press, 1980), pp. 119–45.

famously commented on *Pauline* by pointing out that 'With considerable poetic powers, this writer seems to me possessed with a more intense and morbid self-consciousness than I ever knew in any sane human being'.[25] This was indeed an excruciating experience for Browning, and he was never to repeat writing poetry in an overtly Shelleyan manner.

More recently, a couple of studies have examined Browning's later works;[26] on the whole, however, the emphasis still remains on Browning's early poems. This critical focus, useful and enlightening as it is, sets a limit on identifying the potential influence of Shelley on his other, later texts. My contention is that Shelley continued to influence Browning throughout his life; therefore, I look at a poem—*Fifine at the Fair*—published as late as 1872, to trace that influence.[27]

Browning continued to regard Shelley very highly despite his discovery of the so-called 'Harriet letters', which came to his attention in 1858.[28] Reading the letters, Browning discovered that Shelley and his first wife Harriet Westbrook had not separated on the basis of mutual consent and that Shelley had abandoned her. Browning was later to express his disappointment in a letter to Dr F. J. Furnivall dated 8 December 1885:

For myself, I painfully contrast my notions of Shelley the *man* and Shelley, well, even the *poet*, with what they were sixty years

---

25 Quoted in *Poems of Browning* 1: 17.
26 See Britta Martens, *Browning, Victorian Poetics and the Romantic Legacy: Challenging the Personal Voice* (Farnham: Ashgate, 2011); Porscha Fermanis, 'Anatomising the "Case": Shelley's *The Cenci*, Browning's *The Ring and the Book*, and the Origins of the Dramatic Monologue', in *Legacies of Romanticism: Literature, Culture, Aesthetics*, ed. Carmen Casaliggi and Paul March-Russell (New York: Routledge, 2012), pp. 37–50.
27 John Woolford brings to our attention Browning's Romanticism in *Fifine at the Fair*, but his argument largely draws upon Romantics other than Shelley. See John Woolford, '"Life—That's Venice!" Browning's Romanticism in *Fifine at the Fair*', in *Browning e venezia* (Florence: Leo S. Olschki, 1991), pp. 233–49; 'Browning Rethinks Romanticism', *Essays in Criticism* 43.3 (1993): 211–27.
28 Some private letters between Shelley and Harriet, his first wife, came into Browning's hands in 1858. See *Letters of Robert Browning Collected by Thomas J. Wise*, ed. Thurman L. Hood (New Haven: Yale University Press, 1933), pp. 222–23. It will hereafter be referred to as the *Hood Letters*.

ago, when I only had his works, for a certainty, and took his character on trust.[29]

Browning's rather harsh judgement of Shelley here may well have discouraged critics from pursuing Shelley's influence on Browning's later writings. However, there is early testimony suggesting that, in any case, Browning had never been of one mind about Shelley. There is evidence to suggest that his altered views on Shelley did not entirely change his long-held admiration for the latter. In a letter dated 24 June 1869, addressed to Rossetti, Swinburne refers to Browning's understanding of Shelley in light of the Harriet letters:

> Browning spent an hour here with me yesterday, and of course I tackled him about Forster's reference to Shelley. I am sorry to say he, having seen the papers referred to, and conversed with a man who knew Shelley (at the time) confidentially, says this:
>
> 1°) That Shelley *did* desert Harriet and their child, and the child with which she was then pregnant, without fair warning or fair provision, 'left them 14 shillings altogether', B. says. He has seen Harriet's letter to Shelley on his sudden disappearance, which by his account must be most piteous and touching.
>
> 2ᵈ) That Shelley during that period of his life was not responsible for his actions; was in fact positively insane, through excess of laudanum, taken to allay the pains of his illness.
>
> 3ᵈ) That Lord Eldon distinctly said at the trial that Shelley's atheism had nothing to do with his decision; '*he* had left the children to starve, and the grandfather had taken them up, and had a right to keep them'.
>
> Now of course Browning loves Shelley even as much as you and I do (he said so in concluding) but these, he is certain, are the facts of the case.[30]

As late as 1876, Browning published 'Cenciaja', in which he extolled Shelley's *The Cenci* as 'your superb / Achievement'. We can therefore conclude that, although the Harriet letters were disturbing for Browning, they did not necessarily serve to expunge Shelley's presence in his creative imagination. Bloom similarly asserts that

29 *Hood Letters*, pp. 242–43.
30 *Hood Letters*, p. 371.

'Browning loved Shelley unbrokenly and almost unreservedly from the age of fourteen, when he first read him, until his own death at the age of seventy-seven'.[31]

Mary Shelley's presence in Browning's works is another avenue of critical enquiry that has not been pursued as vigorously as it might have been.[32] This may be due to the fact that Browning said very little about Mary Shelley in his letters, and indeed, when he did mention her, it was in unflattering terms. In one letter to Elizabeth Barrett, Browning refers to Mary Shelley's altered lifestyle after Shelley's death and barely conceals his contempt, whilst, in another letter, he belittles Mary Shelley's translation work as a 'womanly performance'.[33] However, these facts should not deter us from looking for Mary Shelley's presence in Browning's writings. The closest influence at times becomes repressed and silenced without the author's full intention or knowledge. I shall argue that this might well have been the case with regard to Mary Shelley's influence on Browning. Browning and Mary Shelley's profound investment in Shelleyan Romanticism despite their respective critiques of it connects them. By Shelleyan Romanticism, I mean Shelley's belief in reason and imagination as the vehicles to human progress and, in particular, sympathy as a means to identifying oneself with others to enable social solidarity. I also intend to highlight his faith in the good and the beautiful in humankind over self-interest and hatred, and his faith, in line with that of Enlightenment thinkers, in the inevitability of human perfectibility. Mary Shelley was no doubt one of the most sympathetic if not the best of readers of Shelley's works, which is

31 Bloom, *Poetry and Repression*, p. 178.
32 See my *Negotiating History: From Romanticism to Victorianism* (Tokyo: Waseda University Press, 2012), Chapters 2 and 3.
33 See the letter of 11 September 1845: 'Oh that book [Mary Shelley's *Rambles in Germany and Italy, in 1840, 1842 and 1843*]—does one wake or sleep? The "Mary dear" with the brown eyes, and Godwin's daughter and Shelley's wife, and who surely was something better, once upon a time—and to go thro' Rome & Florence & the rest, after what I suppose to be Lady Londonderry's fashion: the intrepidity of the commonplace quite astounds me—.' See *Brownings' Correspondence* 11: 69–70. For Browning's other comment, see the letter of 25 October 1876, to H. Buxton Forman: 'I believe I have seen somewhere that the translation ['Relation' of the Cenci affair] was made by Mrs. Shelley—the note appended to an omitted passage seems a womanly performance' (*Hood Letters*, p. 176).

duly reflected in her own early literary productions. This fact must have been appealing to Browning, whose devotion to Shelley was unparalleled. He devoured Shelley's works in his youth, and Shelley became his idol, to the extent that Browning even adopted Shelley's vegetarianism. Because of Browning's immersion in anything to do with Shelley, it is difficult to conceive that Mary Shelley, as a presence (both as critic and as writer), could have eluded his attention. Indeed, it is my contention that her influence on the young Browning was arguably as significant as that of Shelley himself.

The connection between Elizabeth Barrett and Shelley is one that has been commented upon by critics but not fully explored to date. As for any critical attention to Mary Shelley's influence on Barrett, it is non-existent, as is the case with Browning. In the year preceding their first correspondence, Browning and Barrett were both contributing (without either of them knowing the other) to Richard Hengist Horne's *A New Spirit of the Age* (which included essays on contemporary writers), published in 1844. Barrett offered mottoes for various writers, including Mary Shelley. We can gather from her selection of excerpts (from poems) serving as mottoes that she held Mary Shelley's imaginative qualities in high esteem.[34] As for Shelley, there is evidence to suggest that Barrett was, from early on in her career, familiar with his writings; however, such evidence is still patchy, making it difficult to establish as solid a case for Shelley's influence on the young poet as it is with Browning. Having said that, it is highly improbable that Barrett developed her poetry untouched by Shelley's writings. Indeed, critics have been quick to demonstrate the similarities that exist between the poetry of Shelley and that of Barrett.[35] Consequently, without the wherewithal to make the full biographical case for Shelley's influence on Barrett, I would still like to highlight some of the intertexualities that exist between Barrett's early texts and some of the major poems of Shelley.

In what is known as the Brownings' courtship correspondence, Browning and Barrett are in a dialogue about the nature of Shelley's

---

34 See letters 1545, 1546, 1549 and 1550, in which Barrett makes suggestions for the mottoes for Mary Shelley; *Brownings' Correspondence* 8.

35 Barrett's poem entitled *The Seraphim* (1838) attracted such a comparison in *The Metropolitan Magazine* 22.88 (August 1838), pp. 97–101 (97), in *The Sunbeam* (13 October 1838), p. 295, and in *The Literary Gazette* (1 December 1838), pp. 759–60 (760).

poetry, with Browning, more often than not, bringing Barrett around to his understanding of Shelley. For example, in a letter dated 11 March 1845, addressed to Barrett, Browning insists that she '[r]estore the Prometheus [...] ('Fire-bearer')' in keeping with Shelley's *Prometheus Unbound* when she comes to re-translate *Prometheus Bound*: 'in your poem you shall make Prometheus our way.'[36] As I shall argue further in the chapter on Barrett, the relationship of her poems to Shelley changes (if somewhat subconsciously) from one of allusion to one of influence, with a notable difference, most likely due to her marriage to Browning.

Casa Guidi Windows (1851), because of the political aspect of Barrett's poetry, is (in relation to Shelley) the poem that is in most need of critical attention.[37] Barrett had much in common with Shelley when it came to radical politics. Hence, even whilst her poetry has been compared to that of Wordsworth, whom she worshipped and whose poetry she sought to emulate, her later political ballads, as noted by Marjorie Stone, were 'inclined to be more radically polemical than Wordsworth in appropriating the ballad for political purposes, following Shelley's example more than Wordsworth's'.[38] However, it is not only in the ballads that this is the case but also in her major political effort, *Casa Guidi Windows*. If Shelley's political poems, therefore, did not find a direct heir in Browning's poetry, they did so in Barrett's poetry. This is the hidden genealogy that I would like to bring to light.

If Bloom's theory of influence reads the psychological in the text, namely, the struggle of the latecomer to wrestle with his predecessor, I would like to extend that influence to include the historicist consciousness, which the later poet comes to deploy not by contesting with the forerunner but by collaborating with the precursor. That is to say, the idea is not so much to kill off the father in

36 *Brownings' Correspondence* 10: 119.
37 Most past criticism of *Casa Guidi Windows* has tended to focus on Barrett's reworking of the image of Italy 'as a beautiful but wronged victim of history', which she saw as harmful for the regeneration of Italy. See, for example, Joe Phelan, 'Elizabeth Barrett Browning's *Casa Guidi Windows*, Arthur Hugh Clough's *Amours de Voyage* and the Italian National Uprisings of 1847–9', *Journal of Anglo-Italian Studies* 3 (1993): 137–52 (139–40).
38 Marjorie Stone, *Elizabeth Barrett Browning* (New York: St. Martin's Press, 1995), pp. 106–07.

the Freudian sense, or to play out the family drama at all, but to gain empowerment by engaging with and evoking the cases of historicism in an inherited text. This shift in focus—from the competitive struggle to collaborative empowerment—has some affinity with what Lucy Newlyn teases out in her book on Wordsworth and Coleridge.[39] Among other things, Newlyn focuses on 'allusion' or 'echo' detectable in the writings of Wordsworth and Coleridge that 'can bring with it a context that expands and enriches the immediate frame of reference'.[40] Furthermore, she demonstrates that 'allusion is essentially strategic: a means of recovering strength and revisiting sources of power'.[41] Whilst 'allusion' and 'echo' work well in the case of Coleridge and Wordsworth, given the dialogic nature of their writings, 'influence' better captures Shelley and Browning because of the former's precursory relationship with the latter.

In recent decades, we have seen a burgeoning interest in literary allusions and echoes that cut across the Romantic and Victorian divide.[42] Richard Cronin's *Romantic Victorians* is one of the first attempts at interrogating the lacuna, as it were, of the years between 1824 and 1840—a period when the second-generation Romantics were no longer active and the young Victorians were still unestablished. In addition to the traditional authors, Cronin sheds a fresh light on the previously neglected female poets Felicia Hemans and Letitia Landon, by arguing for the significance of their feminised poetry, which catered to an increasingly commercialised market that was based on female readership. The young Tennyson was among those who appropriated such feminised voices as his own. Another example of Cronin salvaging an important strand of poetic practice (that had previously been neglected) is his identification of realism and the actualisation of the real in John Clare's poetry written on birds' nests. Indeed, over the past decade or so, numerous scholars have followed his line of argument to counter the lack of critical attention paid to these writers. Cronin also provides insights into

---

39 Lucy Newlyn, *Coleridge, Wordsworth and the Language of Allusion* (Oxford: Oxford University Press, 1986).

40 Newlyn, *Coleridge*, p. 17.

41 Newlyn, *Coleridge*, p. 54.

42 See for example, Richard Cronin, *Romantic Victorians: English Literature 1824–1840* (Basingstoke: Palgrave, 2002); *Romantic Echoes in the Victorian Era*, ed. Andrew Radford and Mark Sandy (Aldershot: Ashgate, 2008).

other connections among writers and texts of this period, not limited to poetry but also including the novel, as the most popular genre of the nineteenth century. One that directly relates to my thesis is his identification of Elizabeth Barrett's *Casa Guidi Windows* as the first civic poem, as I shall be elaborating in Chapter Six.

Whilst questioning the artificial nature of literary periodisation, Cronin and others highlighted how the Romantics figure in the writings of the Victorians as a means of self-defining, self-fashioning or self-manoeuvring. In this sense, the Brownings are not unique. In addition, these allusions and echoes manifest themselves in ways that do not necessarily comply with the Bloomian model. In fact, they exist in variegated forms that, at times, even prove to be the opposite of an Oedipal contest.[43] However, despite the prevalence of such literary practice (i.e. drawing on a past icon/text to construct the self) in Victorian literature, I wish to emphasise Robert Browning's unrivalled personal investment in anything to do with Shelley (both his life and his work). The intensity with which Browning engaged with Shelley's texts as well as Shelley's persistent presence throughout Browning's life and oeuvre make the Shelley–Browning relationship a special case that demands a stronger term than 'allusion' or 'echo'. This claim is not to undermine, however, the cultural significance of 'allusion' and 'echo', which at times manifested themselves through not just one but many poets of the nineteenth century, as Mark Sandy's persuasive argument proves.

In his examination of texts written by nineteenth-century poets ranging from Hardy, Arnold and Coleridge to Smith, Clare, Hopkins and Yeats, Sandy alerts us to how their respective engagements with the avian poetry of Shelley and Keats require closer attention. The conclusion he draws is that there is as much continuity as there is a break from Romantic sensibility. It is not simply a case of the replacement of 'Romantic harmonising ideals' by 'a Victorian individuation, separation and tragedy', for the very source of 'tragedy' associated with the nightingale (on which Sandy focuses) is already inherent in the Romantic texts of Keats and Coleridge (through their allusion to Milton). Misidentification of the Romantic nightingale with 'cheerfulness' was not a Victorian construct but a Romantic

---

43 Sarah Wootton writes of Rossetti's relationship with Keats: 'there is no suppressed anguish or anger that leads the inheritor to slay the symbolic figurehead of power'; see Radford and Sandy, *Romantic Echoes*, p. 60.

one. Shelley made that association in his *Defence of Poetry*. Yet, upon careful re-examination of Keats's and Coleridge's texts, Sandy argues for their acute awareness of the dual sense in which their nightingale is meant to figure in their texts. It is through such careful recuperation of the meaning that the nightingale had for the Romantics that Sandy is able to make the continuity between the Romantic and the Victorian texts apparent. Victorians utilised both 'Apollonian harmonies' and the 'Dionysian tragic consciousness' (coexistent in the Romantic texts). If they found it difficult to reconcile the two, at least they left open the possibility of a triumphant unity that the Romantic texts seemed to promise. As Sandy takes Keats's 'Ode to a Nightingale' as a primary example of such a practice, I shall be reverting to this notion when I come to discuss how Prometheus and Romantic texts on Prometheus worked towards similar ends for the Brownings.

Another area of literary criticism that has seen a surge of interest in recent decades is the return-to-history approach that has done much to put 'historical consciousness' or 'historicism' back on the critical map. Historicism has been traditionally associated with the reaction against the Enlightenment 'practice of deducing from first principles truths about how people are obliged to organize themselves socially and politically' in favour of the view that 'human nature is too various for such legislation to be universally applicable'.[44] This 'relativizing of the past by getting to know the different interpretations to which it is open and deciding them on grounds expressing our own contemporary preoccupations'[45] has also led to a heightened awareness of the 'difference' that exists between the past and the present. It is in light of such dialectical understanding of the past that new historicism came to assert itself. Marilyn Butler (who was among the first to advocate this in Romantic studies) provides five principles for such a method, of which three seem relevant here:

- The writings of the past ask for an educated reading, as far as possible from within their own discourse or code or cultural system. [...]
- The modern critic should acknowledge his own position as similar to that of all writers, bound in time and place. [...] The

44 See Paul Hamilton, *Historicism*, 2nd edn (London: Routledge, 2003), p. 2.
45 Hamilton, *Historicism*, p. 16.

aim [of historical criticism] is not to reconstruct the past, which could not be done innocently, even if it were worth doing at all. It is to understand how writing functions in its world, in order to understand writing, the world, and ourselves. [...] But what can be gained in richness of documentation and clarity of perspective is lost if we do not recognize the pastness of the past, the fact that its languages and its purposes are distinctive. The intentions and attitudes which are embedded in past writing can interrogate our own, if we will let them. [...]

• A genuinely historical perspective discourages dogmatism, by obliging us to foreground the difference between our circumstances, aims, and language, and those of the past.[46]

In a book published just over ten years after Butler's essay, James Chandler makes a case for Romantic historicism that is predicated on Butler's thesis. Nevertheless, he is sceptical of the privileged status given to twentieth-century new historicism on the grounds that the originality of this approach may be challenged if 'the complexity and density of historicist thought in Romantic writing' are duly examined. According to Chandler, once we understand that Romantic historicism contains a significant element of self-consciousness, we are able to gain a fuller appreciation of 'the intellectual, political, and even moral stakes of Romantic historiographical operations across a range of representative literary forms'.[47] Romantic historicism, understood to be a British constellation, concerns itself with situating itself (in both time and space) by 'comparing one's own age with former ages, or with our notion of those which are yet to come'.[48] Its 'emphasis on the reflexivity of representation'[49] is related to 'the spirit of the age': 'the period when the normative status of the period becomes a central and self-conscious aspect of historical reflection'.[50]

46 Marilyn Butler, 'Against Tradition: The Case for a Particularized Historical Method', included in *Historical Studies and Literary Criticism*, ed. Jerome J. McGann (Madison: University of Wisconsin Press, 1985), pp. 25–47 (43–44).

47 See James K. Chandler, *England in 1819: The Politics of Literary Culture and the Case of Romantic Historicism* (Chicago: Chicago University Press, 1998), p. 139.

48 Chandler, *England in 1819*, p. 107.

49 Chandler, *England in 1819*, p. 243.

50 Chandler, *England in 1819*, p. 78.

Its 'reliance on the form of the case'[51] would therefore serve to explain the historicity of a given situation. I shall be deploying all of these concepts of Romantic historicism as I come to read the texts.

Each chapter of this book more or less provides an example of such 'influence' or 'intertextuality' at play. In Chapter One, Browning, in *Paracelsus*, historicises Romantic Prometheanism, firstly by appropriating Mary Shelley's use of the Promethean myth, followed by his own development of, or even break from, this usage. That is to say, his own text is charged with the kind of radicalism that *Frankenstein* was first associated with, but deviates from this in his attempt to re-historicise it according to his own Victorian historical consciousness. Browning's choice of an occult Paracelsus, thus, gains a political edge, as Romantics valorised occultism to such an end. His appropriation of Romantic radicalism, mediated by Mary Shelley's feminism, results in something like Browning's own corrective measure to radicalism. When Browning claims that his attempt in *Paracelsus* is radical, he means exactly this: it is rehearsing Romantic Prometheanism. That is not to say that the text endorses Promethean politics, as the poem's tragic ending demonstrates. Rather, Browning's ambivalence towards Romantic Prometheanism should be understood in the context in which Mary Shelley framed hers; he builds on it only to depart from it. The textual relationship between *Valperga* and *Sordello* is a similar case in point. What Browning discerns in *Valperga* is Mary Shelley's historicised view of Europe at the time, which Browning then utilises to create his own. Both of these cases are instances of 'influence' in action, in the sense not only that Browning read Mary Shelley's texts and then deployed similar themes and subject matter, but also that the shaping ideology of his texts is underpinned by his historical situatedness, which was, in turn, a response to that of Mary Shelley. Hence, it is useful to understand 'influence' as bearing historicist significance.

The two chapters on Shelley and Browning bring this thesis to the fore. As noted by critics, Browning's *The Ring and the Book* is, in some sense, a response to Shelley's *The Cenci*. Its exact nature, however, is open to debate. My contention is that Browning's poem is a reworking of Shelley's historicism: 'the sad reality' of *The Cenci* case gleaned from early nineteenth-century Europe (not simply

---

51 Chandler, *England in 1819*, p. 243.

from an Italian perspective but from a pan-European one) is what Browning understands as being the flip side of Romantic idealism. Browning's text is a recasting of Shelley's historical self-awareness into one of his own. In this sense, the latter could be said to be an 'influence'. Shelley's 'The Triumph of Life' and Browning's *Fifine* work similarly. Shelley's understanding of what we have come to call Romanticism in the unfinished poem is the starting point for Browning's own poem—a poem that constitutes, among other things, a statement on Romanticism.

The chapter on Shelley and Elizabeth Barrett differs slightly from the previous ones in my approach to their texts. Barrett's early texts do not suggest her psychological investment in Shelley's texts in the same way that Browning's do; however, as I shall argue in the chapter, her later writings come close to the kind of appropriation of Shelley's historicism that is discernible in those of Browning.

My critical approach for the Brownings (i.e. the application of new historicism to Victorian poetry) is similar to that employed by Antony H. Harrison, who questions the lacuna in 'rigorous interrogations of the historical contexts, particularly the sociopolitical contexts, surrounding the production and reception of Victorian poems'. Thereby, he claims that his 'study is the first extended new historicist project to take Victorian poetry as its subject'.[52] Furthermore, in the process of historicising texts, I examine '[t]he relationship of a work to its literary predecessors' as prescribed by Marilyn Butler to achieve a 'genuinely historical criticism'.[53]

There are several underlying threads that run throughout the various texts by the four writers discussed here. First of all, their literary identities ought to be understood in relation to the idea of exile, as Jane Stabler argues in *The Artistry of Exile*.[54] All four writers were estranged from their own English society—both physically and psychologically; their writing against the backdrop of foreignness and their respective sense of kinship with a foreign cultural heritage combine to make their identities not fixed but constantly negotiating two or more cultures. This aspect of their writings binds them

---

52 Antony H. Harrison, *Victorian Poets and Romantic Poems: Intertextuality and Ideology* (Charlottesville: University Press of Virginia, 1990), p. 6.

53 Butler, 'Against Tradition', pp. 43–44.

54 See Jane Stabler, *The Artistry of Exile: Romantic and Victorian Writers in Italy* (Oxford: Oxford University Press, 2013).

together, as Stabler emphasises, and provides a rationale for treating
them together rather than independently:

> The history of English poetry also tends to overlook the way in
> which the Romantic generation of outcasts is entwined with the
> Victorians who came to Italy a few years later, consciously in
> the footsteps of the Pisan circle, but usually placed in a separate
> category altogether.[55]

The idea of exile not only informs the context of their writings
as an experience that shaped their identities, but also provides a
fresh foundation on which to explore the concepts of influence and
allusion that come into play precisely because of their investment
in, and their utilisation of, the literature of exile that came before
them. In this sense, as Stabler notes, '[p]oetic allusions are stories,
tessellated biographies, and forms of quarrelling and wrangling'
rather than 'a tidy linear narrative'.[56] The constellation of crossroads
discernible among the texts written by these four writers is what this
book seeks to illuminate.

Take, for example, Mary Shelley's *Frankenstein* and Browning's
Paracelsus. Their displaced republicanism finds a voice in the 'Swiss'
identities of both Frankenstein and Paracelsus. It denotes the
beginning of an exile period in Italy for Mary Shelley, which was to
manifest itself in works such as *Frankenstein* and *Valperga*. Although
Browning was still living in England when he wrote *Paracelsus*,
his alienated psyche, as a dissenter in England, channelled itself
through a foreign character, who, likewise, is estranged from his age
and society. The next texts discussed, *Valperga* and *Sordello*, deal
with the idea of exile head-on. The characters not only face exile in
one shape or another—Castruccio in *Valperga* as the member of a
banished political faction and Sordello as a disinherited son of the
warrior Salinguerra—but also reflect, again, the authors' republicanism, displaced from an English context to that of the Italian
political scene of the Middle Ages. Percy Bysshe Shelley's *The Cenci*
and Browning's *The Ring and the Book* are full-blown examples
of texts that bring the notion of exile into play. At the point when
both Shelley and Browning created their respective compositions,

55 Stabler, *Artistry of Exile*, p. 241.
56 Stabler, *Artistry of Exile*, p. 229.

they had been in exile, and their relationship with a foreign subject articulates this most forcefully. Their rendition of Italy as a cultural and political force that oscillates between the Renaissance and the nineteenth century is gleaned through the eyes of an outsider. The authors' own Protestant Englishness complicates, but also enforces, the political message that the two texts convey. Because both texts have a privileged vantage point (that of the outsider) from which to assess the two respective legal cases that form the basis of the texts, they are able to frame each situation as being historically and culturally specific. Shelley's 'The Triumph of Life' and Browning's *Fifine at the Fair* are textualised examples of a psychologically estranged state that might be taken as symptomatic of the exile. They both dramatise what it means to be 'outside' history (if such a vantage point is at all possible) by depicting human society *en masse*. Their respective narrators' dissociated viewpoints enable each to articulate what it means to be psychologically exiled. Elizabeth Barrett's later political poem *Casa Guidi Windows* likewise enacts this dissociation.

The texts also broadly concern the question of gender; specifically, the politicisation of the relationship between, and the respective roles of, man and woman. The Shelleys' thinking on these issues derives, in large part, from Mary Wollstonecraft's *Vindication of the Rights of Woman* (1792). Shelley was of the belief that, unless the female gender was educated to the same standard as the male, there could be no real societal advancement. This is clearly expressed in *The Revolt of Islam* (1818): it is Cythna, the heroine, who leads a revolution to liberate women from the tyrannical rule of a fictional state, Argolis, modelled on the Ottoman Empire. Mary Shelley was equally interested in the education of women and their enlightenment, as attested by Safie's mother in *Frankenstein*, who was betrothed to a sultan but was adamant about giving her daughter a liberal, Christian education. If Mary Shelley was not the radical feminist that her mother was, she at least believed in curbing masculine egotism and fostering domestic sentiments in the opposite gender as the road to happiness for the two genders, as well as for society as a whole.

The Brownings held similar liberal views about the relationship of the genders. Often, for Browning, the very monstrosity of his male characters is indicated precisely through their male egotism and consequent objectification and mistreatment of women. The Duke in 'My Last Duchess' (1842), the speaker in 'Porphyria's Lover'

(1842) and Count Guido in *The Ring and the Book* (1868–69) provide obvious examples. Less melodramatically, Elizabeth Barrett's *Aurora Leigh* (1856) was the first major poem to tackle as its subject matter the question of what it is to be a professional female writer.

To what extent, however, can the Brownings' treatment of these topics be fruitfully regarded as a response to the Shelleys' own treatment? Fundamentally, they were not all that different from one another in that all were liberal thinkers on this issue. However, a closer reading of their respective texts enables us to see them working through different agendas and towards slightly different goals. For example, when treating together the works of Mary Shelley and Browning, Browning is clearly not only taking on Mary Shelley's feminist ideas but also inverting them to suggest that gender roles are socially constructed and hence reversible. Therefore, the power-crazed politician Castruccio Castracani, who embodies masculine egotism in Mary Shelley's *Valperga*, becomes the heroine of Browning's epic poem *Sordello*.

Elizabeth Barrett was a fervent reader of Mary Wollstonecraft, and the latter's feminist ideas find a voice in the celebrated works of the former, such as *Aurora Leigh*. Shelley's radicalism on the question of gender is another influence on Barrett, although this connection has not been examined until now. Of all the Romantics, perhaps Shelley was the most forthright in his feminism, and his ideas on sexual equality are discernible in both his poetry and his prose. What is interesting, however, is how Browning, consciously or unconsciously, dismantles Shelley's feminism by suggesting that Shelley, despite his assertions to the contrary, was not particularly liberated in his thinking. Accordingly, his poetry is imbued with a male egotism, which, in turn, becomes the target of Browning's critique.[57] In this sense, Browning aligns with Mary Shelley, and this is why it is useful to think of Mary Shelley's feminism or anti-Romanticism as a source for Browning's poetics.

If all four writers were liberal in terms of their sexual politics, so too were they, of course, in terms of politics generally. Shelley was infamous at the time as a radical and often mistaken as a revolutionary (although he in fact believed in gradualism). His anonymously published pamphlet, *Necessity of Atheism* (1811), caused him trouble at the University of Oxford, where he had been a student, and

---

57 See Suzuki, *Negotiating History*, Chapter 3.

eventually got him expelled. Shelley was a radical supporter of political issues such as Catholic Emancipation, a cause for which he gave a speech in Ireland. His pamphleteering activity towards liberal ends in Wales was brought to a halt by his hallucinations that spies were trying to kill him. In Italy, where he and Mary lived from 1818 until his death in 1822, he showed great interest in Italian politics and supported Italy's independence from foreign rule. It is, in short, no exaggeration to say that the driving force behind Shelley's poetic career was his 'passion to reform the world'.

For Mary Shelley, such political aspirations were close to home, being the daughter of William Godwin and Mary Wollstonecraft. Her dissenting background, just as that of Godwin, affiliated her with English republicanism, which easily translated to Italian republicanism. Like her husband, she sought to disseminate her radical beliefs through her writings. In Italy, she was to bring both her political thinking and her historical research to a culmination in her composition of *Valperga, or The Life and Adventures of Castruccio, Prince of Lucca* (1823). Although her politics in later life are a matter of controversy, it can be argued that her latent liberalism did not change and that she remained faithful to her early commitment to the cause.

Browning also came from a dissenting background, which made him interested in English republicanism just as Mary Shelley and William Godwin were. His initial phase of emulating Shelley coincided with his radical period in which he wrote *Paracelsus* (1835)—a poem about a Swiss occultist of the Renaissance period. His reference to the peasant uprising in the poem is suggestive of the English equivalent—the Levellers—and his sympathies in the poem are clear. *Frankenstein* and *Paracelsus* both share radical politics as an underlying theme, and the influence of the former's text on the latter's is palpable, as I shall argue in Chapter One. The next poem, *Sordello* (1840), is about the medieval Italian city-states and the struggle between the Guelphs (republican sympathisers) and the Ghibellines (imperial supporters). However, after *Sordello*, Browning never took political struggle as the main theme of his poems again. Rather than developing his radicalism directly in his poetry as Shelley had done, Browning instead sublimated his political ideas into a democratisation of the relationship between reader and writer. According to Browning, the poet and his audience should be on equal terms rather than locked in a relationship that forever depends on the elevation of the poet as a conveyor of supreme wisdom to a grateful and acquiescent readership. His poetry did not necessarily demonstrate this—it was considered difficult at the time and even now can readily baffle the less dedicated reader—but his poetics are based on mutual co-operation between the poet and the reader, requiring work on the reader's side to meet the poet halfway. As attested by his poem 'Why I Am a Liberal' (1886), he remained faithful to the liberal cause until the end of his literary career.

Elizabeth Barrett, like Shelley, came from a monied background. This, however, did not prevent her from sympathising with the underprivileged strata of society. After she married Browning and they took up their abode in Florence, she wrote numerous political poems that evidence her concern for the less fortunate. As well as *Casa Guidi Windows* (1851), in which she expressed her hope for Italian independence, she wrote 'A Plea for the Ragged Schools of England' (1854) and the abolitionist *Poems before Congress* (1860). Her political expressions were as direct as Shelley's had been, and she utilised poetry to advance the liberal cause as Shelley had done. In this respect, when compared with her husband, Barrett is more obviously a disciple of Shelley.

Under the repressive policies of nineteenth-century England, in the aftermath of the French Revolution, it was considered dangerous to talk about contemporary politics, particularly progressive political ideas. This is one reason why writers displaced their argument onto a different cultural setting and a different period. A popular one was Italy: it provided a rich historical background in which writers could work out their political ideas. For example, both Mary Shelley and Browning utilised medieval Italy as a site of contest between republicanism and imperialism, as I have already noted. Shelley and Browning set their works in Renaissance Italy—*The Cenci* (1819) and *The Ring and the Book* (1868–69)—to express obliquely an interest in the contemporary struggle for Italian independence, thereby suggesting that once again the forces of liberty and oppression were at work in Europe as a whole. Elizabeth Barrett took this further to directly voice her hopes for Italian unification in *Casa Guidi Windows*. Thus, their interventions in support of the Risorgimento did not concern Italy alone. Instead, the Risorgimento itself worked metonymically as an emblem of the struggle between liberal and conservative forces. The liberal politics of all four writers projected their hopes and fears onto Italy, where they could be expressed directly.

The Italian exiles who came flooding into England contributed to informing the English public about the political state of Italy. Sympathisers also became interested in Italy as a country and in its history, culture and art. The Shelleys had first-hand experience of all this by actually living in Italy. They read J. C. L. Simonde de Sismondi's *Histoire des républiques italiennes du moyen âge* (1807–18), which informed much of Mary Shelley's *Valperga*. The Shelleys saw a portrait of Beatrice Cenci, thought to be a work by Guido Reni, in Palazzo Colonna in 1818, which inspired Shelley's *The Cenci*. The Brownings followed in their footsteps by going to live in Italy in 1846. There, from her home known as the Casa Guidi, Elizabeth Barrett famously witnessed the celebration parade thanking Leopold II for granting Florentines the right to form a civil guard, as described in Part I of her *Casa Guidi Windows*. Browning found the Old Yellow Book that contained an Italian court case of the seventeenth century at a market in Florence, and this would form the basis of *The Ring and the Book*.

These are just a few examples of works on Italy by the four writers. Other examples include Shelley's meeting with Byron in Venice in 'Julian and Maddalo' (1818–19) and painter- and painting-related poems by Browning, such as 'Old Pictures in Florence', 'Andrea del Sarto' and 'Fra Lippo Lippi' (all included in *Men and Women*, 1855). Browning's interest in medieval and Renaissance Italian painting was part of a vogue in England: Anna Jameson and John Ruskin, amongst others, wrote on the subject. Furthermore, Alexis François Rio's *De la poésie chrétienne* (1836) did much to bring attention to the early Italian painters in England. Whilst Jameson and Ruskin, as well as Mary Shelley, slavishly followed Rio's artistic judgements, Browning wrote against the grain to put forward his own ideas of art, which were connected to his poetics. Italy, therefore, provided much of the material for their writings, and, to understand the background of their art, the significance of Italy as a cultural force has to be appreciated in all tenets of its influence from politics to history and to art.

In fact, Italy not only served as a rich reservoir of creative material for the Shelleys and the Brownings but also attracted a whole host of writers and artists who sought to tap into its cultural and political past and present for their creative expression. Alison Chapman and Jane Stabler explore this aspect of Italy as the location for creativity, particularly for British women in the nineteenth century, in their collection of essays, *Unfolding the South*.[58] What emerges from this analysis of both canonical writers such as Elizabeth Barrett and George Eliot, and less well-known female writers and artists, is the strong attraction which Italy held for female writers as a country for identification and liberalisation:

> The gendered portrait of Italy as 'a woman in distress' was a disturbing legacy for many women writers and artists. In the writing of Felicia Hemans, Mary Shelley, Janet Hamilton and Elizabeth Barrett Browning, however, we can see a determined effort to revise the historical view of Italy's passivity at the hands of 'her' captors.[59]

One example of such embodiment is the fictional heroine of Madame de Staël's novel *Corinne*, who provided a model for nineteenth-century female writers but also posed a problem for them. As much as her artistic role as poetess and *improvisatrice* was vaunted, she was a source of inspiration for many female writers and artists in pursuing their calling in the public sphere. Corinne's doomed fate as a woman was also troubling, and, as Chapman and Stabler note, '[o]ne of the ways in which women artists and writers cope with Corinne's ambiguous legacy is to turn indeterminacy into an aesthetic *forte*'.[60] This aspect of Italy will concern Mary Shelley's *Valperga*, a historical novel, and Elizabeth Barrett's *Casa Guidi Windows*, as the respective chapters on these writers will demonstrate.

It is equally true that, for both men and women (although the focus was on the latter), Italy provided much freedom to exercise their creativity and a contrast against which they could re-think and re-negotiate their own identities, as Chapman and Stabler emphasise:

> Italy is an imaginative and liberating space of possibilities and revelations, opening up the 'travelling heart' to new experiences, pleasures and subjectivities. The idea of Italy's palimpsestic layering of nature and culture recurs in the work of many writers,

---

58 *Unfolding the South: Nineteenth-Century British Women Writers and Artists in Italy*, ed. Alison Chapman and Jane Stabler (Manchester: Manchester University Press, 2003).

59 Chapman and Stabler, *Unfolding the South*, p. 6.

60 Chapman and Stabler, *Unfolding the South*, pp. 6–7.

allowing them to reflect back on where they have travelled from as well as looking towards new horizons.[61]

This land of potential is very much the sense in which writers draw upon Italy for its historical, political and artistic past. To this extent, the Shelleys and the Brownings are no exception.

The six chapters that make up this book can be summarised thus. Chapter One examines Browning's *Paracelsus* in relation to Mary Shelley's *Frankenstein*. *Parcelsus* has been known as the English *Faust* and has been read mainly in that context; however, I suggest that there are more affinities in *Paracelsus* with *Frankenstein* than with *Faust*. For example, Aprile—a character in *Paracelsus*—is a Shelleyan figure, and his manifestation of 'love' contrasts him with Paracelsus, who wants to 'know'. These two types suggest the conflict that Mary Shelley first rehearsed in her creation of Victor Frankenstein and Henry Clerval in *Frankenstein*.

Chapter Two examines Browning's *Sordello* and argues that the text not only displays an awareness of *Valperga* but also constitutes a *response* to it. Whilst *Valperga* suggests that egotism, as a male quality, is gender-specific, *Sordello* challenges such an assumption through its presentation of its heroine, Palma. Politically speaking, Mary Shelley's republicanism finds a successor in Browning's *Sordello*, which confirms Browning's allegiance to the political tradition to which Mary Shelley belonged.

Chapter Three examines Browning's painter poems, namely, 'Fra Lippo Lippi' and 'Old Pictures in Florence'. I place Browning in the context of the art criticism of the nineteenth century to argue that he was working against the critical orthodoxy as represented by people such as John Ruskin, Mary Shelley and Anna Jameson and that he was advocating his own aesthetics through his painter poems.

Chapter Four focuses on Shelley's *The Cenci* and Browning's *The Ring and the Book*, works that have long been acknowledged to have a strong connection but have only recently started to attract critical attention.[62] I see *The Ring* as re-writing *The Cenci*: Browning seems to be altering the case put forward by Shelley, who could only write his poem as a reflection of a 'sad reality'. I argue that both texts reflect the question of Italian independence: *The Cenci* resonates

61 Chapman and Stabler, *Unfolding the South*, pp. 11–12.
62 See Fermanis, 'Anatomising the "Case"', pp. 37–50.

with the pessimistic mood of the post-Napoleonic period, whereas *The Ring* suggests optimism for Italian independence.

Chapter Five looks at one of Browning's later works, *Fifine at the Fair*, in relation to Shelley's 'The Triumph of Life'. Both poems are written as a vision and therefore share certain qualities. For example, they represent society through a pageant in the case of 'The Triumph' and a carnival in *Fifine*. The driving and obstructive forces of the poems are 'desire' and 'anxiety', which coexist in the speaker. These are never resolved in 'The Triumph', owing to Shelley's sudden death, but reach a certain conclusion in *Fifine*. I argue again that Browning is developing some of the issues that Shelley raises in 'The Triumph'.

Chapter Six traces the development of Shelley's influence on Elizabeth Barrett through three sections. The first section argues that Barrett's early poems have some affinities with Shelley's poems, particularly in their conscious determination to participate in the same liberal tradition that Shelley evokes repeatedly in his poetry. The second section examines Barrett's 'A Vision of Poets' and Shelley's 'The Triumph of Life' by focusing on the similarities and continuities of themes in both poems as well as their differences. The final section contends that Barrett's *Casa Guidi Windows* makes use of Shelleyan ideas and tropes for her own political ends.

This book demonstrates how the Brownings engaged with the Shelleys' texts by re-imagining them in their own works, so that they shed fresh light on the subject matter whilst still retaining traces of their influence. My critical interests have much in common with Antony H. Harrison's concerns:

> with the ways in which works of literature perpetually reconstitute themselves, both *as* they are experienced over history by readers with changing horizons of expectations and *in* the works of subsequent writers, where the originary text serves as 'palimpsest'.[63]

Mapping of influence enables us to appreciate how texts operate in myriad ways, sometimes quite independently from the authors in question.

---

63 Harrison, *Victorian Poets*, pp. 7–8.

CHAPTER ONE

Frankenstein and *Paracelsus*

Vigorous, terrible, and with its interest sustained to the last, Frankenstein is certainly one of the most original works that ever proceeded from a female pen. [...] We remember being greatly struck with this work on its first appearance; and our second reading has revived all our early impressions: the romantic excitement of its pages well repays their perusal.[1]

Whether Browning agreed with the anonymous reviewer quoted above remains a moot point; however, Mary Shelley's second edition of *Frankenstein*, published in 1831 (13 years after its original publication), may well have caught Browning's attention. He was, during this period, still steeped in Shelley's poetry; Mary's status as Shelley's wife alone would have been enough to arouse the later poet's interest in her novel. Moreover, there is sufficient evidence in the text of Browning's own *Paracelsus* (1835) to allow us to infer that Browning may well have read and digested *Frankenstein*. Consequently, this chapter reads Mary Shelley's *Frankenstein* and Browning's *Paracelsus* alongside one another, and, in so doing, it investigates whether such a comparison renders the abstruse thematic of Browning's notoriously difficult poem a little clearer.[2] Whilst the Longman editors single

1 From a review of *Frankenstein*, in *London Literary Gazette & Journal of Belles Lettres, Arts, Sciences, Etc.* (19 November 1831), pp. 740–42 (740).
2 See George Myerson, 'Paracelsus: The Science of the Text', *Browning Society Notes* 15.2 & 3 (winter/spring 1985–86): 20–47. Myerson notes that *Frankenstein*, like *Paracelsus*, is a text that also makes the connection between 'neoplatonism and a drive towards experiences' (36), but does not elaborate on the common points of these two texts.

out Shelley's *Prometheus Unbound* as 'a source for P[aracelsus]'s aloof service to mankind',[3] I would argue that *Frankenstein* (which, of course, preceded Shelley's poem) additionally serves as a source for *Paracelsus*. It thus becomes pertinent that the novel's subtitle is 'the modern Prometheus', which features a protagonist who attempts to serve humankind in vain. Just as with Victor Frankenstein, Paracelsus also fails to achieve his Promethean goal. In light of their frustrated efforts to become a Promethean hero, it is my contention that both Mary Shelley's and Browning's protagonists, and their respective fates and failures, are ultimately designed to serve as a critique of (a certain kind of) Prometheanism. Strictly speaking, there are two *kinds* of Prometheanism in question: one that strives after human enlightenment and the betterment of society, and one that seeks to defy both the laws of God and the laws of nature. My emphasis will be on the latter rather than the former, but, before we examine either in relation to the two texts, let us begin by exploring Prometheanism itself.

It is often thought that Shelley's *magnum opus*, *Prometheus Unbound* (1820), is the Romantic text that defines, and is emblematic of, Romantic Prometheanism. This is partly true, but there are other, equally relevant texts, particularly with regard to *Frankenstein*, given that Mary Shelley's novel appeared before her husband's poem. The central texts that inaugurated the Romantic idea of the Promethean myth are Goethe's unfinished drama *Prometheus* and the similarly titled hymn that derives from it, both of which were composed around the same time in 1773, and Byron's poem 'Prometheus' (1816). Although, strictly speaking, Goethe's texts fall outside what we conceive of as the Romantic period, the new paradigm that Goethe created, through his deployment of the Promethean myth, rightly belongs to Romanticism. Goethe not only *humanises* Prometheus but also presents him as an artist like himself.[4] This artistic self-identification with Prometheus is also perceptible in Byron's text, with the difference being that the latter's primary focus is on the punishment of Prometheus by Zeus. What had previously been *godlike* attributes— Prometheus *plasticator* or *pyrophorous*—become de-deified in these new iterations. Thus, Prometheus is humanised and politicised,

---

3 *Poems of Browning* 1: 104.

4 See Caroline Corbeau-Parsons, *Prometheus in the Nineteenth Century: From Myth to Symbol* (Oxford: Legenda Books, 2013), p. 48.

becoming not only an artist but also the possessor of an anti-authoritarian, rebellious spirit and a compassionate heart, who seeks the betterment of humanity even at the cost of his own life.

Prometheus *pyrophorous* (a fire-giver) is emphasised in *Frankenstein* and *Paracelsus* by means of their protagonists' essentially heroic endeavour to better the human condition. The narrative structure of *Frankenstein* enables us to appreciate this. Walton's colossal aspirations echo those of Victor Frankenstein, only to be curbed by the latter's mistakes in pursuing the Promethean ideal at all costs, leading him to accept his own limitations in the face of the dangers posed to his fellow human beings. Whilst Mary Shelley does not condemn Prometheanism outright, she, nonetheless, implies that *self-restraint* is required in order to preserve *domestic* peace and happiness that then extends more generally to societal wellbeing and harmony. Therefore, her text leans towards Burke and Wordsworth in their embrace of tradition and communal solidarity. Whether it can be called a conservative text is debatable, but it is certainly not a radical text in terms of the politics that it endorses.

The politics of *Paracelsus*, however, depart from those of *Frankenstein* inasmuch as Browning uses his protagonist to express his own faith in gradualism:

> 'Tis in the advance of individual minds
> That the slow crowd should ground their expectation
> Eventually to follow—as the sea
> Waits ages in its bed, till some one wave
> Of all the multitudinous mass extends
> The empire of the whole, some feet perhaps,
> Over the strip of sand which could confine
> Its fellows so long time: thenceforth the rest,
> Even to the meanest, hurry in at once,
> And so much is clear gain'd. (3. 883–92)

Whilst 'individual minds' pioneer 'in the advance' of human progress, 'the slow crowd' will 'follow' their example, with 'the meanest' completing that advancement. The failure of Paracelsus is not simply owing to his lack of human sympathy or humility (as I shall argue below); rather, he is ahead of his time. That is to say, his Promethean efforts ultimately will not be in vain because there will always remain (at least the possibility of) others who will assume his role and who will advance his scientific research: 'though I [Paracelsus] sink, another may succeed?' (2. 196). Browning asks us to believe that only an accumulation of scientific endeavours will bring about the societal progress he so desires.

Browning's correlated faith in human perfectibility is also discernible in *Paracelsus* (although he is not as explicit in his endorsement as he is in the later *Sordello*):

> For all these things tend upward—progress is
> The law of life—man is not man as yet:
> Nor shall I deem his object served, his end
> Attain'd, his genuine strength put fairly out,
> While only here and there a star dispels
> The darkness—here and there a towering mind
> O'erlooks its crawling fellows; when the host
> Is out at once to the despair of night;
> When all mankind is perfected alike,
> Equal in full-blown powers—then, not till then,
> Begins the general infancy of man;
> * * *
> When all the race is perfected alike
> As *man*, that is: all tended to mankind
> And, man produced, all has its end thus far (5. 729–58)

In societies where only few individuals excel, 'man is not man'. In other words, human society must wait until every individual becomes as fully enlightened as the *most* enlightened and likewise until all races become similarly equal. This is indeed a rehearsal of Godwinian perfectibility; it is clear that Browning subscribes to it despite his concerns regarding any Romantic transformation of society led by Promethean figures.

Browning's politics have often been discussed, particularly with regard to his later years, but there is no question that, in his early manhood, he adhered to radical politics. *Paracelsus*, for all its religious connotations, is, in truth, a radical text. It not only deals with an occultist as its protagonist but also situates Paracelsus's scientific aspirations within the socio-political context of the time. In other words, the peasant uprising is inscribed as being a precedent to the protests of the English Levellers, whilst, in socio-religious terms, Luther figures as the forerunner of Protestantism. It is in these contexts that we are invited to assess Paracelsus and his laying of the foundations for modern science.

What gives the text a radical edge, however, is the socio-political context not only of sixteenth-century Germany but also of eighteenth-century Europe, culminating in the French Revolution. If we take on board the argument of influence that I delineated in the introduction to this book, it becomes apparent that the kind of radicalism Browning is tapping into, and capitalises on, derives from *Frankenstein*—a text that deliberately evokes the revolutionary milieu of eighteenth-century Europe. The main protagonist of the novel, Victor, is a member of an illustrious family in Geneva (which is also Rousseau's native city and itself a republic at the time), who becomes educated at the University of Ingolstadt, where the revolutionary Illuminati based their activities. He studies natural philosophy via occult science, both of which were associated with radical politics at the time. The setting of the novel and its various references could not have been more explicit in the novel's association with radicalism. The list can easily go on if we consider the books the creature reads as a means to assimilating into human society.[5] There is no doubt that both Victor and the creature are products of the Enlightenment and serve as doppelgangers to each other; therefore, to explore their relationship is to follow the Rousseauist argument of the noble savage vs the civilised man. It is clear that Mary Shelley sought to situate her Promethean hero in the fermenting environment of the 1790s or 'shortly before'.[6]

This connection in *Frankenstein* between occult science and political radicalism, with Germany serving as the hub, is carried over to Browning's *Paracelsus* so that, without the poet's direct discussion of radical politics, the poem comes to be associated with these in the manner of a palimpsest. This reinstatement of radicalism (mediated through the earlier novel) is partly what Browning means by his statement, with reference to *Paracelsus*, that

I shall affix my name & stick my arms akimbo; there are precious bold bits here & there, & the drift & scope are awfully radical,—I

---

5 For example, 'Volney's *Ruins* remained a force in English radicalism throughout the first half of the nineteenth century'; see the notes to *Frankenstein, or The Modern Prometheus: 1818 Text*, ed. Marilyn Butler (Oxford: Oxford University Press, 1993), p. 257.

6 *Frankenstein*, ed. Butler, p. 259.

am 'off' for ever with the other side, but must by all means be 'on' with yours—a position once gained, worthier works shall follow[.]⁷

Browning's condemnation of Paracelsus for his transgression does not negate the latter's role in history; his contribution to science will be carried forth by others to materialise in the future. In that sense, Browning is a radical in advancing progressive history. Unlike Mary Shelley, Browning does not simply condemn but seeks to salvage Romanticism in his own radical gesture. In other words, Paracelsus's aspiration is not entirely disapproved of; rather, it is acknowledged as part of the gradualist progress of humankind. This approbation of political gradualism distinguishes the text from *Frankenstein*'s outright condemnation of the apocalyptic transformations potentially wrought on human society by misguided, 'Promethean' endeavours. Browning is more conciliatory. He does not punish Promethean effort altogether but gently warns the readers that love and humility must accompany any such endeavour.

Let us now turn to the inscription of Prometheus as an over-reacher, one who defies the laws of God, nature and society. It is worth noting that this line of criticism, as it concerns *Frankenstein*, is fundamentally feminist in nature. Although feminist readings of *Frankenstein* tended to focus on the immediate male figures—such as Godwin, Byron and Shelley—as the target of Mary Shelley's critique, it is worth noting that she uses the Promethean artist as a means to explore and critique masculine egotism.

Frankenstein, of course, was dedicated to Mary Shelley's father, William Godwin. The gesture, however, if one reminds oneself of the novel's plot and outcome, is not necessarily a straightforward homage to Godwin: Victor Frankenstein does not change the world for the better as might be expected of a Promethean character. So what did Mary Shelley mean by this dedication? It is hard to disagree with feminist readings of *Frankenstein* that identify an ironic, if not a critical, assessment of the Promethean efforts that Shelley had witnessed first-hand in the men surrounding her.⁸ After

---

7 *Brownings' Correspondence* 3: 134–35.
8 See George Levine, 'The Ambiguous Heritage of *Frankenstein*', in *Endurance of Frankenstein: Essays on Mary Shelley's Novel*, ed. George Levine and U. C. Knoepflmacher (Berkeley: University of California Press, 1979), pp. 3–30

all, it was Godwin who tried to transform society on the basis of the advancement of reason, and it was Shelley who likewise attempted a societal change through politicised concepts of imagination and love. However, unlike the mythological Prometheus, who succeeded in providing fire (knowledge) to humans, thus liberating them, the efforts of both Godwin and Shelley were scorned and condemned. Broadly speaking, one might discern two responses to the failures of the two men. One is to assert that society is at fault for not understanding and embracing those higher aims and principles. The other is to claim boldly that the very exercise of transforming the world is necessarily an act of blasphemy or, at the very least, an act of arrogance. This latter response, to which I now turn my attention, we might term 'anti-Prometheanism'.

Browning's gradual move away from Shelley has been explained in terms of the later poet's gradual detection of, and disenchantment with, the earlier poet's solipsistic and self-elevating conception of the poet, which militated against Browning's less rarified, more socially engaged, idea(l). For example, it has been pointed out that Browning derived his idea of Paracelsus from Shelley's *Alastor* poet, who alienates himself from society to pursue his own idealism.[9] Just as with Paracelsus, the poet is unable to fulfil his mission and is condemned to an early death. However, Browning, as it were, re-socialises this Shelleyan conception, by stressing the futility of such solitary endeavours inasmuch as he claims that their very severance from society and human relationships ensures the spiritual death of the protagonist.

Browning, through his inability to maintain his personal aspirations towards Shelleyan lyricism, has also been accused of a perceived 'failure' to become the visionary poet that Shelley was. For instance, in an earlier poem of his, *Pauline* (1833), Browning indeed tried his hand at self-revelatory lyricism, only to be scorned by J. S. Mill. Browning's next major effort, *Paracelsus* (1835), however,

(4); Peter Dale Scott, 'Vital Artifice: Mary, Percy, and the Psychopolitical Integrity of *Frankenstein*', in *Endurance of Frankenstein*, pp. 172–202 (172, 189); Anne K. Mellor, *Mary Shelley, Her Life, Her Fiction, Her Monsters* (New York: Routledge, 1988), pp. 70–71.

9 See William Hall Griffin and H. C. Minchin, *The Life of Robert Browning, with Notices from His Writings, His Family and His Friends* (London: Methuen, 1938), pp. 66–69.

marks both a move away from, and a continuation of, his attempt at lyricism. There has been a debate as to whether *Paracelsus* succeeds more in dramatic or in lyrical terms. Park Honan, for one, sees the latter: 'It is for its lyrical qualities, surely, and not for its dramatic ones that Paracelsus deserves to be read', whilst John Maynard contends that Browning's swerve away from Shelley took place even before *Pauline*, thereby insisting on the overall 'realistic and dramatic' tone of *Paracelsus*.[10] Browning was to outline this trajectory—from lyricism to drama and then to something else as yet unnamed, which turns out to be dramatic monologue—in his epic poem of 1840, *Sordello*. In light of this progression, we can assume that Browning was consciously moving from one form of poetry to another and that it is therefore not surprising to detect elements of each in *Paracelsus*, if we regard it as a transitional text from lyricism to drama. For Browning, lyricism implied the revelation of one's inner self that was characteristic of Romantic poetry. As he would outline in his 'Essay on Shelley' (1852), Browning intentionally tried to write poetry that was more 'objective' and adhering to 'real' events and characters. Whilst *Paracelsus* is a closet drama that has the inner workings of the protagonist as its central focus, it also employs a detached viewpoint from which the characters can be discerned. In this respect, *Paracelsus* might be called both a Romantic and an anti-Romantic text at once.

We might also discern, in Browning's poem, an alternative source of such anti-Romanticism, in Mary Shelley's writings. Her feminist critique of Shelleyan Romanticism is echoed in Browning's unease with Shelley's idea of masculine sublimity. Moreover, Mary Shelley's condemnation of Victor Frankenstein—whose trajectory closely follows that of Shelley's youth—finds a correlative in Browning's treatment of Paracelsus as the Romantic archetype. He is clearly an outstanding individual who would be entitled to be successful but fails miserably. The storyline of *Frankenstein* alone, with Victor as 'the [failed] modern Prometheus', lends support to the view that Mary Shelley was articulating an anti-Prometheanism in her novel. Furthermore, the treatment of issues of gender in the novel only serves to strengthen this view. Victor neglects his family and his

---

10 See Park Honan, *Browning's Characters: A Study in Poetic Technique* (New Haven: Yale University Press, 1961), p. 24; John Maynard, *Browning's Youth* (Cambridge, MA: Harvard University Press, 1977), p. 229.

fiancée to pursue his own scientific research. The irony of this is that, in the face of a greater cause for which he is working, he neglects the welfare of those who surround him. By doing so, he also fails to achieve his initial goal. The masculine egotism of the Romantic male figure results in the sacrifice of his dependents on the altar of his Promethean project.

Let us turn again to *Paracelsus* (1835), which concerns a Renaissance occultist who seeks to discover the secret of life by dedicating himself to its study. Despite the warnings of his friends—Festus and Michal (Festus's wife to be)—of the danger and futility of such a pursuit, Paracelsus is resolute and determined to achieve his goal without the help of previous scholars. In Part II, Paracelsus attains 'Knowledge', but feels it insufficient when a poet by the name of Aprile presents himself as advocating only 'Love'. In the face of Aprile, Paracelsus realises that he is lacking in the ability to 'Love'. In Part III, Paracelsus becomes the famed scholar of Basil only to be eventually exposed for his quackery. Festus visits Paracelsus in Basil thinking he has at last attained fame and recognition, but is told the truth. Paracelsus decides to pursue 'Knowledge' alone again in Part IV, without 'Love', which he has now come to discard. In Part V, Paracelsus tells Festus on his deathbed of the wisdom he gained by his failure to attain 'Knowledge' alone.

This brief examination of the structure of *Paracelsus* clearly enables us to appreciate how closely it follows that of *Frankenstein*, with the pursuit of scientific knowledge, followed by an outward success that hides the seeds of destruction and, finally, failure to achieve the initial goal. Paracelsus and Frankenstein are both depicted as victims of knowledge, whose inability to love humankind (the monster, in the case of Victor Frankenstein) brings about their ultimate ruin. That this knowledge comes at the expense of their great endeavour, followed by equally great failure, lies at the heart of both texts.

The *Biographie universelle* (1822), which Browning is known to have used for his depiction of Paracelsus, mentions nothing about his mission to serve mankind or his deficiency in Love—the two most significant points that Browning makes in his inscription of Paracelsus. In Part I, Browning clearly states that Paracelsus wishes to serve humankind thus: 'To make some unexampled sacrifice / In their behalf' (1. 470–71). As for his lack of Love, it is not only that a fictional character that embodies Love to illustrate Paracelsus's deficiency is created by Browning but also that the theme of Love runs throughout the whole poem. Paracelsus is clearly inscribed as a Promethean figure. Although Shelley's *Prometheus Unbound* is no doubt a source for Browning's poem, the central themes of *Frankenstein* are so closely aligned to those of *Paracelsus* that it becomes conceivable that the poem is in some way a conscious echo of the earlier novel. For example, one passage suggests Browning's familiarity with the novel.[11] In Part V, where Paracelsus is addressing Festus at his deathbed, Paracelsus refers to what may be 'the making and awaking of the monster':

> For wherefore make account of feverish starts
> Of restless members of a dormant whole—
> Impatient nerves which quiver whilst the body
> Slumbers as in a grave? O long ago
> The brow was twitch'd, the tremulous lids astir,
> The peaceful mouth disturb'd—half-utter'd speech
> Ruffled the lip; sometimes the teeth were set,
> The breath drawn sharp, the strong right-hand clench'd
>   stronger—
> As it would pluck a lion by the maw:
> The glorious creature laugh'd out even in sleep!
>   (5. 740–49)

This brings to mind the scene in *Frankenstein* where the creature comes to life for the first time. Or, to take another example, Festus calls Paracelsus '[t]he thinker, the explorer, the creator' (5. 373), which aligns both Walton and Frankenstein with Paracelsus.

So, to reiterate, I am suggesting not only that Browning had read *Frankenstein* but also that, if one reads *Paracelsus* in tandem with the earlier novel, their points of similarity are thrown into sharp relief. Each features a Romantic protagonist who echoes either Godwin, in his pursuit of human happiness on the basis of reason, or Shelley, in his aspirations after a just society. Mary Shelley, as I have already noted, was familiar with not only the political and literary endeavours of each but also their respective failures. *Frankenstein* can be read as a monument to such futility, insisting that the socio-political context of the time was not propitious enough for the realisation of

---

11 *Poems of Browning* 1: 302.

Godwinian or Shelleyan ideals, and that the failure to recognise this unpropitiousness in itself ensured that such aspirations were doomed never to be realised. As the 1831 edition of *Frankenstein* makes clear, Mary Shelley accentuated the religiosity of the novel. She did this through her suggestion that Victor Frankenstein's aspirations to become the creator of a living being are fundamentally blasphemous. This religious component of *Frankenstein* is echoed in *Paracelsus*, as are the protagonist's efforts to serve humankind. Paracelsus is the Romantic hero on a mission to better humankind, who fails because of his lack of both love and humility.

Paracelsus's ambition and desire to serve humankind are clearly delineated in Part I during his conversation with Festus and Michal. His desire to acquire knowledge is described at length, indicating his single-mindedness and sense of himself as the chosen one. Paracelsus seeks to reign by knowledge, and Browning's characterisation of him arguably owes much to the depiction of those men who sought power or knowledge in various writings of Mary Shelley's. An obvious example might be Castruccio in *Valperga* (1823), whose sole ambition is to become the prince of the region and whose abnormal will to rule suggests from the outset that he will grow to be a tyrant:

> Thus, in solitude, while no censuring eye could check the exuberant vanity, he would throw his arms to the north, the south, the east, and the west, crying,—'There—there—there, and there, shall my fame reach!'—and then, in gay defiance, casting his eager glance towards heaven:—'and even there, if man may climb the slippery sides of the arched palace of eternal fame, there also will I be recorded'.[12]

In similar terms, Paracelsus pursues the knowledge that he hopes will enlighten the world:

> I can devote myself; I have a life
> To give; I, who am singled out for this.
> Think, think; the wide east, where old Wisdom sprung:
> The bright south, where she dwelt; the populous north,
> All are pass'd o'er—it lights on me. 'Tis time
> New hopes should animate the world—new light

12 *N&SW of Mary Shelley* 3: 23.

> Should dawn from new revealings to a race
> Weigh'd down so long, forgotten so long (1. 389–96)

In both quotations, the protagonists' will to acquire and exercise power (whether to reign politically or intellectually) is depicted by their unnatural desire to exert influence over all terrains on earth. Paracelsus's ambition is furthermore characterised by his wish to serve humankind. This thirsting after knowledge, not for his sake but for that of others, is what drives Victor Frankenstein in his scientific enquiry and in the creation of the monster. In this respect, both figures are Promethean characters that seek to promote the welfare of humankind. Frankenstein, in his invocation of occultists such as Cornelius Agrippa, Paracelsus and Albertus Magnus, seeks to 'banish disease from the human frame, and render man invulnerable to any but a violent death'.[13] Paracelsus likewise expresses his wish to save humankind:

> To make some unexampled sacrifice
> In their behalf—to wring some wondrous good
> From heaven or earth for them—to perish, winning
> Eternal weal in the act: as who should dare
> Pluck out the angry thunder from its cloud,
> That, all its gather'd flame discharged on him,
> No storm might threaten summer's azure weather—
>   (1. 470–76)

This clear reference to Prometheus, who gave fire to humankind, thereby provoking the anger of Zeus, imbues both texts with a perceptible anti-Romanticism by implying that *any* human emulation of the gods will necessarily end badly. Unlike Shelley's Prometheus, the effort of the protagonists does not liberate the world or themselves but becomes a curse that takes them to their doom. The figure of a Romantic artist/scientist who stands above humankind in his sublimity is condemned in both texts. In *Frankenstein*, the animation of the creature is presented as a blasphemous act due to Victor's impingement on the realm of God as the Creator of all things. The fact that the monster is fated to be hated by humans is the price of such violation. In *Paracelsus*, the scientist's/occultist's confidence in

13 *Frankenstein*, ed. Butler, p. 23.

revealing the secret of life is in itself arrogance that has to be humbled to accept human limitation in the face of God.

The disappointment and the anguish that both protagonists experience after achieving so-called success—the attainment of knowledge for Paracelsus and the creation of the monster for Frankenstein—are worth noting. Paracelsus communicates the extent of his sorrow to Festus:

> Oh, bitter; very bitter!
> And more bitter
> To fear a deeper curse, and inner ruin—
> Plague beneath plague—the last turning the first
> To light beside its darkness. Let me weep
> My youth and its brave hopes, all dead and gone,
> In tears which burn. Would I were sure to win
> Some startling secret in their stead! a tincture
> Of force to flush old age with youth, or breed
> Gold, or imprison moonbeams till they change
> To opal shafts! only that, hurling it
> Indignant back, I might convince myself
> My aims remain'd supreme and pure as ever!
> Even now, why not desire, for mankind's sake,
> That if I fail, it may be for some fault;
> That, though I sink, another may succeed?
> I cannot! O God, I am despicable!
> Shut out this hideous mockery from my heart! ...
> (2. 182–98)

Although Paracelsus has gained his long sought-after knowledge, he nonetheless feels that he is missing something. In other words, what he has attained will not 'effect the perfect happiness of mankind' as he had originally hoped; and he is forced to face up to this reality as he 'reviews resolutely his Knowledge'.[14] Paracelsus's self-hatred in this passage echoes that of Victor Frankenstein. Upon the latter's creation of the monster, which turns against the maker, Victor is filled with an emotion that manifests itself as a repulsion at his own existence:

---

14 See Browning's own remarks made to his friend Comte A. de Ripert-Monclar to whom the poem was dedicated (*Brownings' Correspondence* 3: 420).

I wandered like an evil spirit, for I had committed deeds of mischief beyond description horrible, and more, much more, (I persuaded myself) was yet behind. [...] I had begun life with benevolent intentions, and thirsted for the moment when I should put them in practice, and make myself useful to my fellow-beings. Now all was blasted: instead of that serenity of conscience, which allowed me to look back upon the past with self-satisfaction, and from thence to gather promise of new hopes, I was seized by remorse and the sense of guilt, which hurried me away to a hell of intense tortures, such as no language can describe.[15]

Although Paracelsus does not share the guilt that Frankenstein suffers from, he nonetheless becomes prey to self-inflicted misery, and certainly, his pursuit of knowledge comes at the expense of sacrificing his own emotional life. Paracelsus's realisation of this comes too late, as follows:

> But were it so—were man all mind—the station
> He gains is little enviable. From God
> Down to the lowest spirit ministrant
> Intelligence exists which casts *our* mind
> Into immeasurable shade. No, no:
> Love, hope, fear, faith—these make humanity;
> These are its sign, and note, and character;
> And these I have lost! gone; shut from me for ever
> (3. 1036–44)

It is emotional, rather than intellectual, life that distinguishes humanity. The fact that Paracelsus sought the 'mind' alone leaves him with the knowledge that he has overestimated its significance. The warning that what Paracelsus pursues is a chimera that is accompanied by danger comes in the voice of a Wordsworthian figure. Festus, who lives the peaceful life of a 'quiet mountain-cloistered priest' (3. 875) in domestic bliss in his native city, suggests the stereotype of the secluded poet that Wordsworth, in his retirement in the Lake District, is so often used to represent. He lectures Paracelsus on the importance of human solidarity, without which man cannot live: 'How can that course be safe which from the first /

---

15 *Frankenstein*, ed. Butler, p. 69.

Produces carelessness to human love?' (1. 626–27). He then proceeds to argue as follows:

> you shall
> Go forth upon your arduous task alone,
> None shall assist you—none partake your toil—
> None share your triumph—still you must retain
> Some one to trust your glory to; to share
> Your rapture with. Had I been chosen like you
> I should encircle me with love (1. 634–40)

What Paracelsus lacks is the only thing that matters to Festus: sympathy with his fellow beings.

It is possible to trace this Wordsworthian figure to a character in *Frankenstein*. Of course, it is more than probable, and even natural, to consider Browning's inscription of this character as being motivated by Wordsworth himself. However, if we attend to the fact that this typecasting of Wordsworth is meant to represent an *idea*, the example from Mary Shelley's novel cannot be ignored, particularly if this character is meant to exist as an antipode to Victor. In *Frankenstein*, we can see how Henry Clerval, Victor's best friend, embodies Wordsworthian qualities, as illustrated in two distinct descriptions. First, his ability to appreciate nature and human ties stands out as his most prominent feature. When they go on an excursion to the outskirts of Ingolstadt, Victor becomes restored to his former self (i.e. as one who is perceptive of natural beauty and human warmth) with the aid of Clerval. We are told that

> [s]tudy had before secluded me from the intercourse of my fellow-creatures, and rendered me unsocial; but Clerval called forth the better feelings of my heart; he again taught me to love the aspect of nature, and the cheerful faces of children.[16]

It is interesting to note that one's salubriousness is measured by using sensitivity towards nature as the yardstick. Victor is conscious of the harmful effects of his scientific research when he admits to Clerval that

---

16 *Frankenstein*, ed. Butler, pp. 50–51.

[a] selfish pursuit had cramped and narrowed me, until your gentleness and affection warmed and opened my senses; I became the same happy creature who, a few years ago, loving and beloved by all, had no sorrow or care.[17]

As I stated earlier, to warm to other human beings is related to one's ability to appreciate nature so that

[a] serene sky and verdant fields filled me [that is, Victor] with ecstasy. The present season was indeed divine; the flowers of spring bloomed in the hedges, while those of summer were already in bud[.][18]

This connection between a healthy mind and receptivity towards nature manifests itself most forcefully when Victor is once again thrown into his own dark, obsessive passion, only this time to fulfil the wish of his creature to make a female partner for him. As we are told:

[f]illed with dreary imaginations, I passed through many beautiful and majestic scenes; but my eyes were fixed and unobserving. I could only think of the bourne of my travels, and the work which was to occupy me whilst they endured.[19]

Victor's mental state stands in sharp contrast to that of Clerval, who 'was alive to every new scene; joyful when he saw the beauties of the setting sun, and more happy when he beheld it rise, and recommence a new day'.[20]

There is another distinction that Mary Shelley introduces between these two characters that underscores the thesis put forward in one of Edmund Burke's first literary works, *A Philosophical Inquiry into the Origins of Our Ideas of the Sublime and the Beautiful* (1757).[21] According to Burke,

17 *Frankenstein*, ed. Butler, p. 51.
18 *Frankenstein*, ed. Butler, p. 51.
19 *Frankenstein*, ed. Butler, p. 128.
20 *Frankenstein*, ed. Butler, p. 128.
21 All quotations from this work are from *The Writings and Speeches of Edmund Burke*, ed. T. O. McLoughlin, James T. Boulton and William B. Todd (Oxford: Clarendon Press, 1997), 1: 210–320.

[w]hatever is fitted in any sort to excite the ideas of pain, and danger, that is to say, whatever is in any sort terrible, or is conversant about terrible objects, or operates in a manner analogous to terror, is a source of the *sublime*.[22]

Victor is repeatedly depicted as being attracted to nature in its exhibition of the sublime as defined by Burke. On one occasion, having taken an excursion to Chamonix with his family, Victor is reminded of his inclinations towards this kind of natural environment, as follows:

I remembered the effect that the view of the tremendous and ever-moving glacier had produced upon my mind when I first saw it. It had then filled me with a sublime ecstacy that gave wings to the soul, and allowed it to soar from the obscure world to light and joy. The sight of the awful and majestic in nature had indeed always the effect of solemnizing my mind, and causing me to forget the passing cares of life.[23]

Mary Shelley, no doubt, gives Victor the Romantic image of a solitary scientist in the midst of nature that has become trite to readers instructed in such iconography. Yet she also makes sure that its antipode, the beautiful, is represented as well. For Clerval expresses his preference for the exact opposite as he travels along the Rhine with Victor, as follows:

The mountains of Switzerland are more majestic and strange: but there is a charm in the banks of this divine river, that I never before saw equaled. [...] Oh, surely, the spirit that inhabits and guards this place has a source more in harmony with man, than those who pile the glacier, or retire to the inaccessible peaks of the mountains of our own country.[24]

In truth, what Burke describes as beautiful is 'a social quality'.[25] Whilst Victor consistently prefers solitude, Clerval seeks society, regardless of whether that is of his family or friends.

22 *Writings and Speeches of Edmund Burke*, p. 216.
23 *Frankenstein*, ed. Butler, pp. 74–75.
24 *Frankenstein*, ed. Butler, p. 129.
25 *Writings and Speeches of Edmund Burke*, p. 219.

The solitary scientist represents one aspect of Shelley as Mary Shelley regarded him. Clerval's approximation to Wordsworth as the nature poet is another association Mary Shelley makes in her novel. We are told that '[h]e was a being formed in the "very poetry of nature"' and that '[t]he scenery of external nature, which others regard only with admiration, he loved with ardour'.[26] What exactly Mary Shelley meant by this is explained in her quote from Wordsworth's 'Tintern Abbey':

> 'The sounding cataract
> Haunted *him* like a passion: the tall rock,
> The mountain, and the deep and gloomy wood,
> Their colours and their forms, were then to him
> An appetite: a feeling, and a love,
> That had no need of a remoter charm,
> By thought supplied, or any interest
> Unborrowed from the eye'.[27]

Although it may be somewhat far-fetched, I wonder if we can read in Clerval's ability to enrich himself through nature the kind of 'second nature' that James Chandler discusses in his book on Wordsworth.[28] In *Wordsworth's Second Nature*, Chandler argues that Wordsworth held both nature and second nature as the sources of a deep-seated passion that instructs the poet, in a way similar to that in which they coexisted for Edmund Burke. What the last four lines above signify comes close to what Burke (and thereby Wordsworth, who was in agreement with Burke) describes as the 'untaught feelings'.[29] In other words, 'a feeling, and a love' are not something gained through 'thought' or metaphysical examination but are attained through intuition that derives from the act of seeing nature and 'a "lore which nature brings" without having to resort to rational method',[30] to quote Chandler again.

Although Clerval does not warn Victor of the futility of his pursuits in the same way that Festus does with Paracelsus, he still

---

26 *Frankenstein*, ed. Butler, p. 130.
27 *Frankenstein*, ed. Butler, p. 130.
28 James K. Chandler, *Wordsworth's Second Nature: A Study of the Poetry and Politics* (Chicago: University of Chicago Press, 1984).
29 *Writings and Speeches of Edmund Burke*, p. 183.
30 Chandler, *Wordsworth's Second Nature*, p. 130.

remains an example of a healthy mind that is in harmony with nature and society. Rather, any such warning comes from Victor himself, to Walton, the adventurer, who is pursuing the dangerous task of going to the North Pole, even at the risk of his fellow sailors' lives: 'Seek happiness in tranquility, and avoid ambition, even if it be only the apparently innocent one of distinguishing yourself in science and discoveries.'[31] Festus similarly persuades Paracelsus to abandon his ambitious aim, lest the following comes true:

> there would be
> A monstrous spectacle upon the earth,
> Beneath the pleasant sun, among the trees,
> A being knowing not what love is. (1. 685–88)

Michal likewise expresses her concern over Paracelsus's aspiration thus:

> cast those hopes away,
> And stay with us: an angel warns me, too,
> Man should be humble; you are very proud!
> And God dethroned has doleful plagues for such!
> (1. 709–12)

Man's challenge to the supremacy of God denotes both in *Frankenstein* and in *Paracelsus* a blasphemy that will bring tragic consequences.

For all the critique of Romantic egotism in both texts, it is also the case that the corrective to the egotistical excesses of both Frankenstein and Paracelsus nonetheless ultimately lies in Romanticism itself. As the monster in *Frankenstein* claims, it is the lack of human sympathy that turns the creature into a vengeful monster. This thematic dramatisation is also prevalent in *Paracelsus*. When Paracelsus encounters Aprile, he realises that his aspirations lack precisely what his alter ego, Aprile, embodies. Aprile, who 'would LOVE infinitely' (2. 345), is, in this respect, a Shelleyan figure, which demonstrates that Shelley still holds a central claim in Browning's philosophy. Indeed, as the Oxford editors note on Browning's 1888 text of *Paracelsus*, there are

---

31 *Frankenstein*, ed. Butler, p. 186.

numerous allusions to Shelley's poetry; they can be classified into poetic echoes on the one hand and engagements with, or invocations of, Shelleyan philosophy on the other.[32] Central to the latter is Love, and William O. Raymond argues that its twin manifestations, in Part II and Part V, are nonetheless different from one another, because its first manifestation is concerned with ideal Love, whereas its second concerns human Love, thereby implying Christian Love. Accordingly, this second manifestation represents Browning's departure from the Shelleyan model. However, it is at least arguable that both these kinds of Love are amply represented in Shelley's writings.[33] Browning himself would note, years later, in his 'Essay on Shelley', that 'the predominating sentiment of Shelley throughout his whole life' was 'sympathy with the oppressed'.[34] Sympathy seems to be the operative word here, denoting one's ability to transcend oneself in order to identify with others, a notion introduced by Adam Smith in his *Moral Sentiments* and used by Browning as the underlying ethos in his poetics, notwithstanding that Smith's conception of the word derives from rationalist principles whereas Browning's derives from Christian ones. If there is a nuanced deployment of the word 'Love' in Parts II and V, it is a question of emphasis rather than one of discrimination. In Shelley's *Prometheus Unbound*, 'love' and 'imagination' transform the world of division to that of oneness. It is initially Prometheus's reiteration of Jupiter's curse that operates to maintain Prometheus's own hatred for himself, thereby effecting division in his psyche. It is only with

32 For the former, see: Part III, line 315, 'scalding tears'; line 542, 'fungous'; line 556, 'The ungracious path'. For the latter, see: Part II, line 334, 'thy speedy ruin'; Part III, line 2, 'time'; line 982, 'the so-heavy chain'; Part V, line 187, 'Oh Persic Zoroaster'; line 228, 'the golden city'. See *The Poetical Works of Robert Browning*, Vol. 1, ed. Ian Jack and Margaret Smith (Oxford: Clarendon Press, 1983). Apart from Browning's mention of 'Zoroaster', all the other references exist in the first edition of 1835. What distinguishes the latter allusions is that Browning dips into Shelley's philosophical musings, such as his critique of solitude in *Alastor*, and his political idealism portrayed in *The Revolt of Islam* and *Prometheus Unbound*.

33 See William O. Raymond, *The Infinite Moment and Other Essays in Robert Browning* (Toronto: University of Toronto Press, 1950), pp. 164–65.

34 See Browning's 'Essay on Shelley' included in *Browning: Selected Poems*, ed. John Woolford, Daniel Karlin and Joseph Phelan (Harlow: Pearson Education, 2010), p. 869.

the power of Asia, who embodies love, plus the imagination of Ion (Asia's sister), that Prometheus is able to liberate himself. The lyrical drama thus succinctly illustrates the significance of love and imagination. This is also the case with Mary Shelley. Despite the anti-Romanticism evident in *Frankenstein*, Shelleyan love and imagination nonetheless constitute an essential part of her ideas, such that the main characters are imbued with Shelleyan qualities. In *Frankenstein*, self-knowledge comes too late to prevent Victor's damnation, but he is still described as 'noble and godlike in ruin'[35] by Walton.

The tragedy that befalls both Frankenstein and Paracelsus is that neither can divert the course of their action. In other words, in spite of their better impulses (to love humankind and the monster), neither can help but spurn the insight that the pursuit of knowledge has given them, and, in both cases, this precipitates their respective downfalls. They reject the consequences of their insight willingly and passionately. As Browning himself commented:

An accident brings the restlessness and unhappiness of Paracelsus to a crisis—he flings away the mask he has been constrained to wear—does not pretend any longer to love men or to care for their love—resolves to continue his pursuit of knowledge, *mere knowledge*, as one to which [h]is soul is wedded past retrieval, but knowledge for his own sake, or rather *its* own sake—without reference to man's welfare, or even his own[.][36]

In a manner similar to Paracelsus's, Frankenstein realises his inability to love his creation and continues to regard him with hatred when the monster seeks his sympathy and compassion by requesting the creation of a female monster as his sole company:

His [the monster's] words had a strange effect upon me. I compassionated him, and sometimes felt a wish to console him; but when I looked upon him, when I saw the filthy mass that moved and talked, my heart sickened, and my feelings were altered to those of horror and hatred.[37]

35 *Frankenstein*, ed. Butler, p. 179.
36 *Brownings' Correspondence* 3: 422.
37 *Frankenstein*, ed. Butler, p. 121.

Although, in *Frankenstein*, this realisation that without love knowledge has no meaning is only implied, it is openly declared in *Paracelsus*:

> I learn'd my own deep error: love's undoing
> Taught me the worth of love in man's estate,
> And what proportion love should hold with power
> In his right constitution: love preceding
> Power—with much power always much more love;
> Love still too straiten'd in its present means,
> And earnest for new power to set it free. (5. 841–47)

>   To sympathize—be proud
> Of their half-reasons, faint aspirings, struggles
> Dimly for truth—their poorest fallacies,
> And prejudice, and fears, and cares, and doubts;
> All with a touch of nobleness, for all
> Their error, all ambitious, upward tending,
> Like plants in mines which never saw the sun,
> But dream of him, and guess where he may be,
> And do their best to climb and get to him:
> All this I knew not, and I fail'd (5. 863–72)

Paracelsus comes to the realisation that 'Power' must be accompanied by 'Love'. He has neglected to reach out from his elevated station (as a scientist) to 'sympathise' with those who may be faulty in themselves but are nonetheless working to attain enlightenment ('do their best to climb and get to him [the sun]'). In this respect, *Paracelsus* responds to such failure by directly engaging the source of failure, unlike *Frankenstein*, which leaves much to be inferred by the reader.

Mary Shelley's nuanced treatment of Prometheanism is carried forward in *Paracelsus*, such that its advancement and its condemnation are embodied simultaneously in both. Perhaps the Promethean effort that leads potentially to societal progress in *Paracelsus* is an echo of other Romantic texts, such as *Prometheus Unbound*, as well; however, its critique is, I would contend, uniquely derived from Mary Shelley's text. Her feminist views gain a voice in *Paracelsus* as a condemnation of a masculine pride and arrogance that seeks to play the role of God. Neither text, however, repudiates Prometheanism completely;

rather, Prometheanism, as it figures in each text, is juxtaposed with the recognition that love and humility must accompany Promethean endeavours if they are even to stand a chance of success. In addition, in the case of Browning, the significance of gradualism is emphasised over the apocalyptic transformation of society advocated by the Romantics. Thus, each text under discussion here broadly conforms to the intellectual preferences of the age in which it was written. Mary Shelley's high Romanticism gives way to Browning's early Victorianism.

CHAPTER TWO

Valperga and *Sordello*

Italy, its history and its culture were enduring objects of fascination to nineteenth-century British writers, enough to make virtually all the leading literary figures of the period feel it necessary to visit.[1] Whilst the civilising ideals of the eighteenth-century Grand Tour had largely been the preserve of the aristocratic class, the more democratic nineteenth-century interest in Europe's cultural heritage was (partially) fuelled by a resurgent fascination with (romanticised) ideas of republicanism.[2] It had its roots in Italian culture and art initially, but it gained political impetus when the Italian exiles flooded into England, thereby informing the English of the state of what was still not a unified country. Indeed, Browning was led to his subject matter through his readings of Dante with the Italian exile and tutor Angelo Cerutti.[3] For those who sought to explore liberal ideas, Italy was particularly appealing for its rich past, which could be exploited without the fear of political censorship.[4]

1 See C. P. Brand, *Italy and the English Romantics: The Italianate Fashion in Early Nineteenth-Century England* (Cambridge: Cambridge University Press, 1957), p. 9.
2 Brand, *Italy and the English Romantics*, pp. 188–89.
3 Angelo Cerutti—'young, self-educated, and imaginative in temperament' as Browning knew him—was a teacher of Italian to middle-class residents of Camberwell, who prided himself on being a grammarian. Browning read Dante, Petrarch, Tasso, Ariosto and Boccaccio with him. See John Maynard, *Browning's Youth* (Cambridge, MA: Harvard University Press, 1977), pp. 304–07.
4 'By the summer of 1820, all the leading radicals, organizers, journalists, publishers, and distributors were confined in prison.' See John Belchem, *'Orator' Hunt: Henry Hunt and English Working-Class Radicalism* (Oxford: Clarendon Press, 1985), pp. 118–19.

Both Mary Shelley and Browning, in their writings, evoke a republican tradition that can be traced from ancient Greece and Rome to medieval Italy and seventeenth-century England, finally culminating in both the American and French Revolutions.[5] Their interest in the republican tradition comes as little surprise, given their dissenting background. Indeed, Godwin suggested to his daughter that she use the English Commonwealth as potential subject matter for her literary endeavours. However, instead of choosing domestic historical context for her writings, Mary turned to medieval Italy for *Valperga*, her historical novel.[6] In a parallel move from the Commonwealth to medieval Italy, Browning would write his play *Strafford* (1837), about the eponymous Thomas Wentworth Strafford (1593–1651), before trying his hand at his epic poem, *Sordello* (1840).

There are a number of striking similarities between *Valperga* and *Sordello*. The historical backdrop of each concerns the medieval city-states that were divided into Guelphs and Ghibellines,[7] but

5 An exhaustive list of writers (if that is at all possible) constituting that 'tradition' would be too long to detail here, but some key persons would be as follows: Aristotle, Polybius, Livy, Cicero, Sallust, Machiavelli, Milton, James Harrington, John Locke, Montesquieu, Rousseau, the founding fathers of America, William Godwin and Mary Wollstonecraft.

6 William Walling brings to our attention Godwin's suggestion to Mary in the summer of 1818 of writing 'a series of biographies that would be called "The Lives of the Commonwealth's Men", a collection that would deal inevitably with the political conflicts of seventeenth-century England'; this, however, might have provided an incentive for Mary to write on Castruccio instead of the 'Commonwealth men'. See William Walling, *Mary Shelley* (New York: Twayne, 1972), p. 62. Godwin took an active part in Mary's composition of *Valperga* (1823), the publication of which was intended to assist him financially; see *Letters of PBS* 2: 352–53. His involvement, however, seems to have been limited to 'mostly just cuts' rather than 'major rewritings or insertions'; see 'Introductory Note' by Nora Crook in *N&SW of Mary Shelley* 3: xiii.

7 Although the two terms do not have simple definitions: 'the Empire had a polarising effect and as communes came to form pro- or anti-imperial traditions so two rival diplomatic systems tended to crystallise. [...] The two words "Ghibelline" and "Guelph", though often used anachronistically by later writers, do not come into the vocabulary of Italian politics until the time of Frederick II (1220–50). [...] There was a tendency to identify an "imperial party" and a "Church party" in some of the cities before these came to acquire

the political clash between the two is also played out between the hero and the heroine. However, while Mary Shelley makes her protagonists emblematic of opposing ideologies and affiliations—her heroine, Euthanasia, is a republican, whilst her hero, Castruccio Castracani, is an imperialist—Browning reverses this so that his hero, Sordello, is associated with republicanism, and his heroine, Palma, conjures up an image of imperialism. Nonetheless, both authors seek to (re-)politicise their central protagonists and to exploit and re-write history for their own ends—the endorsement of democracy in the face of tyranny. However, both texts are also about working through the process of emotional or intellectual trauma; at one level, *Valperga* is about the interiority of emotional life as experienced by its two central female characters; *Sordello*, on the other hand, can be read as Browning's own rite of passage in becoming a poet. In other words, the tension that is created due to conflicting impulses—one to tell a story, and the other to come to terms with the act of writing it—characterises both texts. They also have much to say in terms of gender; Browning's liberty with historical facts enables him to respond to Mary Shelley's gendered argument about masculine egotism.

Mary Shelley conceived the general idea of what was to become the novel as early as 1817, when the Shelleys were still living in England.[8] It was not, however, until two years later, when they moved to Italy, that she began her research on the historical background of the novel.[9] It was another year (excepting the interim period of August 1819 to February 1820, during which she worked on *Mathilda*, a novella) before she began writing it. By the time *Valperga* was completed, four years had passed, and Shelley had

the labels of "Ghibelline" and "Guelph"'. The latter usage seems to have started in Florence around 1242 and then spread rapidly. See Daniel Waley, *The Italian City-Republics* (New York: McGraw-Hill, 1969), p. 201.

8 Mary refers to her conception of the novel and its date in a letter of 30 June 1821 to Maria Gisborne: '[i]t has been a child of mighty slow growth, since I first thought of it in our library at Marlow.' See *Letters of MWS* 1: 203.

9 Mary read J. C. L. Simonde de Sismondi's *History of the Italian Republics* '[i]n January and February, 1819'; 'in the early spring of 1820, she read both Machiavelli's and Niccolò Tegrimi's biographies of Castruccio'; '[i]n the autumn of that same year she read Sismondi again, along with Villani's history of Florence, continuing with the latter through the winter and into the spring of 1821'; see Walling, *Mary Shelley*, p. 53.

already written most of his major works, including *The Revolt of Islam* (1818), 'Julian and Maddalo' (1818–19), *The Cenci* (1819) and *Prometheus Unbound* (1820). Although *Valperga* is often regarded as a novel that breaks away from the dialogical relationship Mary Shelley had with Shelley, it can nonetheless be fruitfully read as constituting one side of an ongoing dialogue with Shelley.[10] Browning, therefore, is responding not only to Mary Shelley's novel but also to an ongoing textual discussion between both Shelleys. Therefore, although *Valperga* has been viewed through a feminist prism by some critics,[11] the central focus of my reading will be on its advocacy of a politicised Shelleyan Romanticism (and its pre-emptive defence of that Romanticism in the face of what would be its eventual defeat as a political movement). In *Sordello*, Browning, for his part, develops Mary Shelley's argument, to offer a politically realisable solution to the seemingly binary choices of republican liberalism and imperialist tyranny. Let me begin by giving a synopsis of both texts.

Valperga, or The Life and Adventures of Castruccio, Prince of Lucca (1823) is loosely based on the life of a *condottiere* of medieval Italy, Castruccio Castracani, and his wholly fictional romantic involvement with two invented female characters, Euthanasia and Beatrice. The political backdrop of the novel is the rivalry between the Guelphs and the Ghibellines that tore apart the Italian city-states as they divided into papal and imperial supporters. The novel opens with the expulsion of the Ghibellines from Lucca, of whom Castruccio Castracani dei Antelminelli, aged 11, was one. Years later, he seeks his advancement at the English court and then returns to the continent and finally to Lucca, where he is made a joint consul with Pagano Quartezzano. During Castruccio's ascent to fame, he revisits Valperga (the castle near Florence), of which Euthanasia becomes the sole heir. Their friendship (that had originated in their childhood) blossoms into love, and Euthanasia familiarises Castruccio with the creed with which she was brought up: love

---

10 As we have seen in Chapter One, Shelley's *Prometheus Unbound* was partly a response to Mary Shelley's *Frankenstein*.

11 See Anne K. Mellor, *Mary Shelley: Her Life, Her Fiction, Her Monsters* (New York: Routledge, 1988), pp. 209–10; Mary Poovey, *The Proper Lady and the Woman Writer: Ideology as Style in the Works of Mary Wollstonecraft, Mary Shelley, and Jane Austen* (Chicago: Chicago University Press, 1984), p. 146.

and peace upheld by wisdom. Castruccio promises Euthanasia that he will restore peace between the two factions. Meanwhile, a plot to restore Ferrara to the marquess of Este is in the process of maturation, and Castruccio is summoned to take part in the handing over of power from the Guelphs to the Ghibellines. There, Castruccio sees Beatrice, is struck by her beauty and is curious to learn of her past, which has been that of a heretic. Beatrice, under the illusion that she is divine, becomes convinced that the emotions she comes to feel towards Castruccio are themselves divinely inspired. These feelings are physically consummated, but, when she finds out that Castruccio is already betrothed to another woman, it shatters her illusion, if not her faith. Beatrice becomes a pilgrim and visits Euthanasia on her journey. Castruccio confesses to Euthanasia when questioned about Beatrice. His story dispels 'the illusion and exaltation of love' that Euthanasia felt for him. Meanwhile, Castruccio is made prince of Lucca and thereupon proceeds to declare war on Florence. It is no longer possible for Valperga to remain neutral, and Castruccio decides to storm the castle when his successive entreaties to Euthanasia prove to be in vain. Euthanasia loses her castle to Castruccio but remains at Lucca, where she is told of an imprisoned heretic, who turns out to be Beatrice. Because of Castruccio's influence, Beatrice is freed and placed under the protection of Euthanasia, who tries to bring her back to Catholicism. Beatrice, however, eventually spurns this guidance by falling under the influence of a witch, who suggests that she exercise her power over Castruccio. She confronts him but also encounters a sadistic, sexually abusive lord and dies of insanity. Whilst Castruccio hardens his ambition to rule over Tuscany, a conspiracy develops in Florence against him. Although Euthanasia has divided loyalties, she ultimately decides to join the conspiracy on the condition that Castruccio's life will be spared. When the plot is uncovered, the conspirators are condemned to death. Euthanasia escapes execution, only to be exiled to Sicily, on the way to which she is lost in a storm. The novel concludes with a brief account of Castruccio's life thereafter.

Browning's *Sordello*, published in 1840, shares the same historical background as Mary Shelley's novel. It was his first attempt at choosing an Italian subject. Like Mary Shelley, he uses as the basis of his plot the conflict between republican Guelph and imperial Ghibelline. This time, the hero of the poem, Sordello, is a Ghibelline, who later converts to the Guelph cause, as he comes to realise that it is more progressive. He starts out as a minstrel to Palma, the daughter of the head of the Ghibelline faction, Eccelin, later becoming emotionally involved with her. Sordello is really the son of Taurello Salinguerra, the right-hand man to Eccelin, but Eccelin's latest wife, Adelaide, disguises his identity, believing that Salinguerra is the better warrior and that he would oust their family should the knowledge of his son's existence lead him to develop dynastic ambitions. Sure enough, Salinguerra, who has been led to believe that his son has died in battle, becomes a loyal servant to the Eccelin family. Time passes, and Adelaide, who has become guilt-ridden at her actions, confesses her deception to Palma. Eccelin overhears part of this conversation and becomes guilt-ridden in turn, retiring to a monastery, arranging for his children to be wed to Guelph families, and devolving his rule to Salinguerra. Sordello, on the other hand, who has witnessed first-hand the devastation of war in Ferrara, decides to work for the people, by supporting the Guelph faction. He tries to co-opt Salinguerra to his cause but fails. An envoy arrives from the emperor, granting full power to rule Lombardy. Salinguerra decides impulsively to give this position to Sordello in order to ensure Palma's co-operation. Now he proposes that Sordello marry Palma and accept the Imperial Perfect. Salinguerra comes to understand his true relationship with Sordello. However, Sordello, torn between his loyalty to the Ghibellines and his preference for the Guelphs, falls insensible and dies.

What Mary Shelley and Browning do in their respective texts is to create a quasi-allegorical history that relates its struggle for democratic ideals. Before elaborating this point further, let us quickly turn back to William Godwin, whose determination to create allegorical histories can be seen as a precursor to both his own daughter and the later Browning. Godwin's *Things As They Are, or The Adventures of Caleb Williams* (1794), by far his most popular novel at the time, is a good example of this. One of the reasons for focusing my argument on *Caleb Williams* is that Godwin exploits history to render 'things as they are'; Gary Kelly similarly reads it as a historical representation of the present:

> Godwin's novel [*Caleb Williams*] was, from the evidence of the natures and names of its characters, an allegory of Protestant, not to say Dissenting history [...] with *Things As They Are* Godwin

had already written a[n] historical novel, set, paradoxically, in the present, but dealing nevertheless with the moral history of man.[12]

While the more overt historical novels written by Godwin, such as *St. Leon* and *Mandeville*, engage in the problematic history of Protestantism, characterised by social alienation and persecution, *Caleb Williams* deals with history as it relates to contemporary Europe.

Caleb Williams tells the story of its eponymous hero, a servant of the aristocratic Ferdinando Falkland. He becomes privy to his master's past; Falkland murdered his neighbour, Barnabas Tyrrel. Caleb flees from Falkland for fear of his own life when Falkland admits to his past crime and threatens him with a penalty of death unless he remains silent. Falkland tries to bribe him into silence but is met with resistance by Caleb, who is determined to bring the case to justice. Eventually, Caleb returns and is reconciled with Falkland, although the ending is controversial as Godwin originally plotted a different conclusion, which would have seen Caleb going mad in prison. The fact that Godwin has Caleb tell the story, thereby placing narrative power in the hands of the democratic hero, signifies his political orientation, which counters that of the status quo by relegating the voice of the ruling class. These radical gestures of exposing not only Falkland's crime, which otherwise would have been concealed, but also his own psychological state form the twin bases of narrative interest. What Godwin does in this novel is not just to confer narrative power onto the democratic hero; he is also keen to demonstrate 'the operation of human passions' and 'the empire of motives', the drama that lies behind human actions. By focusing on these, Godwin believes that the cause of history will be better served. His challenge to the Enlightenment historiographers lies in his presentation of a history fraught with human passions and motives, without which, he contends, we cannot get to the essence of historical 'truth'. General abstraction of facts and events alone cannot, according to Godwin, serve history in a satisfactory way:

> Laying aside the generalities of historical abstraction, we must mark the operation of human passions; must observe the empire

12 See Gary Kelly, *The English Jacobin Novel* (Oxford: Clarendon Press, 1976), p. 208.

of motives whether grovelling or elevated; and must note the influence that one human being exercises over another, and the ascendancy of the daring and the wise over the vulgar multitude. It is thus, and thus only, that we shall be enabled to add, to the knowledge of the past, a sagacity that can penetrate into the depths of futurity.[13]

He insists that a 'mere chronicle of facts, places and dates [...] is in reality no history', and that we 'must then not rest contented with considering society in a mass, but must analyse the materials of which it is composed'.[14] In short, Godwin promotes the status of fictionalised, individual histories over general history; this is partly a reaction to the historiography of writers such as Hume, William Robertson and Gibbon and, more importantly, a means of creating a new *kind* of history. Godwin's insistence on individual history rests on the belief that personal motives and intentions provide us with a clue as to how the past might actually have been, rather than how it became through the abstraction of historical 'facts'. What is discarded in this process of abstraction may just, according to Godwin, be the key to reconstituting such an alternative history.

Accordingly, in her own fictionalised history, Mary Shelley dutifully privileges the private histories of the heroines, Euthanasia and Beatrice, over the public history of Castruccio Castracani. In *Valperga* we see the march of history detailed less through those major events that surrounded the historical figure of Castruccio as through the inner dramas of the female protagonists as they narrate their relationship with Castruccio. Again, we see a shift in control over the story from the conventional male protagonists to the female counterparts. Like Caleb, the humble servant, taking over his master's narrative, Euthanasia and Beatrice overwrite Castruccio Castracani.

This re-focusing, however, does not mean that we are denied access to the inner dramas of Castruccio himself. As a historical account,

---

13 All citations from 'Of History and Romance' are taken from the 'Appendix' to Maurice Hindle's edition of Godwin's *Caleb Williams* (Harmondsworth: Penguin, 1988), pp. 359–74 (363). This previously unpublished essay was composed, according to Godwin's manuscript note, 'while the Enquirer (1797) was in the press, under the impression that the favour of the public might have demanded another volume' (359).

14 Godwin, 'Of History and Romance', pp. 367, 362.

Mary Shelley's novel stands in stark contrast to, say, Machiavelli's *Life of Castruccio Castracani*, which depicts him as one who rose to the height of power from humble origins and distinguished himself as a ruler of great wit, with the aid of Fortune.[15] One of the aims of Machiavelli's book is to emphasise Castruccio as a successful military strategist. John Gibson Lockhart, reviewing *Valperga* in *Blackwood's Edinburgh Magazine*, recalls the terms of Machiavelli's representation of Castruccio by laying emphasis, in turn, on his 'marvellous rise [...] to sovereign and tyrannic power', 'his fiery valour', 'his sportive wit', 'his searing ironies' and 'his untimely death'.[16] Mary Shelley, instead, offers a fresh interpretation of the historical figure as an example of a tyrant who could have potentially worked for a better cause. Thus, it is no wonder that Lockhart complained that 'Mrs Shelley has not done justice to the character of Castruccio' and criticised her for her 'perpetual drumming at poor Buonaparte'.[17] It was apparent to Lockhart that Mary Shelley's Castruccio would inevitably recall, and be coloured by, the recent example of Napoleon, the liberator turned tyrant. Lockhart's attack was aimed at this re-politicisation of Castruccio. The way Lockhart proceeded to criticise Mary Shelley's depiction of the historical figure was to see it pejoratively in terms of gender: 'far too much reliance has been laid on thoughts and feelings, not only modern, but modern and feminine at once.'[18] Lockhart, then, clearly accounts for Mary Shelley's efforts as being derivative of the Godwinian School. By relegating such efforts at democratisation to the realm of the 'feminine', conservatives such as Lockhart sought to discredit what Godwin was attempting to do with history. Moreover, Mary Shelley was in a position to be criticised on her own account for trying her hand at what was considered a masculine genre. This is a double subversion in that she had taken up a subject that traditionally belonged to men and had followed a republican tradition under the influence of her father, Godwin. It is possible to speculate that Godwin changed the very title of Mary Shelley's novel, so that it sounded more like a romance than a history, out of concern for its public reception. The historical novel was still considered a

15 See Niccolò Machiavelli, *Life of Castruccio Castracani*, trans. Andrew Brown (London: Hesperus Press, 2003), p. 3.
16 See *Blackwood's Edinburgh Magazine* 13.74 (Mar. 1823), pp. 283–93 (283).
17 *Blackwood's Edinburgh Magazine*, pp. 283, 284.
18 *Blackwood's Edinburgh Magazine*, p. 284.

masculine genre in which female writers had no right to participate.[19] Indeed, when Anna Barbauld published *Nineteen Hundred and Eleven* in 1812 to criticise Britain's participation in the Napoleonic Wars, the critical reception of the poem was so damning that it ended her poetic career. Mary Shelley's polemical gesture in her own historical novel is intentional, as Betty T. Bennett's comments:

> Mary Shelley's operative theme is political, that her criticism of fourteenth-century Italy differs little from her criticism of fourteenth-century England (and by implication, of nineteenth-century Europe), and that these works [*Valperga* and *Perkin Warbeck*], whatever their stylistic shortcomings, are written in the tradition of social reform, particularly influenced—as were the efforts of so many other reformers of the time—by Godwin and Wollstonecraft.[20]

When Lockhart laments Mary Shelley's portrayal of Castruccio as falling short of Machiavelli's, it is clear that he misses the point. In other words, Mary Shelley is consciously deploying revisionary politics to question, not accept, the traditionally accepted understanding of Castruccio.

Mary Shelley carefully depicts the development of Castruccio's character in relation to his social environment and personal relationships so as to make it apparent to the reader. First, she demonstrates that familial influence has a lasting effect on the protagonist, so that his father's ambition for a political career for Castruccio outweighs the pacifist doctrine of Guinigi, his foster parent.[21] She also emphasises the Guelph–Ghibelline strife, which shapes the lives of those who are implicated in it, as an external force that is partially constituted by, but is also beyond the control of, the individual. She then introduces

---

19 See Lisa Kasmer, *Novel Histories: British Women Writing History, 1760–1830* (Madison: Fairleigh Dickinson University Press, 2012), pp. 5–8.

20 See Donald H. Reiman, Michael C. Jaye and Betty T. Bennett, *The Evidence of the Imagination: Studies of Interactions between Life and Art in English Romantic Literature* (New York: New York University Press, 1978), p. 356.

21 According to Machiavelli, Guinigi, with whom Castruccio came to live, taught him 'how to ride and handle weapons' (*Life of Castruccio Castracani*, p. 6), whereas in Mary Shelley's poem Castruccio's foster father was a priest who sought to make him follow in his footsteps.

power-crazed figures, such as Alberto Scoto and Galeazzo Visconti, who encourage and eventually persuade Castruccio to follow his ambition at all costs. Visconti's objectives are to tarnish the peace compact that Castruccio has made with Florence and to motivate him to further self-aggrandisement. Both prove successful when Galeazzo reminds Castruccio of his initial ambition to defeat Guelph rule altogether. What deserves attention in Mary Shelley's delineation of the character development of Castruccio is that she construes him as willingly discarding every piece of advice and guidance that might potentially have prevented him from becoming a tyrant. In the case of Castruccio, his inability to comprehend and embrace the doctrine of the more enlightened pacifists such as Guinigi and Euthanasia becomes the direct cause of his tragedy.

Browning's protagonist, Sordello, is the antitype of Castruccio, becoming a democratic hero through his political conversion from being born into the Ghibelline faction to eventually embracing Guelph politics. Browning took his character from Dante's *Purgatorio* in the *Divine Comedy*, where Sordello figures in the valley of negligent rulers as observed by Dante and Virgil:

> But lo! a spirit there
> Stands solitary, and toward us looks:
> It will instruct us in the speediest way'.
> We soon approach'd it. O thou Lombard spirit!
> How didst thou stand, in high abstracted mood,
> Scarce moving with slow dignity thine eyes.
> It spoke not aught, but let us onward pass,
> Eyeing us as a lion on his watch.
> But Virgil, with entreaty mild, advanc'd,
> Requesting it to show the best ascent.
> It answer to his question none return'd,
> But of our country and our kind of life
> Demanded. When my courteous guide began,
> 'Mantua,' the solitary shadow quick
> Rose towards us from the place in which it stood,
> And cry'd, 'Mantuan! I am thy countryman
> Sordello'. Each the other then embrac'd. (6. 58–75)[22]

22 See Henry Francis Cary's translation of the *Divina Commedia* (London: The Colonial Press, 1901).

Dante's depiction of Sordello as being solitary and introspective feeds into Browning's characterisation of Sordello. Moreover, Sordello's patriotism, together with his failure to achieve political leadership (being in the valley of negligent rulers), may have had an influence on Browning's depiction of Sordello's story as a cautionary tale about the missed opportunity of seizing political power.

The historical Sordello, as described in the *Biographie universelle*[23] (which Browning is known to have consulted), was born in Goito sometime between 1180 and 1200, abducted the wife of his patron, the count of St Boniface, and lived for some time in Provence. The *Biographie* lists 34 poems in Provençal—half of which are love songs, whilst the rest are dialogues and satires—attributed to Sordello. It is possible that Browning got the idea of Sordello's romantic attachment to Palma (the wife to be of the son of St Boniface) from this account, and that much of his poetical career is partly inferred from precisely those poems that he is claimed to have written. The political trajectory of Sordello, however, is entirely of Browning's own making. He departs completely from accounts of the historical Sordello to pursue his own purpose of writing an epic poem about a democratic hero. However, it is not simply Sordello's political beliefs *per se* that are in question in the poem. The subject of poetics itself, as it relates to Sordello, is also treated. Accordingly, Browning devised a poetical development from lyricism to drama and then to what would be known later as the dramatic monologue. I shall have more to say about this later. Here, I would like to emphasise Browning's depiction of Sordello's character, which puts one in mind of Mary Shelley and Godwin's practice of delineating character in order to write a democratic history. Each deploys a political doctrine (like republicanism, for example) and shows the reader how this doctrine may dictate certain character traits. In fact, Sordello begins his poetic career as a self-serving sensualist. He only comes to embrace the political ideal of his opposite faction when he witnesses the devastation caused by warfare in Ferrara. It is only then that he feels for the people for the first time. His realisation that the people are the ones who suffer under political strife and warfare leads him to adopt the more advanced politics of the Guelphs. His personal tragedy lies in the fact that he is unable to communicate this knowledge to Salinguerra, the right-hand man to Eccelin and the effective leader of

23 Published in fifty volumes between 1811 and 1822.

the Ghibellines. All this is, again, of Browning's own making, and, as he makes clear in the dedication in the 1863 edition, the poem is less about the historical narrative than it is about the inner development of the hero. He says: 'The historical decoration was purposely of no more importance than a background requires; and my stress lay on the incidents in the development of a soul: little else is worth study.'[24] In other words, *Sordello* is less about the historical troubadour than it is about a fictional type whose political ambition was discordant with the political milieu in which he found himself. Browning is not simply narrating Sordello's transition from a hedonistic egotist to a democratic hero. It is Sordello's inner workings and the external influences upon them that are at stake as they take shape in his actions. Browning's downplaying of history in the above quotation is accurate, to the extent that his poem is not about the troubadour as such, but misleading in that he is known to have consulted many historical books to get his descriptions of the context accurate. No doubt Browning takes much poetic licence with his depiction of Sordello; the point is that he is delineating a believable history of one individual who clashes with his immediate environment because he is ahead of his time. There is thus an aesthetic connection to Dante, deriving from an intimation in the *Biographie* that Sordello was the first to conceive of poetry in the Italian vernacular. There is no evidence, however, to suggest that this was actually the case; nevertheless, Browning uses this to suggest that it was Dante who superseded him as the one who established the practice of writing in Italian with his *Divine Comedy*.

Returning now to *Valperga*, we can see that, as its title intimates, Mary Shelley's novel is also about female space. The name Valperga is thought to have derived from Walburga, an English missionary in Germany. According to the *Columbia Encyclopedia*, she settled at Heidenheim to assist St Boniface, where her 'convent became a principal centre of civilisation in Germany and an important shrine'. In the novel, Valperga is the name of a castle that Euthanasia inherits from her mother (as the original heir before her marriage to Adimari). It is worth noting that it may possibly signify a female descent. That 'Valperga' is associated with space, rather than the linear temporality that the other half of the title—'The Life and Adventures of Castruccio'—suggests, is reminiscent of the gendered

24 Reprinted in *Poems of Browning*, p. 353.

demarcation Kristeva makes between the feminine '*space* generating and forming the human species' and masculine '*time*, becoming of history'.[25] Furthermore, based on the female role of motherhood and reproduction, Kristeva names 'repetition' and 'eternity' as the two defining conceptions of time in female subjectivity: 'repetition' as 'cycles, gestation, the eternal recurrence of a biological rhythm which conforms to that of nature' and 'eternity' as a 'massive presence of a monumental temporality' related to the former. For example, the Virgin Mother 'does not die but moves from one spatiality to another within the same time'.[26] In creating an imaginary space to embody an alternative conception of time, Mary Shelley likewise gives Valperga a sense of cyclic continuity as well as that of atemporality or an eternal moment. The former arises from the generational inhabitation of the site, whereas the latter arises from the figurative body of Walburga, with which the name is associated, and, more importantly, from Euthanasia's apocalyptic vision based on 'love' and 'imagination' that permeates the site.

The female space in the novel also denotes the traumatic experiences of the heroines. That is to say, both female protagonists suffer from emotional distress, from which there is no respite, because of the hero's actions. Euthanasia manages to keep her emotions under control more than Beatrice does hers, but they still cannot escape from the trauma wrought by Castruccio. Euthanasia cannot recover from Castruccio's betrayal of trust in his liaison with Beatrice; moreover, his eventual usurpation of her fiefdom to satisfy his political ambition to rule Tuscany proves equally traumatic. Beatrice, who believes that her union with Castruccio is sacred, becomes disillusioned by his attachment to Euthanasia. Because of this, the text invites comparison with *Mathilda*, the novella written midway through Mary Shelley's composition of *Valperga*. In *Mathilda*, the heroine becomes traumatised, first because of the discovery of her father's incestuous love for her and second by his death as a result of his guilt at his passion and its disclosure. That Mary temporarily left *Valperga* to write *Mathilda* in the summer of 1819 is suggestive. The emotional interiority of the two heroines in *Valperga*, which dominates the novel, can be traced back to *Mathilda*. In the novella, not only do the emotions dominate but they also govern the plot:

25 'Women's Time', *Signs* 7.1 (autumn 1981): 13–35 (16).
26 'Women's Time', 16–17.

there is no story independent of Mathilda's emotional outburst, directed at her father and a friend who, at the first instance, appears to hold the potential of becoming a counsellor-lover for Mathilda. Similarly, in *Valperga*, Mary Shelley re-engages with the thematic preoccupation with trauma that leads to the collapse of the narrative in *Mathilda*; the outcome is a disruption of historical continuity that can only be restored by the alternation of private and public histories.

If the tension that exists in *Valperga* is created by this bifurcation of private and public histories, the difficulty of reading *Sordello* lies in Browning's decision to embed his poetic statement in an epic narrative. It is as much a rite of passage for Browning, in establishing his poetics, as it is about the life of a troubadour. In doing so, he is also discovering his own political position (which admittedly had never been in question but which resurfaces in the poem as one that requires reconfirmation), which then becomes reflected in the choices of the main character, Sordello. It is, therefore, impossible to separate the narrative concerning Sordello from Browning's own personal development as a poet. It is also a statement about Romanticism, in which Browning had much investment. Shelley, certainly, figures prominently in the poem (as I have argued elsewhere)[27] but so also do Byron and Wordsworth. The poem should be regarded as a historical testament, in which Browning maps out the transition from Romantic lyricism to a new style of poetic composition.

In Book V, when Browning delineates the transition from the epic to drama, and furthermore to psychological poetry, it becomes apparent that he is conscious of inaugurating a new age. He lists Dante as the proponent of epic poetry and Shakespeare as that of drama. They can be described as 'descriptive' and 'analytical' respectively. Browning continues to tell us, however, that we want a more intercommunicative type of poetry:

> How we attained to talk as brothers talk,
> In half-words, call things by half-names, no balk
> From discontinuing old aids—To-day
> Takes in account the work of Yesterday—
> Has not the world a Past now, its adept
> Consults ere he dispense with or accept

27 See Chapter 3 of my *Negotiating History: From Romanticism to Victorianism* (Tokyo: Waseda University Press, 2012).

> New aids? a single touch more may enhance,
> A touch less turn to insignificance
> Those structures' symmetry the Past has strewed
> Your world with, once so bare: leave the mere rude
> Explicit details, 'tis but brother's speech
> We need, speech where an accent's change gives each
> The other's soul—no speech to understand
> By former audience—need was then expand,
> Expatiate—hardly were they brothers! true—
> Nor I lament my less remove from you,
> Nor reconstruct what stands already: ends
> Accomplished turn to means (5. 605–23)

Browning's poetry of 'brother's speech' is not revolutionary to the extent that it discards past traditions: rather, it builds on and develops them. For example, he is responding to Wordsworth's language of ordinary men[28] by claiming that he likewise believes in equality between poets and other men ('Nor lament my less remove from you'), but does not refute the barrier that exists between them ('Nor reconstruct what stands already'). It is not the simple language of men that Browning is endorsing here but a language of suggestion that is akin to 'brother's speech'. This statement of literary development is also echoed in *Sordello*, where the troubadour himself likewise tries his hand at epic rather than dramatic poetry (2. 521–31, 2. 579–86).

This writer–reader relationship is also a challenge to what Browning perceived as a Shelleyan model of communicating with the audience.[29] In other words, Browning detected a solipsism in the output of the Romantics, and Shelley in particular, who conceived

---

28 Wordsworth famously declared in his 1802 'Preface' to the *Lyrical Ballads* that '[t]he principal object, then, which I proposed to myself in these Poems was to choose incidents and situations from common life, and to relate or describe them throughout, as far as was possible, in a selection of language really used by men'. See *Lyrical Ballads*, ed. Michael Mason (London: Longman, 1992), p. 59.

29 'The subjective poet has, in a sense, no audience; at least, his work is produced without reference to an imagined reader, and gains currency only, so to speak, by accident'; see John Woolford, *Browning the Revisionary* (Basingstoke: Macmillan, 1988), p. ix.

'some kind of vision of the absolute' only available to himself, which he 'then renders as best he can in his work'.[30] Partly because of his awareness of his shortcomings as a visionary, Browning refused to be a solipsistic poet in the Shelleyan sense and committed himself to communicating with men on the same footing. The outcome in the poem, however, is far from straightforward, as Sordello's failure to communicate his ideas to Salinguerra proves. The breakdown of communication between writer and audience suggests an ongoing problem of the ineffectiveness of poets in conveying their message to the general public. To this extent, *Sordello* still remains in the legacy of the Romantics and, in particular, of Shelley.

As the narrator (Browning) interrupts his own narrative to comment on present-day Venice, the political orientation of the poem comes into focus. In other words, Browning has to stop during his narrative because his poem begins to embrace dynastic inclinations. Sordello looks as though he might succumb to imperial aspirations. Just as Rome was saved in time, so Sordello is saved by Browning's reinstatement of his political position: 'Yet not so, surely never so! / Only as good my soul were suffered go / O'er the lagune; forth fare thee, put aside—' (3. 591–93). When Browning meets the 'disheveled ghost' (3. 676), who is a female beggar, in the streets of Venice, he is reminded of the 'suffering humanity' (running title in 1863–75), which he seeks to serve. In a letter to Fanny Haworth, Browning writes as a way of explaining what he meant by 'the sad / Disheveled form wherein I put mankind / To come at times and keep my pact in mind / Renewed me' (3. 942–45):

Why that as I stopped my task awhile, left off my versewriting one sunny June day with a notion of not taking to it again in a hurry, the sad disheveled form I had just been talking of, that plucked and pointed, wherein I put, comprize, typify and figure to myself Mankind, the whole poor-devildom one sees cuffed and huffed from morn to midnight, that, so typified, she may come at times and keep my pact in mind, prick up my republicanism and remind me of certain engagements I have entered into with myself about that same, renewed me, gave me fresh spirit made me after finishing Book 3ᵈ commence Book 4ᵗʰ, what is involved here?[31]

---

30 Woolford, *Browning the Revisionary*, p. viii.
31 *Brownings' Correspondence* 4: 269.

Browning's renewed commitment to the people is thereafter reflected in Sordello's choice of the Guelph party over the Ghibelline party. He realises that the Guelph party is the more advanced of the two and decides to work towards its cause. Despite the reader's potential expectations of an epic romance that concerns the nobility, Browning gestures towards the inclusion of ordinary people to democratise the very conventions and subject matter he seeks to deploy. Such are the radical aesthetics of *Sordello*.

Returning to Mary Shelley's gendered argument in *Valperga* that female participants in history are often victims of male actions, let us now turn to how one might read *Sordello* as a response to such an argument. If Mary Shelley associated imperialism with masculine egotism, Browning reverses this to suggest that women can also be tyrannical. He thus characterises his heroine, Palma, as a power-crazed individual who seeks to make Sordello 'king',[32] whereas his hero, Sordello, is portrayed as a sympathetic youth who feels for the victims of war.[33] This should not be understood as Browning's sole radical gesture; moreover, it ought to be seen in the context of the Foxite radicalism to which Browning subscribed. As Isobel Armstrong argues, the 1830s saw two camps within the newly emerging poetic tradition: one based on the Cambridge Apostles and the other on Fox's *Monthly Repository*. Browning was a disciple of Fox and was a frequent contributor to the journal. The ethos of the journal concerning gender was radical indeed. It maintained that femininity and masculinity were not gender-specific, that they were culturally created and that therefore they were interchangeable between the sexes. This was in contrast to the Apostles, who believed that femininity was specific to women and that women were privileged to exercise emotion and sympathy.[34] Within this rubric of ideas, Browning manoeuvres his way to respond to Mary Shelley's depiction of gender.

Finally, both texts exploit Italy's medieval history to engage in contemporary politics. Whereas *Valperga* concerns itself with

---

32 In a revision Browning undertook in 1855–56, he inserted 'Ghibellinism & selfishness' at 4. 901 after Palma 'spoke'.

33 Sordello is moved by the devastation of war in Ferrara and decides to work for the Guelph cause (i.e. for the people).

34 See Isobel Armstrong, *Victorian Poetry: Poetry, Poetics and Politics* (London: Routledge, 1993), pp. 36–37.

the failure of the Romantic imagination, *Sordello* seeks a practical way out of the impasse into which Browning claims it had fallen. Mary Shelley's attempt at analysing Castruccio's character is driven by the need to offer an explanation as to why he became a tyrant against his best judgement and how Euthanasia's advice had so little effect on him. This has a particularly significant bearing on the Romantics because, if 'imagination' and 'love' cannot deter individuals from embracing tyranny, then the question as to what can remains. To this question, then, Browning responds by offering a more practical solution, suggesting that the liberal individual take political responsibility themselves (even though there is the concomitant risk that such liberal individuals may themselves succumb to tyrannical impulses once installed in power). If we consider the respective political contexts to which Mary Shelley and Browning were responding, this difference becomes readily understandable. *Valperga* is, in a sense, about post-Napoleonic Europe. In other words, the question of why Napoleon could not curb his ambitions for self-aggrandisement and work instead for the people remains the central concern for the liberals of the early nineteenth century. Although Mary Shelley denied the resemblance between Castruccio and Napoleon, the similarities between the two are undoubtedly present, as the *Blackwood*'s critic pointed out. The novel makes sense precisely because it was written after the Napoleonic Wars. With the time lapse of about 20 years, however, Browning's concerns are different: how liberalism can be advanced in English politics on the one hand and how Italian independence can be sought on the other. The solution is more strategic for the English case.[35] That is to say, if the so-called radicals remained faithful to their policies and remained uncompromising, then they would have little chance of winning power. However, if they were to be too compromising, as the Whigs were, they would achieve very little in line with their policies. To solve this dilemma, Browning posed the question of responsibility for the protagonist, Sordello, in giving up the Imperial Perfect too easily:

35 For the situation of the Radicals in the decade Browning was writing *Sordello*, see C. B. Roylance Kent's *The English Radicals: An Historical Sketch* (New York: Burt Franklin, 1971), pp. 347–77; for the relationship between Radicals and Whigs, see pp. 347–49.

Before
He dashes it, however, think once more!
For, was that little truly service? Ay—
I' the end, no doubt; but meantime? (6. 197–200)

While the Romantics argued that such a compromise would have been unacceptable, Browning maintains that it is precisely in such a compromise that political advancement is sought. Such a gesture towards gradualism is what separates him from the apocalyptic transformation of society based on the Romantic imagination—as Browning understood the Shelleys' creed to be.

As I argued in Chapter One, again, the politics of the two texts diverge when confronted with their immediate socio-political situation. Mary Shelley remains firmly entrenched in Romanticism, thereby advocating for the transformation of society based on Love and Imagination, as Shelley had done, however vainly. This can be seen in the central role that Euthanasia is made to play in the novel. The personal and political defeat of her aspirations is the outcome of Romanticism, from whose failure we are meant to gain knowledge. Browning, on the other hand, goes beyond the Romantic transformation of society to intimate a more practical and necessarily gradual means of changing society. As he had done with *Paracelsus*, he does not condemn the efforts of Romanticism as being in vain; rather, he soberly reminds the reader that Sordello's dream of immediately constructing 'Rome' (thereby ideal republicanism) is a fantasy at best, which needs to be worked at if we are to achieve it. Both his politics and his aesthetics look towards a more democratic participation of the people, whereby they have an equal share in the responsibility held by leaders of the enlightened kind. This is the knowledge *Sordello* communicates.

CHAPTER THREE

The Shelleys and Browning on Art, Aesthetics and Poetics

Her [Mary Shelley's] remarks on art, once she lets go of Rio's skirts, are amazing—Fra Angelico, for instance, only painted Martyrs, Virgins &c—she had no eyes for the divine bon-bourgeoisie of his pictures,—the dear common folk of his crowds, those who sit and listen (spectacle at nose and bent into a comfortable heap to hear better) at the sermon of the Saint— and the children, and women—divinely pure they all are, but fresh from the streets & market place—but she is wrong, every where, that is, not right, not seeing what is to see, speaking what one expects to hear. I quarrel with her, for ever, I think.[1]

As Browning's rather negative comments on Mary Shelley demonstrate, he did not look kindly on her post-Shelley life and career. This may well have had something to do with her changed lifestyle,[2] but it may also be indicative of the fact that she had departed from the kind of aesthetic practice she and Shelley had previously embraced, in order to conform to early Victorian tastes. This chapter does not focus on Mary Shelley *per se* but rather maps out Browning's own aesthetics by examining his two poems on art—'Old Pictures in Florence' and 'Fra Lippo Lippi' (1855)—in relation to what both Mary Shelley and Shelley had to say about art.

---

1 Browning to Elizabeth Barrett, dated 11 September 1845, *Brownings' Correspondence* 11: 70.
2 See Introduction, n. 33.

Shelley's preference for classical art (in particular Greek) can be easily gleaned from his comments on the subject in his essays and letters.[3] Mary Shelley shared his praise of, and preference for, classical art, which can be traced to her French translation of Winckelmann's *Geschichte der Kunst des Alterhums* (1764) as *Histoire de l'art chez les anciens* (1802) and her notes to Shelley's essays. Browning likewise showed interest in classical literature throughout his life, although poems dealing with classical themes tended to come later in his life.[4] It is true that he admired Greek writers such as Euripides and that figures from classical Greek literature feature prominently in his oeuvre. One of his most significant 'classical' experiments is arguably 'Aristophanes' Apology' (1875), in which he outlines the aesthetic differences between Aristophanes and Euripides. As is often the case, the Greek context is somewhat overshadowed by Browning's own endorsement of literary realism, which he expresses through Balaustion's preference for Euripides.[5] There is no denying that Browning found a precursor in Euripides with whom he could sympathise; however, it is also a fact that he had identified (in his earlier years particularly) certain limitations in Greek art generally (as I shall argue below) and that he positioned his own aesthetic practice partly in response to such a worldview.

3 For example, 'Notes on Sculptures in Rome and Florence' was published posthumously by his friend Thomas Medwin, and afterwards by Mary Shelley; see *Athenaeum* (1832); *Essays, Letters from Abroad, Translations and Fragments*, ed. Mary Shelley, 2 vols. (London: Edward Moxon, 1840). Relevant letters in praise of ancient Greek art are also found in this volume.

4 Poems with classical themes in the 1840s and 1850s are: 'Artemis Prologizes' (included in *Dramatic Lyrics*, 1842) and 'Protus' (in *Men and Women*, 1855). 'Eurydice to Orpheus' appeared in the catalogue of the Royal Academy Exhibition of 1864. Later poems are *Balaustion's Adventure* (1871), *Aristophanes' Apology* (1875), 'Pheidippides' (included in *Dramatic Idyls*, 1879), 'Echetlos' and 'Pan and Luna' (in *Dramatic Idyls*, 1880), 'Apollo and the Fates' (in *Parleyings with Certain People of Importance in Their Day*, 1887), 'Imperante Augusto Natus Est—' and 'Development' (in *Asolando: Fancies and Facts*, 1889). See Edmund D. Cressman, 'Classical Poems of Robert Browning', *The Classical Journal* 23.3 (Dec. 1927): 198–207.

5 For a discussion that maps out the two different aesthetic camps, not only in ancient Greece but also in Victorian England, see Jane A. McCusker, 'Browning's "Aristophanes' Apology" and Matthew Arnold', *The Modern Language Review* 79.4 (Oct. 1984): 783–96.

Let me begin with Mary Shelley, whose commentary on Italian art comes most forcefully in her *Rambles in Germany and Italy, in 1840, 1842, and 1843* (1844). In the chapters on the art scene in Florence, she makes it explicit from the very beginning that what she seeks in the works of the 'elder Florentine painters' is 'their souls', conceived of as being 'sublime and holy in the face of man'.[6] In other words, the aesthetically successful rendering of these painted religious subjects was precisely due to the religious zeal that governed the artists' aesthetic impulse in the first place. Fra Angelico, for example, is reviewed in the following terms:

> surpasses all his contemporaries in the celestial sweetness he fuses into the countenances of his saints and angels. We may believe ourselves regarding the blessed in the kingdom of heaven, as we look at these creations / of a mind cradled in love, charity, and devotion. [...] The delicacy and softness for which he is remarkable never degenerates into insipidity. His pure taste made him conceive the highest beauty, his faith gave him a foretaste of beatitude, and he adorned with / these attributes the beings whom alone he consented to represent, the saints and angels of Paradise.[7]

Fra Angelico is worthy of praise precisely because his artistic endeavours represent the application of his Christian faith. Browning openly, if privately, challenged Mary Shelley's views by criticising her in the letter quoted at the beginning of this chapter. Browning's comments make explicit a type of aesthetics predicated on realism rather than idealism, which he would then go on to put into practice in his own writings. Browning apostrophises Mary Shelley in the very same letter:

> but why don't you tell us that at Rome they eat roasted chestnuts, and put the shells into their aprons, the women do, and calmly empty the whole on the heads of the passengers in the street below; and that at Padua when a man drives his wagon up to a house and stops, all the mouse-coloured oxen that pull it from a beam against their foreheads sit down in a heap and rest.[8]

6 *N&SW of Mary Shelley*, p. 303.
7 *N&SW of Mary Shelley*, p. 305.
8 *Brownings' Correspondence* 11: 70.

The charge is straightforward: if Mary Shelley had expanded her attention to include real things and people, she would have done better aesthetically. There is evidence to suggest that Browning is not doing full justice to Mary Shelley's aesthetics, as her book reviews published in the *Westminster Reviews* of 1829 prove. She was more than capable of appreciating the realistic descriptions of Roman life found in L. Simond's *A Tour in Italy and Sicily* (1828). In the very same review (including that of Best's *Italy as It Is*), Mary Shelley makes it clear that appreciation of art requires as much attention and study as a novel. She challenges Simond on the following lines:

> If we were at all inclined to quarrel with him, it would be with his opinions concerning works of art;—he does not sufficiently admire—and this arises from not having sufficiently studied—the productions of the great masters.—The knowledge of beauty is not a simple perception gained by the eyes; it requires refinement and education merely to perceive the intention of an artist, to pass judgement; we must not only, as it were, turn over the leaves hastily, reading merely the heads of the chapters, and table of contents, we must scan each page, peruse each line. A good picture requires at least as much time for its perusal as the volume of a novel.[9]

It is clear from her comments that taste requires refinement and improvement, which is not available to everyone because some people are unwilling to put in the effort and attention required. Just as this quotation demonstrates Mary Shelley's independent view of art—that she is not slavishly following others—her commentary on the different manners detectable in various parts of Italy (described by Simond) indicates a close connection to her own interest in political systems. Given Mary Shelley's distinct voice in these reviews, Browning in his comments had arguably fallen prey to the general assumption that Mary Shelley was only able to shine with the assistance of Shelley, without whom she could not escape mediocrity. This is indeed a case of gross misreading of Mary Shelley.

The critical orthodoxies about Browning's aesthetics and the way he put these aesthetics into practice have tended to focus on 'Fra Lippo Lippi'. William DeVane made the connection between

9 *The Westminster Review* II.12 (1829–30), pp. 127–40 (133).

Lippi's artistic attributes and Browning's own poetry back in 1927, followed by critics such as Thomas J. Collins, who claimed that 'he [Fra Lippo Lippi] serves as a mouthpiece for Browning's ideas on the nature of art' (for the justification of which assertion Collins quotes from the 'Essay on Shelley'). This particular line of critical argument subsequently fell out of favour. The ironic detachment with which Browning treats Lippi problematises a straightforward acceptance of Lippi's pronouncements on art as necessarily endorsed by the poet himself. Nonetheless, one does not need to deny the ironic attitude with which Browning treats Lippi to argue that, within the context of contemporary debates on aesthetics, Browning might well use Lippi as his mouthpiece for his views on art. The quotation from Browning's letter to Elizabeth Barrett shows that he sought to map out his own views on art and that he took his incipient challenge to contemporary assumptions about art very seriously.[10]

The idea of the marriage of religion and art as the yardstick against which to evaluate art originated in the nineteenth-century art critic Alexis-François Rio.[11] A French Catholic, Rio, in his *De la poésie chrétienne* (*The Poetry of Christian Art*), praised painters such as Giotto and Fra Angelico, whose purity and idealism matched their religious zeal:

> The compunction of the heart, its aspirations towards God, ecstatic raptures, the foretaste of celestial bliss—in short, all those profound and exalted emotions, which no artist can express

10 See William Clyde DeVane, Jr., *Browning's Parleyings: The Autobiography of a Mind* (New Haven: Yale University Press, 1927), p. 229; *A Browning Handbook* (New York: Appleton-Century-Crofts, 1955), pp. 218–19; Thomas J. Collins, *Robert Browning's Moral-Aesthetic Theory 1833–1855* (Lincoln: University of Nebraska Press, 1967), p.143; for a more recent account, see Stefan Hawlin, 'Browning, Shelley, and "On Worming Dogs"', *Essays in Criticism* 40.2 (Apr. 1990): 136–55. For Browning's ironic attitude in the poem, see Susan Hackett and John Ferns, 'A Portrait of the Artist as a Young Monk: The Degree of Irony in Browning's "Fra Lippo Lippi"', *Studies in Browning and His Circle* 4.2 (autumn 1976): 105–18.

11 See David J. Delaura, 'The Context of Browning's Painter Poems: Aesthetics, Polemics, Histories', *PMLA* 95.3 (May 1980): 367–88. He claims that 'Rio's thesis is the indispensable framework within which to interpret Robert Browning's painter poems of the forties and fifties' (367).

without having previously experienced them, formed, as it were, a mysterious cycle for the exercise of the genius of Fra Angelico, and afforded him never-failing delight.[12]

In truth, it was not only Mary Shelley but also a whole host of art critics who came under the influence of Rio. They all took their cue from Rio's work, which won much critical acclaim in Britain, as J. B. Bullen writes:

> By the 1840s A. F. Rio's book *De la poésie de l'art chrétienne* [sic] (1836) had become the most widely read history of early art in Britain, and was the single most influential authority for Browning, Ruskin, Lord Lindsay, Anna Jameson, Francis Palgrave, Mary Shelley, and all those who made artistic pilgrimages to the sites of medieval Italy.[13]

Browning was, therefore, proving himself an exception to the critical norm in repudiating Rio's aesthetics in the above-quoted letter.

The early Italian Masters, however, gave way to a new age of painters, such as Fra Lippo Lippi, who did not meet with Rio's approbation; accordingly, Mary Shelley echoes Rio's unease with this burgeoning, worldly naturalism:

> Then it was that their imagination so degenerated, that they had recourse to portraits to represent Christ, the Virgin, and the Saints; some of them even fell so far from the ideal of sinless chastity, as to paint their mistresses and women of unworthy life; offering to the worship of the pious, the image of mere physical beauty, without the superior grandeur of moral excellence.[14]

These are the lines that arguably ignited Browning's defence of the likes of Fra Lippo Lippi. As Browning makes the painter say, in the eponymously titled poem, 'If you get simple beauty and nought else / You get about the best thing God invents' (ll. 217–18).

---

12 Alexis-François Rio, *The Poetry of Christian Art*, trans. from the French (London: T. Bosworth, 1854), p. 148.

13 J. B. Bullen, *The Pre-Raphaelite Body: Fear and Desire in Painting, Poetry, and Criticism* (Oxford: Clarendon Press, 1998), p. 22.

14 *N&SW of Mary Shelley*, p. 307.

Before examining 'Fra Lippo Lippi' in detail, I would like to look at the aesthetic milieu in which Browning wrote his credo on art. Despite Rio's popularity, Protestant readers nonetheless felt uncomfortable with the overt religiosity of his tone. As J. B. Bullen explains, the unease with which they regarded Catholicism was partly because Catholics were seen to be gaining more influence since the passing of the Catholic Emancipation Act of 1829 in Britain.[15] It is in this political climate that Rio's art criticism came to be associated with certain aesthetic, rather than religious, principles. Henry Drummond and Francis Palgrave were representative figures who stressed 'higher and purer forms' of medieval art as opposed to the glorification of 'bodily display and voluptuousness' of the high Renaissance.[16] Such re-writing of the significance of medieval art into fastidiousness was best summed up in Palgrave's denunciation of the 'wretchedly profligate' Fra Lippo Lippi.[17] Browning, by contrast, used his choice of Lippi as his subject matter to unleash his attack on the Protestant demonisation of the body.

As is well known, Browning based much of his information on Lippi on Vasari's *Lives of the Artists*.[18] The poem begins with Lippi being caught by a night guard on the streets for seeking to court a prostitute. Lippi entreats the guard to let him off lightly because he is a painter under the patronage of Cosimo de' Medici. He goes on to give a broadly conventional account of the function and purpose of art, which, in the words of the Prior, is 'to paint the souls of men—' (l. 182). This idealistic style had long been associated with painters such as Fra Angelico and Giotto di Bondone. Lippi refutes this traditional view by arguing that, unless there is 'flesh', there can be no soul:

> Now, is this sense, I ask?
> A fine way to paint soul, by painting body

---

15 Bullen, *The Pre-Raphaelite Body*, p. 22.
16 Bullen, *The Pre-Raphaelite Body*, p. 24.
17 Bullen, *The Pre-Raphaelite Body*, p. 25.
18 The Brownings owned a copy of Giorgio Vasari, *Le Vite de' più eccellenti architetti, pittori et sculptori italiani da Cimabue insino a' tempi nostri, Rezeption* (Florence: Lorenzo Torrentino, 1550), and *The Life of Giovanni Angelico da Fiesole*, trans. Giovanni Aubrey Bezzi (Chiswick: C. Whittingham, 1850). See *The Browning Collections: A Reconstruction with Other Memorabilia*, compiled by Phillip Kelley and Betty A. Coley (Winfield, KS: Wedgestone Press, 1984), p. 200 (A2377, A2378).

> So ill, the eye can't stop there, must go further
> And can't fare worse! (ll. 198–201)

Tied in with Lippi's insistence on the aesthetic presence of the 'flesh' is his physical desire to court a prostitute. Browning makes a bold statement by rejecting any bourgeois morality that might judge Lippi's art on the basis of his actions; that is to say, his amorous affairs do not make him a debased artist.[19]

> For me, I think I speak as I was taught—
> I always see the Garden and God there
> A-making man's wife—and, my lesson learned,
> The value and significance of flesh,
> I can't unlearn ten minutes afterward. (ll. 265–69)

In other words, without mastering the 'flesh' one cannot possibly hope to express the 'soul'.[20] Material physicality is just as important as spirituality, which painters seek to communicate through their paintings.

Returning to Shelley, we can glean something of the poet's view of the classics from his poems based on Greek myths (*Prometheus Unbound* [1820] and *Adonais* [1821]); a poem with a Greek theme (*Hellas* [1822]); his translations of Plato; and, as I have already mentioned, his essays and letters. In a letter to Thomas Love Peacock, dated 22 December 1818, Shelley extols the Greek statues[21] in the museum in Naples:

> Since I wrote this I have seen the museum of this city. Such statues! There is Venus; an ideal shape of the most winning loveliness. A Bacchus, more sublime than any living being. A Satyr, making love to a youth, in which the expressed life of the sculpture, and

19 Lawrence Poston III makes a similar point by saying that '[b]oth of these poems ['Fra Lippo Lippi' and 'Andrea del Sarto'], too, reconfirm Browning's insistence that the artist's private life is, finally, a matter separate from his art'. See 'Browning Rearranges Browning', *Studies in Browning and His Circle* 2.1 (spring 1974): 39–54 (52).

20 Thomas J. Collins makes a similar point in *Browning's Moral-Aesthetic Theory*, pp. 143–44.

21 As it is unclear which statue Shelley is referring to in the museum, it is hard to determine whether it was an original or a replica.

the inconceivable beauty of the form of the youth, overcome one's repugnance to the subject.[22]

The fact that the 'expressed life of the sculpture' and 'inconceivable beauty of the form of the youth' 'overcome one's repugnance to the subject' is telling in that Shelley exalted beauty as surpassing any moral objections to subject matter. It is also telling in the sense that the Greeks, 'who turned all things, superstition, prejudice, murder, madness—to Beauty',[23] are to be credited for their accomplishments in aesthetics. The praise with which Shelley showers the Greeks cannot be exaggerated:

> I now understand why the Greeks were such great poets: and above all, I can account, it seems to me, for the harmony, the unity, the perfection, the uniform excellence, of all their works of art. They lived in a perpetual commerce with external nature, and nourished themselves upon the spirit of its forms. Their theatres were all open to the mountains and the sky. Their columns, the ideal types of a sacred forest, with its roof of interwoven tracery, admitted the light and wind; the odour and the freshness of the country penetrated the cities. Their temples were mostly upaithric; and the flying clouds, the stars, or the deep sky, were seen above. O, but for that series of wretched wars which terminated in the Roman conquest of the world; but for the Christian religion, which put the finishing stroke on the ancient system; but for those changes that conducted Athens to its ruin,—to what an eminence might not humanity have arrived![24]

Greek art excels precisely because of its paganism, in harmony with nature. It is the introduction of Christianity that 'put the finishing stroke on the ancient system'. Unlike Rio, Shelley embraces the opposite idea; the *absence* of (Christian) religion enabled Greek art to flourish. What attracted Shelley to ancient Greece was not just to do with art. As he states in 'A Discourse on the Manners of the Ancients', '[t]he history of ancient Greece is the study of legislators, philosophers, and poets' as opposed to '[t]he study of modern history',

22 Shelley, *Essays* 2: 181.
23 See 'A Statue of Minerva', *Athenaeum* 256 (22 Sep. 1832), p. 617.
24 To T. L. P. dated 26 January 1819. Shelley, *Essays* 2: 192.

which 'is the study of kings, financiers, statesmen, and priests'.[25] The appeal of ancient Greece for Shelley is not exclusively to do with art but more importantly to do with the political and legislative structure of ancient Greece with which it is inextricably bound. As his fully developed argument in *A Defence of Poetry* testifies, he did not see 'legislators, philosophers, and poets' separately but rather as the same, under the nomenclature of *legislator*, which he was to celebrate as the guide of society. As much as Browning shared and sympathised with Shelley's ideas, he was to divert from his secular republican ideal as the overarching principle. Before examining this aspect of Browning's views on art, the social context within which he articulated them is worth attending to.

Maureen McCue advances the notion that 'by the 1830s, the visual and the verbal arts were increasingly interdependent', thereby signifying an interchangeability among the different genres of art.[26] This is certainly true of the Browning text I discuss below: although, in 'Old Pictures in Florence', Browning focuses on paintings and sculptures, there is little doubt that his views on, and theories about, Greek and modern aesthetics extend well beyond the visual and plastic arts. In other words, the ideal perfection that Greek statuary embodies is the same principle that guides classical literature generally.

A brief outline of 'Old Pictures in Florence' may be helpful here. Browning begins his discourse on art by invoking Giotto's never-completed bell-tower. He explains why the medieval and Renaissance artists deserve attention. In short, this is because they epitomise human limitations in the face of eternity, whereas Greek art represents perfection, but only of this world. After he makes this contrast, he moves on to talk about various artists of medieval and Renaissance Italy. During the course of his description of these artists, his argument veers into the political when he suggests that the liberation of Italy from foreign powers would elevate the arts still further. A healthy political system is thus an important ingredient for a nation's health and cultural advancement. At this juncture, he returns to Giotto, whose bell-tower represents the pinnacle of imperfect art.

25 *The Complete Works of Percy Bysshe Shelley*, ed. Roger Ingpen and Walter E. Peck, 10 vols. (New York: Gordian Press, 1965), 7: 226.

26 Maureen McCue, *British Romanticism and the Reception of Italian Old Master Art, 1793–1840* (Farnham: Ashgate, 2014), p. 127.

In delineating what made medieval and Renaissance artists special, Browning dramatises the moment 'eternity' came to play a crucial role in their psyche:

> Growth came when, looking your last on them all,
> You turned your eyes inwardly one fine day
> And cried with a start—What if we so small
> Are greater, ay, greater the while than they?
> Are they perfect of lineament, perfect of stature?
> In both, of such lower types are we
> Precisely because of our wider nature;
> For time, theirs—ours, for eternity. (ll. 113–20)

Browning is depicting a moment when artists came to perceive themselves as being not necessarily *less* than the ancient Greeks, but *more*, because of the conception of 'eternity', a conception that did not enter the minds of the ancient Greeks, who only entertained the thought of this world. The oft-quoted passage from August Wilhelm von Schlegel in his lectures on the dramatic arts and literature argues for this bifurcation of Greek and modern arts:

Among the Greeks human nature was in itself all-sufficient; they were conscious of no wants, and aspired at no higher perfection than that which they could actually attain by the exercise of their own faculties. We, however, are taught by superior wisdom that man, through a high offence, forfeited the place for which he was originally destined; and that the whole object of his earthly existence is to strive to regain that situation, which, if left to his own strength, he could never accomplish. The religion of the senses had only in view the possession of outward and perishable blessings; and immortality, in so far as it was believed, appeared in an obscure distance like a shadow, a faint dream of this bright and vivid futurity. The very reverse of all this is the case with the Christian: every thing finite and mortal is lost in the contemplation of infinity; life has become shadow and darkness, and the first dawning of our real existence opens in the world beyond the grave. Such a religion must waken the foreboding, which slumbers in every feeling heart, to the most thorough consciousness, that the happiness after which we strive we can never here attain; that no external object can ever entirely fill our souls; and that every mortal enjoyment is but a fleeting and momentary deception. When the soul, resting as it were under the willows of exile, breathes out its longing for its distant home, the prevailing character of its songs must be melancholy. Hence the poetry of the ancients was the poetry of enjoyment, and ours is that of desire: the former has its foundation in the scene which is present, while the latter hovers betwixt recollection and hope.[27]

Schlegel's description shows how the two kinds of art developed under two very different worldviews. In other words, 'poetry of enjoyment' derives its aesthetics from a governing principle that ruled all the Greek arts and focuses on the present. The post-lapsarian Christian worldview, on the other hand, obliges one to contemplate the idea of immortality, thereby making poetry 'melancholy'. Browning, who was familiar with Schlegel's writings, preserves and reiterates this distinction between Greek and modern arts in writings other than 'Old Pictures in Florence'. For example, in *Sordello* (1840), he suggests that the medieval poet is engaged in a task that extends beyond the present to the next life:

> What do we here? Simply experiment
> Each on the other's power and its intent
> When elsewhere tasked, if this of mine were trucked
> For thine to either's profit,—watch construct,
> In short, an engine: with a finished one
> What it can do is all, nought how 'tis done;
> But this of ours yet in probation, dusk
> A kernel of strange wheelwork thro' its husk
> Grows into shape by quarters and by halves;
> Remark this tooth's spring, wonder what that valve's
> Fall bodes, presume each faculty's device,
> Make out each other more or less precise—
> The scope of the whole engine's to be proved—
> We die: which means to say the whole's removed,

27 August Wilhelm von Schlegel, *Vorlesungen über dramatische Kunst und Literatur* (*Lectures on Dramatic Art and Literature*; delivered at Vienna 1808; published 1809–1811; trans. J. Black, London: Baldwin, Cradock and Joy, 1815). Quoted in *English Romantic Hellenism 1700–1824*, ed. Timothy Webb (Manchester: Manchester University Press, 1982), pp. 214–15.

Dismounted wheel by wheel that complex gin,
To be set up anew elsewhere, begin
A task indeed but with a clearer clime
Than the murk lodgment of our building-time (3. 811–28)

Browning here uses 'engine' as a metaphor for life, which we 'construct' in our lifetime. When we die, however, we restart the entire process in the afterlife, using the knowledge we acquired during our lifetime. It is, therefore, the *process* of understanding the parts that is important and not the resultant understanding itself. This is, in fact, what Browning argues in his delineation of modern artists in 'Old Pictures in Florence':

'Tis a life-long toil till our lump be leaven—
The better! what's come to perfection perishes.
Things learned on earth, we shall practise in heaven.
Works done least rapidly, Art most cherishes. (ll. 129–32)

Whilst classical art only concerns itself with the present, modern art 'seethes with' (l. 122) the prospect of change and development ('be leaven') in the afterlife, which gives meaning to art.

Where Shelley's understanding differs from Schlegel's is that he deliberately sidelines religion as the driving force of modern art and sees the lack of religion as providing classical art with its motivation and impetus, as shown above. In other words, as I mentioned before, the ideal guiding principle for Shelley is the secular republican model of ancient Greece, whereas, for Browning, religion holds a higher authority than human institutions; thus, it follows that his preference for medieval and Renaissance art outweighs the appeal of classical art.

In 'Old Pictures in Florence', Browning observes a distinction not only between the different outlooks on art but also in terms of the artists' subject matter:

the early painters,
To cries of 'Greek Art and what more wish you?'—
Replied, 'Become now self-acquainters,
And paint man, man,— whatever the issue!' (ll. 145–48)

Browning had already done this using a different argument in his 'Essay on Shelley', where he distinguishes between two areas of poetry: one 'subjective' and the other 'objective'.[28] The former is concerned with '[n]ot what man sees, but what God sees—the *ideas* of Plato, seeds of creation lying burningly on the Divine Hand', whereas the latter is concerned with 'the doings of men'.[29] In other words, the 'subjective' poet sees the world through the eyes of God, whereas the 'objective' poet sees it through those of men. It follows that the former kind of poetry beholds 'the universe, nature and man, in their actual state of perfection in imperfection',[30] unlike the latter, which 'get[s] at new substance by breaking up the assumed wholes into parts of independent and unclassed value'.[31]

Browning's 'Essay on Shelley' was published as an introduction to a cache of letters attributed to Shelley that turned out to be forgeries. Edward Moxon intended to publish them 'as a pendant to his earlier collection of Shelley's prose (*Essays, Letters from Abroad, Translations and Fragments*, ed. Mary Shelley, 1840)'.[32] As the story goes, it soon became clear that these letters were not written by Shelley but by a man who called himself 'Major'—a self-styled illegitimate son of Byron. Accordingly, Moxon withdrew the volume from sale, and only a handful of copies survive. Nonetheless, because the volume was intended as a 'pendant' to the 1840 volume of Shelley's essays and letters, Browning had this volume in mind as well as the forged letters when writing his 'Essay on Shelley'.[33] When one examines the 'Essay', it is clear that for Browning the main interest of the volume is in its views on ancient Greek art and literature.[34] Browning, having read the letters (quoted above) in praise of ancient Greece, must have been impressed. This is because

---

28 All quotations from the 'Essay on Shelley' are from *Browning: Selected Poems*, ed. John Woolford, Daniel Karlin and Joseph Phelan (Harlow: Pearson Education, 2010).

29 *Browning: Selected Poems*, pp. 858–59.

30 *Browning: Selected Poems*, p. 864.

31 *Browning: Selected Poems*, pp. 861–62.

32 See the introduction to the 'Essay', *Browning: Selected Poems*, p. 852.

33 The Brownings owned a copy of *Essays, Letters from Abroad*. See *The Browning Collections*, p. 178 (A2102).

34 The first volume includes 'Essay on the Literature, Arts, and Manners of the Athenians—A Fragment', 'Preface to the Banquet of Plato', 'The Banquet—translated from Plato', 'Ion, or The Iliad—translated from Plato', 'Menexenus, or The Funeral Oration—A Fragment', 'Fragments from the Republic of Plato' and 'On a Passage in Crito'. The second volume consists mainly of

the conception of poetics that he would later endorse in the 'Essay' was exactly in response to, and a reaction to, Shelley's enthusiasm for Greek art and literature generally, and for Platonic idealism in particular (as specified by Browning himself). The 'subjective' poetry is what Browning sheds in favour of 'objective' poetry. This polarisation feeds into a larger narrative of taste that was being created around the difference between classical and medieval or Renaissance art.

McCue argues that classicism flourished during the time of the Grand Tour, when privileged young men would have their education 'finished' by touring the continent with the help of the classical education they received at university.[35] They were in a position to appreciate the classical artworks based on literature they had read in the original Greek and Latin. In post-Napoleonic times, however, opportunities for middle-class people to go to the continent became more common. In great numbers, members of the bourgeoisie flocked to European cities to satiate their taste for art. However, the role played by classical art did little towards shaping middle-class tastes; rather, there was a marked preference, by these new travellers to the continent, for medieval and Renaissance art, simply because that was the art with which they were most familiar. In post-Napoleonic Britain, an increasing number of medieval and Renaissance paintings were making their way into galleries and private collections; therefore, the middle classes were given the chance to view these medieval and Renaissance paintings more frequently.

Browning was one of these middle-class connoisseurs of art, often visiting Dulwich Picture Gallery in his younger days.[36] This

letters from Italy, but, there again, Shelley refers repeatedly to ancient Greek art and civilisation as the origin of southern Italian culture.

35 See her chapter on 'Connoisseurship'.

36 Dulwich Picture Gallery was founded in 1811 as England's first public art gallery. Located in south London, it gave a unique opportunity for residents of Camberwell (where Browning grew up) or Dulwich to visit the museum. The first collection of paintings was left by a Francis Bourgeois—an art dealer turned collector—when he died in 1811. The collection boasts a remarkable array of painters such as Rembrandt, Rubens, Watteau, Canaletto, Poussin, Claude, Ruisdael, Gainsborough, Reynolds, Van Dyck, Reni, Raphael, Murillo and many more. See John Maynard, *Browning's Youth* (Cambridge, MA: Harvard University Press, 1977), p. 17; Ian Dejordin, *Dulwich Picture Gallery, London* (London: Scala, 2009), pp. 4–5.

issue of class, in fact, is another element in the 'Essay on Shelley' to which sufficient critical attention has not been paid. Browning is carving out a niche for himself that is distinctively non-aristocratic and more middle-class. The sublimity with which Shelley's poetry is associated denotes 'power', as Burke argued in his work on the sublime.[37] Browning's poetry, on the other hand, shies away from such 'power' by either abdicating it thematically or abandoning it stylistically (as in the case of *Sordello*), so that he is seen to be on the same footing as the reader.[38] Whether the outcome is what Browning had intended is a different matter, but his reworking of Romantic poetics suggests that he was seeking to democratise poetry in a way similar to Wordsworth, but through different means.

Browning's challenge to the Shelleys' aesthetics reveals his own poetics as seeking to accomplish what one aspect of Romanticism, and in particular Shelleyan Romanticism, had failed to do. Romanticism had successfully conceptualised the ideal but had neglected to give expression to the real world of people and actions.[39] Here is what he says:

> [The 'subjective' poet] is impelled to embody the thing he perceives, not so much with reference to the many below as to the one above him, the supreme Intelligence which apprehends all things in their absolute truth,—an ultimate view ever aspired to, if but partially attained, by the poet's own soul. Not what man sees, but what God sees—the *Ideas* of Plato, seeds of creation lying burningly on the Divine Hand—it is toward these that he struggles. Not with the combination of humanity in action, but with the primal elements of humanity he has to do; and he digs where he stands,—preferring to seek them in his own soul as the

37 '[P]ower is undoubtedly a capital source of the sublime'; see Edmund Burke, *A Philosophical Enquiry into the Sublime and Beautiful* (London: Routledge, 2008), pp. 195–201 (201). Burke traces 'power' in the 'sublime' from nature, monarchy to God—anything that exercises 'terror' or 'awe'.

38 As I have argued in the previous chapter, Sordello abdicates or dies before taking on 'power', and he also repudiates the kind of poetry that is associated with 'power' after realising that it is egotistical.

39 It is more nuanced than this, as my article on Leigh Hunt and Browning demonstrates. See 'Browning on Romanticism: "Fra Lippo Lippi" and Leigh Hunt', *Keats-Shelley Review* 27.1 (Apr. 2013): 31–38.

nearest reflex of that absolute Mind, according to the intuitions of which he desires to perceive and speak.[40]

Shelley fits the above description, as his poetry is mainly concerned with concepts such as 'Good' and 'Beautiful', which he extracts from his own mind to communicate to the reader. For example, in the 'Preface' to *Prometheus Unbound*, his *magnum opus*, Shelley sought the following:

> to familiarize the highly refined imagination of the more select classes of poetical readers with beautiful idealisms of moral excellence; aware that until the mind can love, and admire, and trust, and hope, and endure, reasoned principles of moral conduct are seeds cast upon the highway of life, which the unconscious passenger tramples into dust, although they would bear the harvest of his happiness.[41]

Browning then goes on to describe the second type of poet, who 'chooses to deal with the doings of men'. The 'objective poet' is of equal value, '[f]or it is with this world, as starting point and basis alike, that we shall always have to concern ourselves'. Browning was to execute this in his dramatic monologues, which allowed an insight into the psyche of speakers from all walks of life, from an egotistical bishop to a bloodthirsty patriot. There is no hierarchical relationship between the two types of poets, and they complement each other in what they seek to communicate.

The 'Essay' inaugurates a new age based on dramatic rather than visionary principles, and it is as much a means of promoting the values it espouses as it is a homage to Shelley. Browning chose to write about real people and their actions in *Men and Women*, the work in which both 'Fra Lippo Lippi' and 'Old Pictures in Florence' appear. His art criticism reflects his own poetic practice and its relationship with Romanticism, the literary legacy that he inherited. It is hard not to reach the conclusion that his preference for realism in art is expressed in the kind of material he chose for his own poetry.[42]

40 *Browning: Selected Poems*, pp. 858–59.
41 *Poems of Shelley* 2: 475.
42 Leonee Ormond in 'Browning and Painting' concludes that 'Old Pictures in Florence', 'Andrea del Sarto' and 'Fra Lippo Lippi' are 'about the crafts

If one reads the 'Essay on Shelley' in this light, it becomes clear that Browning sees himself as an exponent of a poetry that works on 'the raw material it [spiritual comprehension] operates upon'.[43] Thus, like Lippi, he is the latecomer who advances art not by the spirituality that previous painters such as Fra Angelico have attained, but by focusing on the physical reality. Browning's stress on the significance of the physicality of painting counters his predecessor, who believes solely in the value of the 'soul'. This is not to say, however, that Browning endorses the 'flesh' alone, as both 'flesh' and 'soul' complement each other.[44]

In conclusion, I would like to emphasise the significance of Shelley's role in the formation of Browning's taste. That is to say, Shelley's total immersion in Greek art and literature (substantiated by its secular republican polity) arguably prompted a counter-reaction in Browning, who found that his own interest lay rather in medieval and Renaissance art (which drew much of its inspiration from Christianity). It was a shift in taste that was seen generally in the nineteenth century; however, in Browning's case, it was a shift that derived from a deeply personal decision to move away from, and displace, Shelley. In addition, Browning distanced himself from the overtly religious tone adopted by Rio and others (including Mary Shelley), arguably due to their moralising tendency, but also because he saw in naturalists such as Lippi material for a new kind of art that he could develop. His views on art prove that he was wrestling with different kinds of artistic tastes; however, as his 'Essay on Shelley' demonstrates, he was about to inaugurate a completely new type of poetry that would go down in history as such. What seems like a trite comment on Mary Shelley's slavish praise of Fra Angelico unlocks the key to Browning's deep-rooted conviction that in realism lay the next step to poetic progress.

---

of poetry, and about Browning as its practitioner'; see *Writers and Their Background: Robert Browning*, ed. Isobel Armstrong (Athens: Ohio University Press, 1975), pp. 184–210 (210).

43 *Browning: Selected Poems*, p. 860.

44 In 'The Context of Browning's Painter Poems', Delaura makes a point about the Protestant emphasis on 'realism', which Browning took on board, as did Charles Kingsley (378); he also cautions readers not to take Lippi's thesis on 'flesh' literally, as Browning ultimately did not endorse 'beauty for its own sake' (383).

CHAPTER FOUR

The Cenci
and
The Ring and the Book

As Browning's later poems, such as 'Memorabilia' (1855) and 'Cenciaja' (1876), attest, Shelley remained an active influence upon Browning's middle and late writing periods with respect to creative imagination. Accordingly, this chapter reads Browning's narrative poem *The Ring and the Book* (1868–69) as constituting an ongoing dialogue with Shelley's verse drama *The Cenci* (1819). It argues that Browning's poem is a direct response to the historical context of the earlier work: Browning even suggested, at an early stage, that what was to become *The Ring and the Book* should be called *The Franceschini*, perhaps by analogy with Shelley's *The Cenci*.[1]

Browning is known to have owned a copy of *The Cenci*,[2] and we can assume that he knew it well. In his 'Essay on Shelley' (1852), he lists *The Cenci* together with 'Julian and Maddalo' and 'Ode to Naples' as examples of the 'objective poetry' of Shelley's output.[3] Whilst assigning the role of subjective poet to Shelley, Browning nonetheless argues that Shelley was equally able to write objectively.[4]

---

1 See *The Ring and the Book*, ed. Richard D. Altick and Thomas J. Collins (Peterborough, ON: Broadview Press, 2001), p. xi.

2 See *The Browning Collections: A Reconstruction with Other Memorabilia*, compiled by Phillip Kelley and Betty A. Coley (Winfield, KS: Wedgestone Press, 1984), p. 177 (A2097).

3 See *Poems of Browning* 3: 731.

4 For Browning's 'Essay on Shelley' and the distinction between 'subjective' and 'objective' poetry, see Chapter Three.

Whilst Browning was working on *The Ring and the Book*, he came across a reference to the Cenci case in the Old Yellow Book (the original case proceedings for *The Ring*), which he later introduced in 'Cenciaja'. Therefore, the association of the Cenci case with the Franceschini case is a matter of documented fact. Although the relationship between *The Cenci* and *The Ring* has been noted by many critics, the direct influence of the former on the latter has not been discussed fully;[5] it is my contention that Browning tried to not only emulate Shelley but also 'overcome' him by re-writing Shelley's drama. The result is that Browning produced a work that is highly subjective in its idealistic appeal, particularly in the way that the Pope's views take centre stage, as opposed to Shelley's objective reality that falls short of any idealism.[6] It is the 'sad reality', as Shelley put it, which dominates his drama. My focus here is less on the 'subjective' and 'objective' aspects of their output but rather

5 For the similarities between *The Cenci* and *The Ring*, see: Betty Miller, *Robert Browning: A Portrait* (New York: Charles Scribner's Sons, 1952), pp. 246–48; *Browning's Major Poetry*, ed. Ian Jack (Oxford: Clarendon Press, 1973), pp. 275–76. Criticism that compares *The Cenci* and *The Ring* includes: Shigeko Kurobane, '"Scorpion Ringed with Fire" and "A Rose for the Breast of God": *The Cenci* and *The Ring and the Book*', *Studies in Browning and His Circle* 24 (June 2001): 68–77; Mary E. Finn, 'In the House (of Cards) that Rome Built: Shelley's *The Cenci* and Browning's *The Ring and the Book*', in *Influence and Resistance in Nineteenth-Century English Poetry*, ed. G. Kim Blank and Margot K. Louis (New York: St. Martin's Press, 1993), pp. 188–202; Paul Cundiff, *Robert Browning: A Shelley Promethean* (St Petersburg, FL: Valkyrie Press, 1977), pp. 145–97; and Richard C. Keenan, 'Shelley's Influence on the Poetry of Robert Browning' (unpublished PhD thesis, Temple University, 1974), pp. 142–78. More recent scholarship on the relationship between the two works includes Porscha Fermanis's 'Anatomising the "Case": Shelley's *The Cenci*, Browning's *The Ring and the Book*, and the Origins of the Dramatic Monologue', in *Legacies of Romanticism: Literature, Culture, Aesthetics*, ed. Carmen Casaliggi and Paul March-Russell (New York: Routledge, 2012), pp. 37–50.

6 Whether *The Ring* is a work of objective or subjective poetry is open to debate. The multiple voices that comprise the poem are arguably a reason for thinking that it is objective; however, if one were to take into account the poet-speaker of Book I, who effectively tells the reader how to understand the case, it offers grounds for the latter. For the oscillation of Browning's narrative device, see Britta Martens, *Browning, Victorian Poetics and the Romantic Legacy: Challenging the Personal Voice* (Farnham: Ashgate, 2011), Chapter 5.

on the revisionary scheme which Browning adopts in his writing of *The Ring*. It is also a common critical practice when discussing Browning's poetry to focus on the dramatic monologue and its relation to previous forms, such as the Romantic lyric (particularly the conversation poems) and Romantic drama.[7] Instead, I emphasise the revisionary aspect of *The Ring* in relation to *The Cenci*, with a consequent focus on the historicity of each.

In discussing Browning's attempt to re-write *The Cenci*, I would like to focus on four points. First, I note the polarisation of characters into good and evil that Browning was drawn to in his depiction of the characters in *The Ring*—Pompilia, Caponsachi, Guido and the Pope.[8] In addition to the simple Manichaeanism at work, I argue that Browning was influenced by *The Cenci*, in which Shelley draws upon a similarly clear distinction between two opposing natures. Second, Browning plays with the idea of casuistry, which Shelley makes the central idea governing the dramatic action of the main character, Beatrice, and her lover Orsino. Whilst Shelley dramatises the process by which Beatrice falls prey to casuistic reasoning for the killing of her father, and thereby to her tragic fall, Browning makes Guido the casuist whose character remains consistent throughout. Third, I discuss what James Chandler argues as a 'case' for *The Cenci*. Shelley presents a situation that is morally problematic and transforms it so that the moral dilemma is resolved by sympathy for the victim-turned-aggressor.[9] My contention is that Browning, likewise, re-created his own 'case' on the basis of the Old Yellow Book but with Shelley's

---

7 Fermanis argues for the significance of the Romantic drama ('Anatomising the "Case"', p. 39).

8 Browning writes: 'I was struck with the enormous wickedness and weakness of the main composition of the piece, and with the incidental evolution of good thereby—good to the priest, to the poor girl, to the old Pope who judges anon, and I would fain hope, to who reads and applies my reasoning to his own experience, which is not likely to fail him.' See *Robert Browning and Julia Wedgwood: A Broken Friendship as Revealed in Their Letters*, ed. R. Curle (London: John Murray and Jonathan Cape, 1937), p. 159. Ian Jack claims that 'one of the most striking things about the principal characters in *The Ring and the Book* is that they are depicted in black and white' (*Browning's Major Poetry*, p. 295).

9 See James K. Chandler, *England in 1819: The Politics of Literary Culture and the Case of Romantic Historicism* (Chicago: Chicago University Press, 1998), pp. 498–507.

The Cenci in mind. Whilst Shelley left his drama with 'no moral solution to the dilemma of Beatrice's guilt or innocence',[10] Browning emphasised the rescue theme to combat such irresolution. Last, *The Cenci* is a historical play in both senses of the word; that is to say, it is based on a historical event but also necessarily represents the time in which Shelley composed the play. The significance of the year 1819 has been brought to critical attention by Chandler. The force with which Shelley wrote of the political milieu of his times in other poems of 1819 is discernible in how Browning responded to Shelley's historical message by re-writing it according to his own sense of historicity.

Beatrice Cenci's case concerns a court trial held in Rome 'during the Pontificate of Clement VIII, in the year 1599'.[11] Beatrice was the daughter of Count Cenci, of an illustrious family, who was tried, along with her brother Giacamo and her stepmother Lucretia, for the murder of her father. Beatrice, who was the main victim of Count Cenci's perverted passion and hatred, pleaded for deliverance from the hands of her father, only to be spurned. When she was subjected to incest (although never explicitly stated in *The Cenci* but only implied), Beatrice decided to take action, supported by her brother and mother, who were equally cruelly treated by the Count. They hired two men to execute the task, but their plot was discovered when the two men were captured and tortured. Beatrice, along with Giacamo and Lucretia, was sentenced to death for the murder of Count Cenci.

Similarly, Robert Browning's *The Ring and the Book* is a reworking of an actual Roman murder story, in which Pompilia figures as the tragic heroine. Having been married off to Guido Franceschini, a middle-aged man from an illustrious family, for mercenary reasons on Guido's part and for social status on the part of Pompilia's parents, Violante and Pietro Comparini, Pompilia suffers from her husband's retribution and ill treatment because of her parents' actions. After finding out that Guido is impoverished and had only feigned his wealth, Violante and Pietro sue him for the return of Pompilia's dowry. Violante also discloses the fact that Pompilia is not her real child and that she had bought her from a prostitute, thereby nullifying Pompilia's dowry. If she is not their daughter, they cannot be asked to provide her with a dowry. Pompilia, oppressed by the

10 Fermanis, 'Anatomising the "Case"', p. 43.
11 *Poems of Shelley* 2: 727.

tyranny of her husband, flees with the help of a priest, Caponsacchi, but is overtaken by Guido on her way to Rome. At that point, Caponsacchi is charged with adultery whilst Pompilia is sent off to a nunnery for penitent women. Pompilia, however, being pregnant at the time, is placed in the custody of her parents and gives birth to a son, Gaetano, eight months later. Guido turns up at their house and successfully pretends to be Caponsacchi, gains entrance and murders Violante and Pietro and fatally wounds Pompilia. Guido and his hired men are caught afterwards and tried for murder.

The Ring consists of ten testimonies or monologues by nine different people or groups of people, each of whom offers their account of the story: 'Half-Rome', 'The Other Half-Rome', 'Tertium Quid', 'Count Guido Franceschini', 'Giuseppe Caponsacchi', 'Pompilia', 'Dominus Hyacinthus de Archangelis', 'Doctor Johannes-Baptista Bottinius', 'The Pope' and 'Guido'.[12] Therefore, Browning allows differences to emerge through their varying perspectives. Although critics have argued that this is why the poem embraces relativism,[13] it is also true that the poem reveals its own preferences for the accounts given by Pompilia and the Pope, with both of whom we are invited to sympathise by the poet-speaker of Book I. Each testimony is weighed against the others so that, by the time the poem reaches the Pope's monologue, there is very little room to contradict the Pope's verdict. The over-riding notion is that Pompilia is 'the perfect paragon' (3. 81). This depiction of her by 'the other half-Rome' (who represents the opinion of the Romans that Pompilia was innocent) is supported by Caponsacchi, Bottinius and the Pope. The epithets 'the perfect soul Pompilia' (6. 1162), 'martyr and saint' (6. 1992), 'a faultless nature in flawless form' (9. 195), 'the worth of perfect chastity' (9. 1179), 'our paragon' (9. 1211) and 'the marvel of a soul like thine' (10. 1018) all attest to Pomilia's purity.[14]

---

12 'Half-Rome' speaks on behalf of Guido while 'The Other Half-Rome' speaks on behalf of Pompilia. 'Tertium Quid', a representative of a privileged class, thereby slightly partial to Guido, maintains a somewhat neutral position. Archangelis is the defender and Bottinius the prosecutor.

13 See Robert Langbaum, *The Poetry of Experience: The Dramatic Monologue in Modern Literary Tradition* (New York: Norton, 1957), Chapter 3.

14 While I do not wish to simply rehearse the Victorian understanding of Pompilia, from which we have moved on, especially in recognising her as someone who is not simply naïve and innocent but fully aware of her agency,

It has been said that the historical Pompilia was not the kind of saint portrayed by Browning but 'an ordinary girl, deprived of advantages in childhood, with sufficient good looks to attract, and insufficient character to resist temptation, and with instincts stronger than her principles'.[15] It cannot be denied that Browning infused the tale with his own idealism, even if we take seriously his insistence on his faithfulness to the Old Yellow Book.[16] The question, then, is as follows: where did Browning get the idea of Pompilia's being a 'paragon of virtue and purity'?[17] Critics have argued that he based his heroine on his memories of Elizabeth Barrett: 'I am convinced that it [Mrs Browning's spiritual presence] entered largely into the conception of Pompilia, and, so far as this depends on it, the character of the whole work.'[18] Even if this were the case, however, there is no reason for not exploring other means by which Browning created his heroine. For example, one might add to these a model for Pompilia in Beatrice Cenci, who, likewise, proved her purity and innocence through her endurance of hardship and oppression. In fact, the tragedy of *The Cenci* is emphasised by Beatrice Cenci's inner integrity, as the 'Preface' to *The Cenci* included in *Poems of Shelley* says: 'Beatrice Cenci appears to have been one of those rare persons

I emphasise the earlier approach for understanding Browning's strategic use of Shelley's characterisation in *The Cenci*. See, for recent argument on the character of Pompilia, Katherine Anne Gilbert's 'The Politics of Character: The Lawyers and Pompilia in Robert Browning's *The Ring and the Book* (1868–69)', *Victorian Poetry* 49.3 (autumn 2011): 317–45.

15 John Marshall Gest, *The Old Yellow Book: Source of Browning's The Ring and the Book* (Boston: Chipman Law, 1925), p. 624. See also Michael Meredith, 'Flight from Arezzo: Fact and Fictions in *The Ring and the Book*', *Studies in Browning and His Circle* 25 (2003): 101–16.

16 Paul Cundiff argues for Browning's divergence from the Old Yellow Book. See 'Robert Browning: "Our Human Speech"', *Victorian Newsletter* 15 (spring 1959): 1–9. Browning claims that he had found Pompilia in the Old Yellow Book 'just as she speaks and acts in my poem'. See John W. Chadwick, *The Christian Register* (19 Jan. 1888): 37.

17 Gest, *The Old Yellow Book*, p. 624.

18 Mrs Sutherland Orr, *Life and Letters of Robert Browning* (London: Mith, Elder & Co., 1891), p. 281. For recent debate on the significance of Elizabeth Barrett in Browning's characterisation of Pompilia, see Charles Laporte, '"Sacred Legendary Artists": Anna Jameson and Barrett Browning in the Hagiography of Pompilia', *Victorian Poetry* 39.4 (winter 2001): 551–72 (567).

in whom energy and gentleness dwell together without destroying one another.'[19] Unlike Beatrice, however, Pompilia forgives Guido for his actions, and her forgiveness closely corresponds to Shelley's insistence that 'no person can be truly dishonoured by the act of another; and the fit return to make to the most enormous injuries is kindness and forbearance'.[20] Browning's characterisation of Pompilia in this way can thus be read as another instance of his revisionary attempt at re-writing *The Cenci*. In *The Ring*, the polarisation of characters into good and evil follows that of *The Cenci*. Beatrice *is* the epitome of goodness, whereas Count Cenci is that of evil. Likewise, in Browning's characterisations, Guido is 'a human monster, sunk to the level of a brute', set against the 'whiteness' of Pompilia.[21] In a manner similar to that in which Count Cenci seeks to destroy the purity of Beatrice, Guido 'tortured [Pompilia] with due care' (3. 718). Guido turns to vengeance 'since hate was thus the truth of him' (7. 1727).[22]

The Pope of *The Cenci* represents the corrupted Church; preferring to maintain a good relationship with the socially and economically powerful Count Cenci, he does not grant Beatrice her plea to prosecute her father. Browning's Pope, however, symbolises a spiritual force that is commensurate with Browning's own religious beliefs as a Christian. Although Browning's dissenting background complicates his depiction of the Catholic faith, he nonetheless uses the Pope to express a broad set of ethics to which he can subscribe. Again, it is possible to read this as evidence of Browning's revisionary re-writing of *The Cenci*.

Another change that Browning made in his work was in the figure of Caponsacchi: 'the real Caponsacchi was as much at home in Arezzo's red-light district as in its aristocratic drawing-rooms' and 'clearly possessed a dangerous attraction for women'.[23] In *The Ring*,

19 See the 'Preface' to *The Cenci* included in *Poems of Shelley* 2: 735.
20 *Poems of Shelley* 2: 730.
21 Gest, *The Old Yellow Book*, p. 624.
22 Algernon Swinburne makes an extensive comparison of Count Cenci and Guido in 'Notes on the Text of Shelley', *The Fortnightly Review* (1 May 1869): 539–61. The comparison also occurs in the *Saturday Review* 27 (3 April 1869): 460–61.
23 Meredith, 'Flight from Arezzo', 110. Meredith's reading derives from material that Browning either had no access to or repudiated as pro-Guido propaganda.

however, Caponsacchi is idealised like Pompilia; he becomes a priest-knight who risks his position by rescuing the oppressed victim. In *The Cenci*, Beatrice befriends a prelate, Orsino, who turns out to be false. Caponsacchi is the ignoble Orsino of *The Cenci* re-configured and purified. Whilst Orsino acts selfishly, Caponsacchi transcends his own self-interest by sympathising with the victim. Browning followed Shelley's example by clearly dividing his characters into good and evil, but also revised Shelley's delineation of 'sad reality' by creating the Pope and Caponsacchi as the spiritual supporters of the oppressed victim, Pompilia.

Casuistry lies at the heart of both works, which are both set in sixteenth- and seventeenth-century Rome. Casuistry has a long history, originating in antiquity, reaching its pinnacle during the Renaissance and falling into disrepute because of Pascal's attack on the Jesuits in *Les Provinciales* in 1657.[24] Both Shelley and Browning utilise the force of casuistry in the realms of ethics and jurisprudence in which it came to exercise its power. Their understanding of casuistry is unequivocally negative, reflecting the pejorative connotations it had acquired by the nineteenth century. However, the practice of casuistry was a significant means of dealing with the complex moral problems that presented themselves in Renaissance Italy. To rehearse its broad definition:

> Casuistry involves the following elements: (1) A particular (typically ethically complicated or troublesome) situation; (2) Accepted general moral principles; (3) A discussion of how the moral principles may be rationally applied in the particular circumstances.[25]

Casuists 'approached moral questions in the spirit of Aristotle and Aquinas rather than of Plato and Augustine' by choosing 'a course of action prudently and virtuously, rather than [...] ascend[ing] to a vision of eternal truth'.[26] By allowing exceptions, however, rather

---

24 See Albert R. Jonsen and Stephen Toulmin, *The Abuse of Casuistry: A History of Moral Reasoning* (Berkeley: University of California Press, 1988).

25 See Guido Calabresi, *Ideals, Beliefs, Attitudes, and the Law: Private Law Perspective on a Public Law Problem* (Syracuse: Syracuse University Press, 1985), p. 120.

26 Jonsen and Toulmin, *Abuse of Casuistry*, p. 148.

than adhering to rules, casuistry led to moral laxity. Pascal claimed that casuistry was used to excuse those who were rich and powerful. Thus, casuistry became equated with 'a quibbling, evasive way of dealing with difficult cases of duty; sophistry' (*OED*).

Orsino, a prelate in love with Beatrice, is an exemplar of the casuistical thinking that Shelley believed was prevalent among Catholics at the time. Because Orsino fears that, if Beatrice is wedded to some relative by the arrangement of the Pope, he 'should be debarred from all access' (1. 2. 71), he is determined to keep things as they are, despite Beatrice's petition to the Pope. Tragedy befalls Beatrice, then, not when she conceives of the act of killing her father, but when she falls prey to the casuistic justification of her action. It is Orsino who first conceives of the idea of Cenci's murder, but he makes others commit the act:

> Now what harm
> If Cenci should be murdered?—Yet, if murdered,
> Wherefore by me? And what if I could take
> The profit, yet omit the sin and peril
> In such an action? Of all earthly things
> I fear a man whose blows outspeed his words;
> And such is Cenci: and while Cenci lives
> His daughter's dowry were a secret grave
> If a priest wins her.—Oh, fair Beatrice! (2. 2. 120–28)

> and he prospers best,
> Not who becomes the instrument of ill,
> But who can flatter the dark spirit, that makes
> Its empire and its prey of other hearts,
> Till it become his slave—as I will do. (2. 2. 157–61)

Orsino is depicted as a calculating villain who seeks to reap the fruit of others' actions without having to involve himself in their wrongdoing. On the other hand, Beatrice becomes convinced that killing her father is the only way to redeem the ill that has befallen her:

> As I have said, I have endured a wrong,
> Which, though it be expressionless, is such
> As asks atonement, both for what is past,
> And lest I be reserved, day after day,

> To load with crimes an overburdened soul,
> And be—what ye can dream not. I have prayed
> To God, and I have talked with my own heart,
> And have unravelled my entangled will,
> And have at length determined what is right. (3. 1. 213–21)

Although killing her father is a grave crime, under the circumstances—
that is, of being subjected to incest—Beatrice justifies her action in the
presence of God. Her conviction that she is doing right is maintained
until the end, so that, when the two hirelings kill Count Cenci, she
insists on their innocence as she persuades her mother:

> Mother,
> What is done wisely, is done well. Be bold
> As thou art just. 'Tis like a truant child
> To fear that others know what thou hast done,
> Even from thine own strong consciousness, and thus
> Write on unsteady eyes and altered cheeks
> All thou wouldst hide. Be faithful to thyself,
> And fear no other witness but thy fear.
> For if, as cannot be, some circumstance
> Should rise in accusation, we can blind
> Suspicion with such cheap astonishment,
> Or overbear it with such guiltless pride,
> As murderers cannot feign. (4. 4. 34–46)

In other words, Beatrice is convinced through casuistic reasoning that
their conduct is 'guiltless' and that they are not to be classed as other
'murderers', who have no such conviction. She takes the law into her
own hands, thereby confusing its sanction with her own retribution.

Browning revises the role of casuistic reasoning in *The Ring*.
The main characters—Pompilia and Caponsacchi—are free from
casuistic thinking, which is reserved exclusively for Guido and the
lawyers. Guido paints a picture of himself as someone who has fairly
entered into a bargain—'Being the exchange of quality for wealth'
(5. 502)—but who has been cheated by Pietro and Violante when
they reclaim their daughter's dowry. It is *he* who has been injured
by the pact, and, therefore, *he* has good reasons to treat Pompilia
with scorn. When he pursues his wife and Caponsacchi, he argues,
he would have been justified in killing them on the spot for adultery

but decides instead to resort to the law, which sees Caponsacchi assigned to another town and Pompilia confined to a nunnery. Let down again, Guido decides to take action, but only because the law has denied him justice: 'No more of law; a voice beyond the law / Enters my heart, *Quis est pro Domino?*' (5. 1548–49). At this point, when Guido imagines that the Lord is on his side, he takes matters into his own hands just as Beatrice does. He thinks that his case will exonerate his actions. Killing an adulterous wife was considered excusable by the casuists because adultery injured a gentleman's honour;[27] however, if the killing were done in cold blood, which was the case with Guido, because he waited several months before acting, then the qualification would not apply to him. Guido tries to argue around this so that his prolonged injury somehow gives him the right to take action. The Pope sees through this when he says: 'There's Loyola adapted to our time! / Under such guidance Guido plays his part' (10. 1942–43). St Ignatius Loyola was the founder of the Jesuit order, notorious for its worldliness and casuistry.[28] Guido's defender Archangelis argues, in terms similar to those used by Guido himself, 'that Honour is man's supreme good' (8. 585) and 'Whenever honour and repute are touched / Arrives at term of fury and despair, / Loses all guidance from the reason-check' (8. 603–05). Therefore, Guido's case is to be treated as an exception to the law because it was an act of injured honour. This casuistic reasoning is overturned because the story that Pompilia tells gains conviction, as Guido testifies:

> She too must shimmer through the gloom o' the grave,
> Come and confront me—not at judgment-seat
> Where I could twist her soul, as erst her flesh,
> And turn her truth into a lie,—but there,
> O' the death-bed, with God's hand between us both,
> Striking me dumb, and helping her to speak,
> Tell her own story her own way, and turn
> My plausibility to nothingness! (11. 1682–89)

Pompilia's story is so revealing of the truth that the prosecutor, Bottinius, objects to her statement: 'Leaving a lawyer nothing to

---

27 See 'Pride: The Case of the Insulted Gentleman', in Jonsen and Toulmin, *Abuse of Casuistry*, pp. 216–27.

28 *The Ring*, ed. Altick and Collins, p. 639.

excuse, / Reason away and show his skill about!' (9. 1441–42). Thus, casuistry is condemned in *The Ring* and is replaced with 'truth' as communicated through Pompilia, Caponsacchi and the Pope.[29]

Shelley dramatises the case of Beatrice Cenci as one example whereby a 'falling off' from the 'high road of Catholic morality' necessitates casuistry to come into play:[30] '[i]t is in the restless and anatomizing casuistry with which men seek the justification of Beatrice, yet feel that she has done what needs justification.'[31] The case of Beatrice Cenci is presented to us not as one of casuistic reasoning but as a 'case of the heart' that requires 'sympathy' from the masses, a sympathy that could not have been obtained if Beatrice had been 'wiser and better'. As Chandler argues, it is an example of the 'subordination of casuistry to sensibility': 'it is a tragedy which has already received, from its capacity of *awakening and sustaining the sympathy* of men, approbation and success.'[32] The play has a power to *move* people, that is, to encourage them to transfer their position to that of Beatrice Cenci, through the act of 'sympathy'. We are solicited to pity the heroine, whose 'gentle and amiable being' was 'thus violently thwarted from her nature by the necessity of circumstance and opinion'; therefore, we 'feel that she has done what needs justification'.[33] Browning takes this case further; he says that it is not the oppressed victim who should suffer, as Shelley suggests with Beatrice Cenci, but those responsible for the lack of help in delivering her from her difficult circumstances, which also makes for the tragedy of the play. It is because Beatrice is reduced to a cold, self-anatomising mind that she becomes a monster herself.[34] Browning re-humanises the tragic heroine by rescuing her from that destiny; by doing so, he revolutionises the sentiment that had become stifled because of the cold, rationalising mind.

29 Laura Struve argues that '[t]he most stringent attacks on the law in Browning's poem revolve around its relation to fiction and artistic creation'. See '"This Is No Way to Tell a Story": Robert Browning's Attack on the Law in *The Ring and the Book*', *Law and Literature* 20.3 (autumn 2008): 423–43 (433).
30 Chandler, *England in 1819*, p. 198.
31 *Poems of Shelley* 2: 731.
32 Chandler, *England in 1819*, p. 504.
33 *Poems of Shelley* 2: 727–28.
34 Orsino talks about the 'self-anatomy' that is detectable in the Cenci family (2. 2. 110).

In *The Ring*, Browning likewise conceives of a 'case' that calls for the exercise of casuistry: the lawyers both argue casuistically, for example. However, the ultimate resolution moves away from this. Readers, together with members of the court, are solicited to be *moved* by Pompilia's testimony, thus leaving little room for casuistic reasoning to operate. The sympathy which readers are invited to feel for the oppressed Pompilia also encourages them to exonerate her from her crime. In a parallel move, of course, readers are equally solicited to feel antipathy towards Guido and his actions. Whilst, in *The Cenci*, Shelley paints Beatrice as the victim of casuistry, Browning releases his own heroine from it, thereby allowing sympathy to take centre stage, enabling 'subordination of casuistry to sensibility' to become complete.

Browning was inspired to write *The Ring* by the Old Yellow Book of court proceedings which he found in a market in Florence. In Book I, he tells us how he 'disappeared' and 'the book grew all in all' (1. 687). Even if we are not to take his words at face value, the significance of the 'gold' (that is, 'crude fact') with which he 'interfused' 'alloy' (fancy) cannot be overlooked. He is not fabricating a story; rather, he is resuscitating an event of the past:

> Yet, something dead may get to live again,
> Something with too much life or not enough,
> Which, either way imperfect, ended once:
> And end whereat man's impulse intervenes,
> Makes new beginning, starts the dead alive,
> Completes the incomplete and saves the thing. (1. 729–34)

Browning is talking here about his own attempt to bring the content of the Old Yellow Book alive. However, if we consider for a moment the rich array of texts (both literal and metaphorical) that go into resuscitating a past that is made jointly by Browning and his reading of the Old Yellow Book, it is possible to read *The Cenci* as one of the texts that he was trying to bring to life. *The Cenci* was a 'sad reality' that Shelley was confronted with, which Browning inherited along with *Prometheus Unbound*.[35] If the 'falling off'

---

35 Shelley refers to *The Cenci* as 'a sad reality' in his dedication to Leigh Hunt (*Poems of Shelley* 2: 726). Browning mentions both *The Cenci* and *Prometheus Unbound* in a letter dated 2 October 1845 to Elizabeth Barrett, after talking

from the 'high road' is what has made a 'case' for *The Cenci*, the text remains 'incomplete', a haunting presence that must be rectified or normalised by the act of 'saving'. This is exactly what Browning does in *The Ring*: 'I enter, spark-like, put old powers to play, / Push lines out to the limit' (1. 755–56). Beatrice in *The Cenci* pleads in vain for help to escape from her monstrous father, whereupon she is made into a complete victim of her father's perverted passions. With no way of escape, she despairs, fears for her own life and therefore kills her own father. She is tried by the court and sentenced to death. There is no room for salvation in the story that Shelley tells as a reflection of 'sad reality'. Pompilia, who, likewise, pleads for help, is successful in getting assistance from the warrior-priest Caponsacchi. By introducing the trope of the rescued damsel, Browning 'saves' the inherited text from the lack of moral resolution in *The Cenci* and creates 'a successful female Promethean figure, thus rewriting the Shelleys' more pessimistic renditions of violent revolt and female defeat'.[36]

The Cenci case, as it turns out, is not only about a parricide for which Beatrice gets the death sentence: it is also specifically concerned with the historicity of that event. In a Catholic world in which religion is 'interwoven with the whole fabric of life', the Church 'pervades intensely the whole frame of society, and is, according to the temper of the mind which it inhabits, a passion, a persuasion, an excuse, a refuge; never a check'.[37] The murder of Count Cenci is not weighed against his tyranny and evil actions towards his immediate family as would be the case in present-day society (thereby acting as a 'check'), but is instead assessed according to the patriarchal order which upholds religion in so many ways:

> Paolo Santa Croce
> Murdered his mother yester evening,
> And he is fled. Parricide growth so rife,
> That soon, for some just cause no doubt, the young
> Will strangle us all, dozing in our chairs. (5. 4. 18–22)

about Shelley's early work *Zastrozzi*: 'And now, please read a chorus in the "Prometheus Unbound" or a scene from the "Cenci"—and join company with Shelley again.' See *Brownings' Correspondence* 11: 108.

36 Fermanis, 'Anatomising the "Case"', p. 47.

37 *Poems of Shelley* 2: 732.

The Pope's example is revealing of the yardstick by which he is measuring the Cenci case: to pardon the murder of Count Cenci will only encourage the disobedience of children against their parents, which will, in turn, sanction their (potential) rebellion against the Church. Furthermore, the Pope knows that he is the upholder of an evil system: 'for some just cause no doubt'. When entreated to respond to the grievances of the Cenci family against the Count, Cardinal Camillo reminds them that the Pope 'holds it [the Cenci case] of most dangerous example / In aught to weaken the paternal power / Being, as 'twere, the shadow of his own' (2. 2. 54–56). To the Pope, then, the Cenci case is only an example of the need for the authority of the Church to be upheld at all costs.[38]

Shelley wrote a series of political poems in 1819 that, as a group, might be represented emblematically by 'England in 1819'. In the poem of that name, England is represented as comprising all ills 'from which a glorious Phantom may / Burst to illumine our tempestuous day'.[39] The year 1819 figures as the symbolic year in which the state of England is represented: it was of course the year of the Peterloo Massacre, which prompted Shelley's major effort in *The Mask of Anarchy*. As Chandler argues, it became a pivotal year on which the destiny of a nation hinged. Shelley's historicism allows him to assess it both in the light of history, and also in the context of its projection into the future. In other words, England can become either a relic of what it once was or a revelation 'to illumine our tempestuous day'.[40] This sense of self-consciousness in the writings of 1819—seeing themselves in the light of past, present and future— makes them historicist texts.

The Romantic historicism that emerged in the wake of pan-European calls for liberty and independence is another, broader context in which to place *The Cenci*. If England was suffering under an incompetent king and politicians, Italy was subjected to foreign governance that would not allow Italian independence. After the Napoleonic Wars, England had acceded to the reactionary politics that placed Italy in the grip of the Austrian Empire. The Shelleys

38 Browning was later to add this anecdote concerning the reason for the failure of Beatrice's defence in the Cenci case in his 'Cenciaja'.
39 *Shelley's Poetry and Prose*, selected and ed. Donald H. Reiman and Neil Fraistat, 2nd edn (New York: Norton, 2002), p. 327.
40 Chandler, *England in 1819*, pp. 23–33.

were as concerned with the fate of Italy as they were with the fate of England. Shelley composed the 'Lines Written among the Euganean Hills, October, 1818' and 'Stanzas Written in Dejection—December 1818, near Naples', whilst Mary Shelley embarked on *Valperga, or The Life and Adventures of Castruccio, Prince of Lucca*, which dealt with contemporary European politics in the guise of the Italian politics of the Middle Ages. In 'Lines Written among the Euganean Hills', Shelley contemplates the fate of Venice and other Italian cities, which suffered under Austrian tyranny ('Celtic Anarch'), in a manner similar to that of England in 'England in 1819':

> But if Freedom should awake
> In her omnipotence, and shake
> From the Celtic Anarch's hold (ll. 150–52)

> Thou and all thy sister band
> Might adorn this sunny land,
> Twining memories of old time
> With new virtues more sublime (ll. 156–59)

Should such a transformation fail, however, 'perish thou and they'.[41] Again, Shelley posits the case of Italy as one of being on the brink of either mummification or regeneration. Shelley appeals to his contemporary audience to make this choice, as a nation, whether to remain in moral degeneration or to '[b]urst to illumine our tempestuous day'.

Shelley perceived a tidal change on a pan-European scale that would either make countries and regions into modern nation-states based on the sovereignty of the people or cause them to relapse into the dark ages of feudalism.[42] This consciousness informs his writing,

---

41 *Poems of Shelley* 2: 160.

42 See Shelley's 'A Philosophical View of Reform', in *The Complete Works of Percy Bysshe Shelley*, ed. Roger Ingpen and Walter E. Peck, 10 vols. (New York: Gordian Press, 1965), Vol. 7. In the first section of the essay, he outlines the changes that have taken place on a more international level (including the Americas and India); in the second part, he argues for the 'sentiment of the necessity of change': 'Two circumstances arrest the attention of those who turn their regard to the present political condition of the English nation—first, that there is an almost universal sentiment of the approach of some change to be

and *The Cenci* is no exception. Michael Rossington, discussing the title-page of *The Cenci* in his 'Introduction', writes:

> It is worth noting that his [Shelley's] earlier idea, expressed to Peacock, that anonymity would be 'essential, deeply essential to [the play's] success' [...] had been abandoned, and that the word 'ITALY' allows itself to be read not simply as a statement of the provenance of the printed text but as a pointed reference to *C[enci]*'s relevance to the contemporary nationalist struggle in the Italian peninsula.[43]

It is, therefore, significant that Shelley should place his drama in the Italian context of the nineteenth century. The publication of 'the first full-length unexpurgated version' of the Cenci story was ascribed 'to the climate of political instability in the Italian peninsula in 1821', and, as one contemporary critic put it, 'the tragedy means the beginning of Italian liberty'.[44] The Cenci story had further resonance in Italy: it 'surfaced in the early nineteenth-century as a result of the legacy of the Napoleonic occupation of Italy during which, according to many observers, the authority of the Church had been challenged, especially in Rome'.[45] The corruptibility of the Catholic Church and the casuistic reasoning that had become the trademark of Jesuit Catholicism are subjected to scrutiny. It is nothing new that Shelley engages in an onslaught on institutionalised religion; however, his success in depicting a society that is entirely dependent on a religious code is worth critical attention. The tragedy of the play lies not in the fallibility of the Church (which he nonetheless makes explicit) but in the justification of revenge by casuistic reasoning. One can locate the historical message of this play in the contrast between the 'sad reality' of how things are and how things should be. When it is situated among the texts of 1819, marked by anger and despair at the incompetence and tyranny of the English government, it is easy to read *The Cenci* as a gentle reminder of the danger and futility of vengeance in the face of adversity and oppression.

wrought in the institutions of the government, and secondly, the necessity and desirableness of such a change' (p. 21).

43 *Poems of Shelley* 2: 717.
44 *Poems of Shelley* 2: 870–72.
45 *Poems of Shelley* 2: 870.

Just as Shelley's *The Cenci* can be taken as a statement on the condition of England and Italy in 1819, so Browning can be seen to encode the situation of Italy in his writing of *The Ring*. Unlike Shelley, Browning did not express his political views directly in his poems but rather probed the character of historical figures, such as Napoleon III.[46] It is possible to argue that Browning does this to some extent with *The Ring* in his characterisation of Pope Innocent XII.[47] The Pope is depicted as a modern Pope who is open to heresy:

> —do they, these Molinists,
> At peril of their body and their soul,—
> Recognized truths, obedient to some truth
> Unrecognized yet, but perceptible? (10. 1869–72)

The Pope's seeking of the truth in the character of Pompilia—'Perfect in whiteness' (10. 1006)—and of Caponsacchi—'my warrior-priest' (10. 1096)—proves that he understands the 'case' to be that of the 'heart'. He does not question the purity of Pompilia and the motive behind Caponsacchi's rescue, accepting it as being based on his 'pity' for 'the oppressed' (10. 1558). The Pope whom Browning uses as his mouthpiece is not the Pope of *The Cenci* who represents the corrupted Church; rather, this Pope symbolises a spiritual force that is commensurate with Browning's own religious beliefs.[48]

Furthermore, Browning encodes the destiny of Italy in *The Ring* as Shelley had done in *The Cenci*. The 'sad reality' of the foreign domination under which Italy suffers is turned into the unification of Italy through the efforts of heroes such as Garibaldi (although this is never mentioned in the text). The help that was so desperately sought, but was not granted, is finally given to the heroine in the figure of a 'warrior-saint', Caponsacchi. Browning's alteration of their characters to accentuate this motif (that is, rescue as spiritual

---

46 See his *Prince Hohenstiel-Schwangau, Saviour of Society* (London: Smith, Elder, 1871).

47 See Flavia Alaya, 'The Ring, the Rescue, & the Risorgimento: Reunifying the Brownings' Italy', *Browning Institute Studies* 6 (1978): 1–41; also included in *Critical Essays on Elizabeth Barrett Browning*, ed. Sandra Donaldson (New York: G. K. Hall, 1999), pp. 42–70.

48 It should be noted that, as a Protestant, citing the Pope as a religious authority would have posed some problems for Browning.

salvation) reflects the significance of spiritual regeneration in Italy at the time he was writing *The Ring*. The possibility of some future Pope (not Pius IX) being seen as a leader to unite Italy is again foreshadowed in the privileged place given to the Pope in *The Ring*. Browning's *Sordello* (1840) can be cited as an earlier instance of this. In the conflict between the republicans and the imperialists, the papacy is seen as the upholder of a more advanced party. As Browning dedicates *The Ring* to his deceased wife, he is also encoding her efforts towards the achievement of Italian unification that resulted in the publication of *Casa Guidi Windows* (1851).

Browning not only understood the 'case' that Shelley was making in *The Cenci* but also understood it as a case of Romantic historicism. Shelley's plea for a future that was projected in his poetry as the workings of an 'unacknowledged legislator of the world' was responded to by Browning, who, in his works, laid out what Shelley had only foreseen and intuited. If the key word in Shelley's works of 1819 is 'oppression', then Browning makes that his central theme in *The Ring* by introducing a rescue motif so that the heroine, in the end, is liberated. This coincides with Browning's reading of Shelley as someone whose 'predominating sentiment [...] throughout his whole life' was 'his sympathy with the oppressed'.[49] The political urgency with which Shelley warned his audience of the state of England is carried forth in Browning's writings such as *Sordello*, in which he makes the protagonist choose between progress and regress. Sordello is compelled to choose between the Ghibelline faction (which will enable his full reign) and the Guelph party (which he believes to be more progressive). Just as Sordello is unable to make that choice but has to be killed off in 1840 because of the lack of a resolution, so radicalism fails, only to make way for middle-of-the-road Whiggism.[50] As this failure to realise the ideal in the real became one of the legacies of Shelley that Browning inherited and subsequently deployed in his own poetics, I would argue that such a failure also meant that he internalised that political aspiration and made it into a personal one, which is what I would term the revolutionising of sentiment. Although Shelley had already done this with

---

49 'Essay on Shelley', in *Browning: Selected Poems*, ed. John Woolford, Daniel Karlin and Joseph Phelan (Harlow: Pearson Education, 2010), p. 869.

50 See John Woolford and Daniel Karlin, *Robert Browning* (London: Longman, 1996), pp. 157–65.

figures from Greek mythology in *Prometheus Unbound*, Browning attempted the same in *The Ring*.

There is no question that Browning's personal history with Elizabeth Barrett shaped *The Ring*, but I would argue that the said history contains more than a simple story of elopement and rescue. That which he sought in his rescue of the invalid poetess contained the seed/s for his own salvation in his response to Shelley's legacy.[51] Browning had failed in his political radicalism, falling short of Shelley's attempts; his visionary poetry came to nothing, in the same way that Sordello failed to reveal himself. Browning could not live up to Shelley's presence, which, as Harold Bloom would argue, was dramatised in 'Childe Roland to the Dark Tower Came'.[52] Browning had not simply abandoned the Shelleyan cause by moving away from his poetic idol to establish his own poetics based on objective poetry; rather, he had found his Shelleyan Muse, whom he literally rescued and restored to life and vitality. The interchange-ability of Barrett and Shelley has been noted by past critics, but its importance to Browning's writings is still under-appreciated.[53] Rescuing the poetess becomes Browning's way of revolutionising the world.

To read the rescue theme beyond the biographical and treat it as a trope enables us to appreciate its ramifications in *The Ring*: the story concerns not only Pompilia's rescue by Caponsacchi but also the rescue of Italy itself (which the oppressed Beatrice represents) from the rule of the Austrian Empire. That Beatrice does not get the help she seeks to release herself from the oppression of Count Cenci translates clearly into the Italian situation of 1819. Browning takes up Italian politics in *The Ring* by way of advancing the cause that came

51 Paul Cundiff, in his *Robert Browning*, argues: '*The Ring and the Book* is Browning's magnum opus in advancement of Prometheanism' (p. 145).

52 See 'Browning: Good Moments and Ruined Quests', in *Poetry and Repression* (New Haven: Yale University Press, 1976), pp. 175–204.

53 Daniel Karlin, for example, quotes from Browning's 'Essay on Shelley' a description of Shelley that applies also to Elizabeth Barrett: '[h]er [Barrett's] poetry was perfectly blank to him, and this blankness was [...] "the very radiance and aroma of [her] personality, projected from it but not separated".' Karlin also comments on the affinity between Barrett and Shelley: '[i]t is Elizabeth Barrett, not Browning, who is akin to Shelley, who is the divine messenger.' See *The Courtship of Robert Browning and Elizabeth Barrett* (Oxford: Clarendon Press, 1985), pp. 182, 188.

to be known as the Risorgimento. Thus, an allegorical reading of *The Ring* is possible, as Flavia Alaya demonstrates:

> a Roman girl of ambiguous lineage (the old Italy, 'Juliet among nations') is forced into a repressive marriage with a foreign nobleman ambitious of shooting up his shaky dynasty (the Austrian Tyrant); but prompted finally by the stirring of new life within her (Young Italy), she seeks liberation through both her own (revolutionary) defiance of the accepted order and the sympathetic intervention of others (the foreign libertarian powers).[54]

The 'rescue', then, can be read in multiple ways: as a figuration of Browning's own rescue of Elizabeth Barrett, as Beatrice Cenci re-envisioned as Pompilia, and as Italy itself. Whilst Shelley was only able to imagine the independence of Italy, Browning was able to conceive of it more optimistically. Shelley's encoding of politics in 1819 in *The Cenci* is translated in *The Ring* as its counterpart of the future: just as Shelley envisioned the future wherein 'a glorious Phantom may / Burst to illumine our tempestuous day', Pompilia responds to such hope for the future by saying, 'And I rise', thereby gesturing towards both her and Italy's salvation.

---

54 Alaya, 'The Ring, the Rescue, & the Risorgimento', p. 24.

CHAPTER FIVE

'The Triumph of Life'
and
Fifine at the Fair

By the time Browning published his poem *Fifine at the Fair* (1872), 37 years had passed since the publication of *Paracelsus*, and he had established himself as an eminent Victorian poet with the successful publication and reception of *The Ring and the Book*. It is perhaps surprising to find Browning revisiting Romanticism in his later years, when his Victorian sensibility had been firmly consolidated, as had his preferred poetic form, the dramatic monologue. Nevertheless, there is evidence to suggest that his dialogue with his Romantic predecessors was not fully concluded and that he still had things to say on the subject. John Woolford has argued that Browning is both commenting on (in order to supersede) and accepting Romanticism in *Fifine*. Whilst Byron comes under attack in the poem for his belittling view of humanity in the face of nature,[1] Keats and Wordsworth are cited as sources of influence for the poem because the relationship between dream and reality is exploited.[2] Woolford argues that, whilst 'Browning rejects Romanticism' in *Sordello* (1840), he nonetheless 'rejects his own rejection' in *Fifine*.[3] Whilst agreeing with Woolford that the influence of Byron, Keats and Wordsworth can be discerned in the poem, this chapter argues for another influence: Shelley.

1 John Woolford, '"Life—That's Venice!" Browning's Romanticism in *Fifine at the Fair*', in *Browning e venezia* (Florence: Leo S. Olschki, 1991), pp. 233–49.
2 John Woolford, 'Browning Rethinks Romanticism', *Essays in Criticism* 43.3 (1993): 211–27.
3 Woolford, 'Browning Rethinks Romanticism', 211.

Browning made it clear that *Fifine* was 'the most metaphysical and boldest' poem he had written since *Sordello*,[4] which provides ample reason to assume that he is back in his old territory, which was his engagement with Romanticism, as Woolford rightly points out. As I have argued elsewhere, Shelley, as a poetic influence, is not dismissed at the beginning of *Sordello* but remains a prominent source throughout the poem.[5] I would like to argue that Shelley returned to haunt Browning once again in *Fifine*.

This chapter discerns two areas of interest that come into focus when one reads Shelley's 'The Triumph of Life' (1822) and *Fifine* in tandem: firstly, the dream vision, which lies at the heart of both poems, and secondly, the underlying theme of conflict between feelings for a wife and feelings for another woman, which is dramatised less obviously in 'The Triumph' but more explicitly in *Fifine*. With regard to the latter, I focus my analysis on another Shelley poem, *Epipsychidion* (1821), comparing Shelley's ideas on Love with the argument on 'falsity' and 'truth' that Browning elaborates in *Fifine*. Finally, I conclude that Shelley's pessimism (which pervades 'The Triumph') owes much to his failure to win an audience. Browning addresses this discrepancy between the poet's intended audience and the reality by recasting the writer–reader relationship on the basis of his altered attitude towards the masses.

The dream vision has a long history which originated in classical literature and the Scriptures and was developed in the Middle Ages by writers such as Guillaume de Lorris, Geoffrey Chaucer, William Langland, the *Pearl* poet, Dante Alighieri and Giovanni Boccaccio. It follows a quasi-formulaic pattern: the dreamer is usually under a specific condition that precipitates the dream. In the narrative of the dream, the speaker-narrator and dreamer-character become split so that the reader is able to discern the mistake that the dreamer-character makes in the dream and the imagery that is being communicated to us becomes self-evident. The dream is sometimes revelatory in nature and concludes in the realisation of the dreamer that it was only a dream.[6] Both Shelley and Browning follow the

---

4 Alfred Domett, *Diary of Alfred Domett*, ed. E. A. Horsman (London: Oxford University Press, 1953), p. 52.

5 See my *Negotiating History: From Romanticism to Victorianism* (Tokyo: Waseda University Press, 2012), Chapter 3.

6 See J. Stephen Russell, *The English Dream Vision: Anatomy of a Form*

structure of the traditional dream vision only in a loose sense, as there is no split between the speaker-narrator and the dreamer-character as such. However, Shelley does faithfully exploit the characteristic framing of the dream vision in which 'the dreamer was distressed or concerned about some unnamed problem or worry, such that he found it hard to get to sleep on that fateful night':[7]

But I, whom thoughts which must remain untold

Had kept as wakeful as the stars that gem
The cone of night, [...] (ll. 21–22)

And then a Vision on my brain was rolled.... (l. 40)[8]

Both poems include instances in which the speaker undergoes a mental transformation during 'a half slumber', at the scene of a sunrise in the case of 'The Triumph', and by listening to Schumann's *Carnaval* in the case of *Fifine*. Both Shelley and Browning utilise the dream vision to reach a certain kind of truth about themselves and the world at large. They are both beset by moral dilemmas, which are worked through in each text, with 'The Triumph' truncated by the author's sudden death and with *Fifine* reaching closure by the speaker-narrator's playing out his passions and finally settling on emotional constancy for the now-deceased wife. Although 'The Triumph' is not the only Romantic text with a dream vision, as Woolford illustrates with Keats's *Hyperion* poems and parts of Wordsworth's *Prelude*, it is particularly compelling that 'The Triumph' and *Fifine* are both poems about being torn between fidelity towards the wife and passion for another woman.

In 'The Triumph', the speaker witnesses a pageant on a public road, with historical figures chained to a 'chariot' as it overtakes the massed crowd. It is perceived as a 'ghastly sight' in which the masses partake in an orgiastic dance to keep up with and supersede the 'chariot'. At the wayside, a figure, who turns out to be Rousseau, appears, to warn the speaker of the effects of the spectacle. He then goes on to give an

(Columbus: Ohio State University Press, 1988), Chapter 4.

7 Russell, *The English Dream Vision*, p. 5.

8 All citations of 'The Triumph of Life' are from *Shelley's Poetry and Prose*, selected and ed. by Donald H. Reiman and Neil Fraistat, 2nd edn (New York: Norton, 2002).

account of his origin and the process whereby he came to be reduced to a 'root', for which he was originally mistaken by the speaker. The enigmatic narrative of his initial harmony with nature, which has culminated in his encounter with the 'shape all light', and his final destruction by her, ends abruptly because of Shelley's untimely death.

This dream vision in 'The Triumph' functions as a means to seeing a certain kind of reality—life as a tragic repetition of wrongdoing. For instance, the historical figures are not seen to be great and almighty actors on the world stage; rather, they are fallible and liable to self-deception, thinking mistakenly that they possess self-knowledge. When the speaker-narrator asks Rousseau about the figures chained to the 'chariot', he answers:

> 'The Wise,
>
> 'The great, the unforgotten: they who wore
> Mitres and helms and crowns, or wreathes of light,
> Signs of thought's empire over thought; their lore
>
> 'Taught them not this—to know themselves; their might
> Could not repress the mutiny within,
> And for the morn of truth they feigned, deep night
>
> 'Caught them ere evening'. (ll. 208–15)

'The Wise, / The great, the unforgotten', in other words, 'bishops, warriors, kings and sages',[9] have all been subdued to the 'chariot' (except for Socrates and Jesus), through not being able to 'know themselves' or control their inner struggles. They are seen to be just as prone to the devastating effect of the 'chariot' as the masses are, equally ignorant in that they do not know where they come from, where they go and why. In other words, their actions are completely purposeless; passions such as 'fear' are the only driving force that leads them onwards:

> a great stream
> Of people there was hurrying to and fro
> Numerous as gnats upon the evening gleam,

---

9 *Shelley's Poetry and Prose*, ed. Reiman and Fraistat, p. 461.

All hastening onward, yet none seemed to know
Whither he went, or whence he came, or why
He made one of the multitude, yet so

Was borne amid the crowd as through the sky
One of the million leaves of summer's bier.—
Old age and youth, manhood and infancy,

Mixed in one mighty torrent did appear,
Some flying from the thing they feared and some
Seeking the object of another's fear (ll. 44–55)

The folly of the crowd intensifies as they approach the chariot. Their orgiastic dance to keep up soon becomes subjected to its own devastating effects and dies out, only to be taken over by the chariot itself:

                              Swift, fierce and obscene
The wild dance maddens in the van, and those
Who lead it, fleet as shadows on the green,

Outspeed the chariot and without repose
Mix with each other in tempestuous measure
To savage music.... Wilder as it grows,

They, tortured by the agonizing pleasure,
Convulsed and on the rapid whirlwinds spun
Of that fierce spirit, whose unholy leisure

Was soothed by mischief since the world begun,
Throw back their heads and loose their streaming hair,
And in their dance round her who dims the Sun

Maidens and youths fling their wild arms in air
As their feet twinkle; now recede and now
Bending within each other's atmosphere

Kindle invisibly; and as they glow
Like moths by light attracted and repelled,
Oft to new bright destruction come and go:

Till like two clouds into one vale impelled
That shake the mountains when their lightnings mingle
And die in rain—the fiery band which held

Their natures, snaps… the shock still may tingle
One falls and then another in the path
Senseless, nor is the desolation single,

Yet ere I can say *where* the chariot hath
Past over them; nor other trace I find
But as of foam after the Ocean's wrath

Is spent upon the desert shore. (ll. 137–64)

As '[t]he carnal sinners of the Second Circle in Dante's Inferno (Canto V) are blown about by whirling winds',[10] the youths are seen to be caught up in 'the rapid whirlwinds' in the 'agonizing pleasure' of their sexual attraction to each other, until 'the fiery band which held / Their natures, snaps'. This ghastly spectacle is what becomes revealed to the speaker through the dream vision.

In *Fifine*, the speaker, identified as Don Juan, takes his wife, Elvire, to visit a fair at the seaside town of Pornic in Brittany. As they stroll through the fair, the speaker encounters, and becomes attracted to, a gypsy dancer, Fifine. Much of the poem is devoted to his shifting emotions towards these two very different women, who are made to speak for themselves. This is essentially the speaker's device for defending his emotional inconstancy. Then, the speaker relates a dream initiated by Schumann's *Carnaval*. He imagines seeing the carnival in Venice from the air. At first, he is repulsed by what he sees, but a closer look has him realise that the crowd holds intrinsic value. He is taught that we should accept reality as it is, as opposed to what it should be ideally. At the end of this dream, he finds himself back where he had started. He resolves to stay with his wife, until Fifine places a letter in his hand that prompts him to go with her instead. In the 'Epilogue', the speaker is left on his own with the memory of his dead wife, whom he misses.

Although the story of *Fifine* could not be more different from that of 'The Triumph', a similar kind of revelation is brought about

10 *Shelley's Poetry and Prose*, ed. Reiman and Fraistat, p. 459.

by the speaker's dream vision. The speaker in *Fifine* is transported
to Venice, where he finds himself overlooking a crowd of people.
Initially, his condescending view of the people is reflected in how
he sees them as being characterised by the wrong kind of passions,
in a manner similar to how the speaker sees the people in 'The
Triumph': 'my late disgust / At the brute-pageant, each grotesque
of greed and lust / And idle hate, and love as impotent for good—'
(ll. 1861–63). Soon after, however, he recognises that his own attitude
in seeing them in such a way might also be problematic: 'I found /
Somehow the proper goal for wisdom was the ground / not the sky'
(ll. 1866–68). He learns that, if he comes closer to them, they then
become worthy objects of observation. His altered view of the people
is thus an important outcome of the dream vision.

The two visions share certain similarities—one depicts a pageant,
the other a carnival—in that they effectively conceive of people
en masse. These crowds can be taken to represent humanity, as
the narrator in *Fifine* comes to realise, and as the pageant in 'The
Triumph' illustrates through its depiction of the course of Western
history:

> There went
> Conviction to my soul, that what I took of late
> For Venice was the world; its Carnival—the state
> Of mankind, masquerade in life-long permanence
> For all time, and no one particular feast day. (ll. 1856–60)[11]

The intrinsic qualities of humankind are under scrutiny, and thus these
qualities bear different manifestations. The very act of masquerading
becomes a useful means by which humankind's driving passions
become transposed onto the masks that people wear. Whilst, in
Fifine, people literally wear masks, in 'The Triumph', the over-riding
passions become so strong that they become the masks themselves.

The notion that passions, which individuals embody, become
transposed onto the masks, thereby becoming identifiable by them,
is a well-formulated one in *The Masque of Anarchy*, the famous poem
Shelley wrote in the wake of the Peterloo Massacre. In the poem, the

---

11 All citations of *Fifine at the Fair* are from *Robert Browning: The Poems*, Vol. 2,
ed. John Pettigrew and supplemented and completed by Thomas J. Collins
(New Haven: Yale UP, 1981).

government is under attack for the devastation caused on St Peter's Fields in Manchester. Shelley's criticism not only targets the incident but also extends further to the foreign and domestic policies of the Tory government: the Foreign Secretary, Castlereagh, is known as 'Murder' for 'his bloody suppression of unrest in Ireland'[12] and the Home Secretary, Sidmouth, as 'Hypocrisy' for his use of spies for domestic security.[13] Shelley is putting forward the idea that we do not simply embody certain passions but that these passions become us, by taking over our identity in their intensity, as succinctly summarised in *Fifine*: 'man pampers till his mood / Becomes himself, the whole sole face we name him by' (ll. 1715–16).

This idea recurs in 'The Triumph'. People wear masks that show their inner passions, such as 'fear' and 'lust'. In Shelley's earlier poem *Prometheus Unbound*, unmasking denotes liberation from such passions:

> The loathsome mask has fallen, the man remains,
> Sceptreless, free, uncircumscribed:—but man:
> Equal, unclassed, tribeless and nationless,
> Exempt from awe, worship, degree,—the King
> Over himself; just, gentle, wise:—but man (3. 4. 193–97)

In 'The Triumph', the act of unmasking does not result in such liberation but leaves one in perpetual sorrow at the loss of 'joy':

> thus, on the way
> Mask after mask fell from the countenance
> And form of all, and long before the day
>
> 'Was old, the joy which waked like Heaven's glance
> The sleepers in the oblivious valley, died,
> And some grew weary of the ghastly dance
>
> 'And fell, as I have fallen by the way side,

12 *Shelley's Poetry and Prose*, ed. Reiman and Fraistat, p. 316.

13 *The Masque of Anarchy* was included in *The Poetical Works*, 3 vols. (London: 1867). Browning owned a copy of the 1857 edition. See *The Browning Collections: A Reconstruction with Other Memorabilia*, compiled by Phillip Kelley and Betty A. Coley (Winfield, KS: Wedgestone Press, 1984), p. 179 (A2112).

Those soonest from whose forms most shadows past
And least of strength and beauty did abide'.— (ll. 535–43)

Liberation from 'fear' or 'lust' does not materialise in 'The Triumph'; rather, the force of these drives and emotions plays out in a perpetual cycle.

In *Fifine*, people are likewise marked by the passions that they wear on their faces:

> These, you are to understand,
> Were the mere hard and sharp distinctions. On each hand,
> I soon became aware, flocked the infinitude
> Of passions, loves and hates, man pampers till his mood
> Becomes himself, the whole sole face we name him by,
> Nor want denotement else, if age or youth supply
> The rest of him: old, young,—classed creature: in the main
> A love, a hate, a hope, a fear, each soul a-strain
> Some one way through the flesh—the face, an evidence
> O' the soul at work inside; and, all the more intense,
> So much the more grotesque. (ll. 1711–21)

This grotesque masquerading of the inner passions causes the speaker to feel contempt towards the people. This is precisely the attitude criticised by Browning in the ensuing part of *Fifine*:

> Whence
> 'Twas easy to infer what meant my late disgust
> At the brute-pageant, each grotesque of greed and lust
> And idle hate, and love as impotent for good—
> When from my pride of place I passed the interlude
> In critical review; and what, the wonder that ensued
> When, from such pinnacled pre-eminence, I found
> Somehow the proper goal for wisdom was the ground
> And not the sky,—so, slid sagaciously betimes
> Down heaven's baluster-rope, to reach the mob of mimes
> And mummers; whereby came discovery there was just
> Enough and not too much of hate, love, greed and lust,
> Could one discerningly but hold the balance, shift
> The weight from scale to scale, do justice to the drift
> Of nature, and explain the glories by the shames

Mixed up in man, one stuff miscalled by different names
According to what stage i' the process turned his rough,
Even as I gazed, to smooth—only get close enough!
—What was all this except the lesson of life? (ll. 1860–78)

The speaker's 'disgust' at 'the brute-pageant, each grotesque of greed and lust / And idle hate, and love as impotent for good' can be read as an echo of 'The Triumph', in which the speaker-narrator is '[s]truck to the heart by this sad pageantry'. The speaker of *Fifine* subsequently realises, however, that it is his attitude towards the crowd that is the problem and not the crowd itself. In other words, the speaker's elevated position is a sign of 'pride', and he must descend to the 'ground' if he really wants to engage with the people. Such a gesture enables one to 'explain the glories by the shames / Mixed up in man'. In fact, working with humanity is exactly what Browning did in the dramatic monologues. To Shelley's unanswered question of 'The Triumph', 'Then, what is life?', Browning arguably responds by saying 'What was all this except the lesson of life?'

In 'The Triumph', eminent men and women are characterised as being unable to 'repress the mystery [mutiny] within'[14] and 'know themselves', whilst the ignorant masses are described as being sterile in their 'dance' following the 'chariot'. Despite the expectations one would have from reading traditional dream visions such as Dante's *Divina Commedia* or Petrarch's *Trionfi*—the models from which 'The Triumph' derives—the speaker-narrator is not saved in the end by love or God's grace but is disheartened: 'why God made irreconcilable / Good and the means of good' (ll. 230–31). The speaker-narrator is exempt from participating in such a pageant because of his elevated status as an onlooker. Even in this state, the speaker-narrator is scornful of the people and looks down upon them ('numerous as gnats'). Rousseau, his guide, on the other hand, has in fact woken up to reality (which is the pageant) and urges him to 'follow' 'and from spectator turn / Actor or victim in this wretchedness' (ll. 305–06). Rousseau's failure as a visionary, leading to him

14 There is an ambiguous word in the manuscript, which Mary Shelley reads as 'mystery', whereas the later editors have replaced it with 'mutiny'. See *Peter Bell the Third and The Triumph of Life: Bodleian Shelley MS. Shelley adds. c. 5, folios 50–69, and Bodleian Shelley MS. Shelley adds. c. 4, folios 18–58*, ed. Donald H. Reiman (New York: Garland, 1986).

being consumed by the masses, suggests that the speaker-narrator's role in history is at best problematic; pessimism becomes the poem's dominant tone.

What I have argued thus far does not necessarily mean that Browning is rejecting the idealism professed by Shelley in earlier texts, such as *Prometheus Unbound*, in which characters do actually live up to such an elevated status; rather, he is rejecting Shelley's pessimism concerning humanity. The dream vision in *Fifine* leads the speaker to a deeper understanding of himself and human nature. That is to say, we must learn 'how from strife / Grew peace—from evil, good', which leads to the

> knowledge that, to get
> Acquaintance with the way o' the world, we must not fret
> Nor fume, on altitudes of self-sufficiency,
> But bid a frank farewell to what—we think—should be,
> And, with as good a grace, welcome what is—we find.
> (ll. 1880–84)

Shelley's central concern was with what 'should be' rather than 'what is'. If we think of *Prometheus Unbound*, his *magnum opus*, this becomes immediately clear. One might also recall Shelley's father-in-law, William Godwin, who entitled his book *Things As They Are, or The Adventures of Caleb Williams*. This discrepancy between reality and the idealised state of being was particularly acute for Romantics such as Shelley and Godwin. However, rather than despairing over the fact that reality falls short of the ideal, as Shelley and Godwin were prone to doing, Browning, on the other hand, embraces reality and attempts to mediate between the two, in the belief that working with reality will enable him to discern the ideal *within* it.

This negotiation between two opposing states is played out in *Fifine*. First, the land and the sea are placed in opposition to each other in the prologue. The 'amphibian' is able to manoeuvre between both land and sea without being confined to one or the other. The air is the only sphere to which he has no access: only those that can fly, such as the butterfly, can '[own] the sky instead' (l. 19). The speaker can reach out but is unable to obtain the bird's-eye view: 'I never shall join its flight, / For, naught buoys flesh in air' (ll. 21–22). After this symbolic prologue follows the text, the underlining argument of which is the conflict between 'spirit' and 'flesh'. Elvire, the wife of the speaker, is associated with '[l]and the solid and safe' (l. 69); Fifine, the dancer to whom Don Juan is physically attracted, is linked with the sea, which '[g]ives flesh such noon-disport' (l. 58). The solid land provides security and comfort, whilst the ever-shifting sea offers movement and excitement. The speaker finds himself oscillating between these two poles throughout the poem.

If *Fifine* is about the conflict of passions, the same can be said of 'The Triumph', which can also be read biographically, as being about Shelley's personal conflict between his fidelity to Mary Shelley and his passion for Jane Williams. What is significant in the manuscript of 'The Triumph' is that Shelley deliberately separates his feelings towards Jane Williams and his loyalty to Mary Shelley by allowing a disruption of the text to occur in the guise of lyrical poems addressed to Jane. In other words, his complex inner drama is played out in two different domains: one as an epic and the other as lyric poetry. The two are mutually exclusive, and, because they stand in opposition to each other, the poem arguably never reaches a resolution.[15]

15 For the relationship between 'The Triumph' and lyric poetry, see my chapter 'Shelley's "The Triumph of Life": A Resistance to History and the Art of Forgetting', in *The Influence and Anxiety of the British Romantics*, ed. Sharon Ruston (Lampeter: Edwin Mellon, 1999), pp. 89–107. Shelley drafted numerous poems addressed to Jane Williams, with whom he was infatuated, just before and during the time he was composing 'The Triumph'. 'To Jane. The Invitation' and 'To Jane. A Recollection' (1822) were originally published in Shelley's *Posthumous Poems* (1824), a copy of which Browning owned. 'The Serpent Is Shut Out from Paradise' first appeared in John Ascham's two-volume pirated edition of 1834 and under an altered title as 'To Edward Williams' by Michael Rossetti in his edition of 1870. Given the content of the poem, it is likely that it was composed with Jane in mind. 'With a Guitar. To Jane' was first published in the *Athenaeum* (20 Oct. 1832), entitled simply 'With a Guitar', and was included in the one-volume edition of *Poetical Works* (1840) entitled 'To a Lady with a Guitar'. 'To Jane', 'written at Lerici during the last month of Shelley's life' (*Shelley's Poetry and Prose*, selected and ed. Donald H. Reiman and Sharon B. Powers, 1st edn [New York: Norton, 1977], p. 451), was first published by Thomas Medwin as 'An Ariette for Music' in its incomplete version in the *Athenaeum* (17 Nov. 1832) and later republished by Mary Shelley in *Poetical Works* (1839), but was later published as a complete text in the one-volume edition of *Poetical Works* (1840) as 'To — '. 'Lines Written in the Bay of Lerici', written 'two or three weeks before his [Shelley's] death' (*Shelley's Poetry and Prose*, ed. Reiman and Powers, p. 452) with Jane Williams as the main subject, was first published with the same title by Richard Garnett in a shortened

All the Jane poems largely concern pleasure, which Shelley gained in her company, as opposed to grief in the Mary poems. It can be surmised that these poems were painful for Mary Shelley to read. It is perhaps due to such feelings on her part that she made sure that readers did not associate Shelley's last months with the strong presence of Jane in his texts. She altered the order of the poems she decided to publish so that they did not seem like Shelley's final sentiments, by putting them towards the beginning of the poems written in 1822, and she made the addressee of the poems anonymous so that Jane would not feature as the object of Shelley's passion. Even Thomas Medwin followed the example of omitting 'Jane' in the title. It was only after Mary Shelley's death (1851) that 'Lines Written in the Bay of Lerici'—by far the most explicit of Shelley's poems about Jane—was published by Richard Garnett in 1862.

Did Browning know that Shelley wrote a cluster of poems for a woman other than Mary Shelley in the very final days of his life? It would have taken some effort on Browning's part to patch together the scattered fragments in which they existed, but these texts were certainly available to him. There are also hints in 'The Triumph' to suggest that all is not right. For example, the opening of 'The Triumph' begins with a sunrise, which the speaker claims to have stayed awake for the entire night to watch. We are presented with a troubled psyche, although the cause of the speaker's trouble is not named. Further on in the text, when Rousseau gives his account of his past, the culminating incident is his encounter with the 'shape all light'—the embodiment of Eros. In effect, we are presented with a public vision of Western history on the one hand and private emotions on the other.

Let us map out the dichotomous relationship between 'The Triumph' and the Jane poems, particularly the poem cluster 'Lines Written in the Bay of Lerici'.[16] 'The Triumph', as I have already noted, is a view of Western history given by the speaker-narrator and then by the historical figure of Rousseau. Its preoccupation is with time, the horizontal axis that takes us from the past to the present and possibly to the future. As the masses and the Car of Life are in constant motion towards the future, and as the *terza rima* rhyme

version in *Macmillan's Magazine* 6 (June 1862), pp. 122–23, and with the missing first lines in *Relics of Shelley* (London: 1862), under the same title.

16 All citations from 'Lines Written in the Bay of Lerici' are from Richard Garnett's text in *Macmillan's Magazine*.

scheme of the poem compels us onwards, there is no moment that is at a standstill, save for Rousseau's encounter with the 'shape all light'. 'Lines', however, offers a different kind of time frame, whereby the moment is dramatised in its eternity as comprising the vertical axis. 'The past and future were forgot, / As they had been, and would be, not' (ll. 31–32). Shelley is reflecting on his rendezvous with Jane and reminiscing about her presence with thoughts 'I dare not speak' (l. 35). He ends the poem with a sentiment that is potentially echoed in the last line of 'The Triumph':

> Too happy they, whose pleasure sought
> Extinguishes all sense and thought
> Of the regret that pleasure [...]
> Destroying life alone, not peace. (ll. 55–58)

This is a Shelleyan crux in that for all his liberal views on Love (on which I shall have more to say below), 'pleasure' alone will not restore him to 'peace', and choosing one or the other will entail sacrifice. In 'The Triumph', the speaker-narrator's question 'Then, what is Life?' (l. 544) is answered by Rousseau, who responds 'Happy those for whom the fold / Of' (ll. 547–48), whereupon the poem breaks off. There is an echo of the 'Lines' here, in that Rousseau is one of those who were not granted spiritual salvation as the line might have continued to suggest, thereby implying the similar fate of the speaker-narrator, who may well be a version of Shelley himself. It is worth noting that, in Mary Shelley's edited version of 'The Triumph', the poem simply ends with 'Then, what is life? I cried'. Mary Shelley's versioning of Shelley's texts is a familiar topic among modern Shelley scholars,[17] but how much it registered for Victorian readers is a question open to debate. It may be asking for too much to suggest that Browning, for example, would have noticed this to the extent that we notice it today; nonetheless, it is not impossible that Browning might have had some knowledge of Shelley's divided passions, as Clyde de L. Ryals points out.[18]

---

17 See Lisa Vargo's 'Close Your Eyes and Think of Shelley: Versioning Mary Shelley's Triumph of Life', in *Evaluating Shelley*, ed. Timothy Clark and Jerold E. Hogle (Edinburgh: Edinburgh University Press, 1996), pp. 215–24.

18 Clyde de L. Ryals, 'Browning's "Fifine at the Fair": Some Further Sources and Influences', *English Language Notes* 7.1 (Sept. 1969): 46–51.

A more explicit text that reveals Shelley's complex passions at work is *Epipsychidion* (1821). In this poem, Shelley addresses Teresa (or 'Emilia')[19] Viviani on the nature of love, which no doubt would have caught Browning's attention. The poem manifests Shelley's ideas about free love:

> I never was attached to that great sect,
> Whose doctrine is, that each one should select
> Out of the crowd a mistress or a friend,
> And all the rest, though fair and wise, commend
> To cold oblivion, though it is in the code
> Of modern morals, and the beaten road
> Which those poor slaves with weary footsteps tread,
> Who travel to their home among the dead
> By the broad highway of the world, and so
> With one chained friend, perhaps a jealous foe,
> The dreariest and the longest journey go. (ll. 149–59)

There had been rumours about Shelley's personal life, which Browning would probably have been familiar with, but this account substantiates the idea that Shelley was involved (at least platonically) with more than one woman. What deserves attention here is the line of argument that Shelley puts forward in defence of such a position, which is not one of libertinism. It is love of the 'truth', not 'morals', that guides him; consequently, this 'kills / Error', leading him to enlightenment ('fills / The Universe with glorious beams'):

> Love is like understanding, that grows bright,
> Gazing on many truths; 'tis like thy light,
> Imagination! which from earth and sky,
> And from the depths of human fantasy,
> As from a thousand prisms and mirrors, fills
> The Universe with glorious beams, and kills
> Error, the worm, with many a sun-like arrow
> Of its reverberated lightning. (ll. 162–69)

---

19 See *Shelley's Poetry and Prose*, ed. Reiman and Fraistat, p. 392. Teresa's biographer has argued that the Shelleys called her 'Emilia' because her position in a triangle involving two suitors was analogous to that of Emilia, the heroine of Boccaccio's *Teseida* (the story that was the model for Chaucer's *Knight's Tale*).

Browning takes on a similar argument in *Fifine*; however, he does not limit himself to the discovery of love alone (as Shelley would have it) but is open to the discovery of other truths. As 'True Love' would lead to the extinction of 'Error', so would love for the 'truth' reveal the 'false' nature in people. In *Fifine*, the speaker is interested in how appearances can disguise the true nature of people, arguing that what seems to be the 'truth' can turn out to be 'false' and vice versa:

> Because the man who wept the tears was, all the time,
> Happy enough; because the other man, a-grime
> With guilt, was, at the least, as white as I and you;
> Because the timid type of bashful maidhood, who
> Starts at her own pure shade, already numbers seven
> Born babes and, in a month, will turn their odd to even;
> Because the saucy prince would prove, could you unfurl
> Some yards of wrap, a meek and meritorious girl—
> Precisely as you see success attained by each
> O' the mimes, do you approve, not foolishly impeach
> The falsehood! (ll. 1493–1503)

In other words, appearances can be deceptive, and one has to detect the 'falsehood' first (without necessarily criticising it) if one wishes to delve deeper into 'truth'. Browning goes on to elaborate on how we eventually attain 'truth':

> That's the first o' the truths found: all things, slow
> Or quick i' the passage, come at last to that, you know!
> Each has a false outside, whereby a truth is forced
> To issue from within: truth, falsehood, are divorced
> By the excepted eye, at the rare season, for
> The happy moment. Life means—learning to abhor
> The false, and love the true, truth treasured snatch by snatch,
> Waifs counted at their worth. And when with strays they
>   match
> I' the parti-coloured world,—when, under foul, shines fair,
> And truth, displayed i' the point, flashes forth everywhere
> I' the circle, manifest to soul, though hid from sense,
> And no obstruction more affects this confidence,—
> When faith is ripe for sight,—why, reasonably, then
> Comes the great clearing-up. (ll. 1503–16)

As 'Love' was in Shelley's poem, 'truth' is an emanation of light that kills 'falsehood', and such a process of 'great clearing-up' is privileged over simple categorisation into what is true and what is false through the adoption of neat formulae. Whilst, for Shelley, 'Love' is simply a profusion of light that eclipses any 'Error', thereby suggesting a natural process for those who are attuned to it, for Browning, discovering the 'truth' entails a discerning subject ('the excepted eye') who can discriminate truth from falsehood. Browning's formulation is less immediate and more methodological, whereas Shelley simply conveys what he experiences to his reader. Browning breaks down that process so that readers can potentially re-enact it themselves.

This trajectory of reaching the 'truth' through 'falsehood' is one that the speaker takes as well. In *Fifine*, Browning brings together the two polarities that stand in conflict with each other: Elvire and Fifine. His solution is not to settle on moralistic judgement or to paint a 'Don Juan' character of profligacy. The speaker's love for the 'truth' will not allow him to discard his passion for Fifine as immoral and thereby truncate his desire for her. That said, however, he cannot become the libertine that the legendary Don Juan was, because he is also loyal to his wife. In his inability to decide between the two women, his philosophical meanderings take him on to consider womanhood in general: they 'giving all and taking naught in turn' whilst man 'takes all and gives naught' (ll. 1214–15). With her pale and ghostly presence, Elvire never quite becomes a real, embodied woman, whilst Fifine's physicality is accentuated to the point that she becomes 'flesh'. Perhaps the boldest part of the poem is that the speaker does not remain entirely faithful to Elvire, as he goes off with Fifine towards the end, but, as the 'Epilogue' suggests, he returns to Elvire. In other words, what appeared to be infidelity to his wife (leaving for his assignation with Fifine) turned out to be 'false', thereby reinforcing his loyalty to his wife in the 'Epilogue'. Browning is depicting a complex process through which we ascertain the 'truth' in the face of tempting 'falsehood'. The poem seems to suggest that we cannot shirk from confronting this reality by merely upholding morality or abandoning it. It is only through the 'hate' of 'falsehood' that we derive the 'truth'. In this sense, Browning is addressing a dilemma that Shelley faced in 'The Triumph of Life', only to overcome it by gesturing towards a synthesis that would materialise through his living up to reality and seeing the process through.

It is impossible to surmise how Shelley would have ended 'The Triumph'; however, given the overall pessimism of the poem, it is highly unlikely that the moral dilemma would have been resolved into a neat solution. As the messy condition of the manuscript reveals, human passions are often complex and resistant to being incorporated into some coherent system. What Shelley knew all along is perhaps something that came later for Browning. There have been interpretations that relate Browning's personal life to the poem. W. O. Raymond, for instance, has claimed that '[t]he connection between the personal background of Browning's life in 1872 and the theme and mood of *Fifine at the Fair* seems to be unmistakable'.[20] What Raymond is specifically referring to is Browning's emotional involvement with Lady Ashburton, which culminated in his proposal of marriage to her, followed by her refusal. Raymond further argues that the guilt Browning experienced in his involvement with another woman, and inconstancy towards his dead wife, governs and accounts for many of the similes and metaphors of *Fifine*. More recently, Samuel B. Southwell, in *Quest for Eros*, has endorsed a similar view when he suggests that 'the quest [of Don Juan in the poem] might be considered an exploration of personal failure in that affair'.[21] While still cherishing the memory of his wife, Elizabeth Barrett, who had passed away 11 years before the publication of the poem, it could not have been a pleasant experience for Browning to be attracted to other women. That, however, may have been the 'truth' that he confronted as a source of the speaker's attraction to Fifine, and which he worked out through this poem.

Although both 'The Triumph' and *Fifine* engage in the personal, that is, the emotional life of the respective poets, it is also the case that they are public manifestations of history, or, more specifically, Shelley's articulation of Romantic history, on the one hand, and Browning's corrective account of it, on the other. As Shelley described Mary Shelley's *Valperga* as 'a romantic truth of history',

20 See William O. Raymond, *The Infinite Moment and Other Essays in Robert Browning*, 2nd edn (Toronto: University of Toronto Press, 1965), pp. 115–28 (117). William Whitla, on the other hand, asserts that 'Browning was not Don Juan, nor was Lady Ashburton a Fifine'; see 'Browning and the Ashburton Affair', *The Browning Society Notes* 2 (July 1972): 12–41.

21 Samuel B. Southwell, *Quest for Eros: Browning and 'Fifine'* (Lexington: University of Kentucky Press, 2014), p. 185.

Romantic history was never given a happy ending, contrary to what we might expect from the poet who wrote *Prometheus Unbound*— idealism par excellence. Shelley's relationship with his contemporary readers was an outright failure. His letters written during the last two years of his life clearly demonstrate this, referring not only to the hostility of critics and indifference of the public but also to his own disappointment.[22] It is in response to this failure of Shelley's to capture an audience that would enable his ideas to disseminate through society and cause transformative change that we should understand his pessimistic final poem. Therefore, it is somewhat misguided to conclude (as some have done) that Shelley's idealism gave in to pessimism as a course of its own development or regression. Rather, his pervading pessimism (if we can call it that) comes from the material fact that he could not gain the kind of readership he had in mind in order for his poetry to have an effect on society. Browning clearly saw this sharp discrepancy between a poet of Shelley's type and the average member of society, which is why he focuses on shrinking that distance (as we have seen earlier when Browning corrects his attitude towards the masses) as a means of forwarding Shelleyan Romanticism. This, presumably, is what Woolford meant by 'rejecting his own rejection' of Romanticism.

22 All the letters are quoted from *The Complete Works of Percy Bysshe Shelley*, ed. Roger Ingpen and Walter E. Peck, 10 vols. (New York: Gordian Press, 1965). 'I am, speaking literally, infirm of purpose. I have great designs, and feeble hopes of ever accomplishing them. [...] To be sure, the reception the public have given me might [go] far enough to damp any man's enthusiasm' (10: 222; Nov. 1820); 'My "Cenci" had been, I believe, a complete failure [...] at least the silence of the book seller would say so [...] With no strong personal reasons to interest me, my disappointment on public grounds has been excessive' (10: 266; May 1821); 'As to the Poem I send you, I fear it is worth little. Heaven knows what makes me persevere (after the severe reproof of public neglect) in writing verses; and Heaven alone, whose will I execute so awkwardly, is responsible for my presumption' (10: 285; July 1821); 'I write nothing, and probably shall write no more. It offends me to see my name classed among those who have no name. If I cannot be something better, I had rather be nothing, and the accursed cause to the downfall of which I dedicate what I powers I may have had—flourishes like a cedar and covers England with its boughs' (10: 307; Aug. 1821); 'I try to be what I might have been, but am not successful[l]' (10: 333; Oct. 1821); 'Or who acted as midwife to this last of my orphans [*Hellas*], introducing it to oblivion, and me to my accustomed failure?' (10: 370; Apr. 1822).

Furthermore, Browning offers a corrective of the writer–reader relationship from the Romantic model to a more democratic one that depends on co-operation with the reader (as in the dramatic monologue). In this active participation of the reader lies, according to Browning, the seed for poetry to enact change in the minds of readers, as well as wider societal change. Shelley knew that this had been the case with the *philosophes* and French citizens, as he states in the 'Preface' to *Laon and Cythna* (later renamed as *The Revolt of Islam*):

> The French Revolution may be considered as one of those manifes-tations of a general state of feeling among civilized mankind, produced by a defect of correspondence between the knowledge existing in society and the improvement, or gradual abolition of political institutions.[23]

It is the collapse of communication endemic in the writer–reader relationship of Shelley's type that motivates Browning's revisionary endeavours; in this sense, Browning is actively enacting that failure (in the guise of a historicist consciousness that knows its limitations) in order to rework it into something else. This collaborative deployment of Shelley's failure in order to achieve his own ends is what I mean by Shelley's influence on Browning.

23 *Poems of Shelley* 2: 35.

CHAPTER SIX

Elizabeth Barrett and Shelley

Romantic Politics: *The Battle of Marathon, Prometheus Bound* and *The Seraphim*

I had promised my own prudence to shut close the gates of Eden between Milton and myself, so that none might say I dared to walk in his footsteps. He should be within, I thought, with his Adam and Eve unfallen or falling,—and I, without, with my EXILES,—I also an exile! It would not do. The subject, and his glory covering it, swept through the gates, and I stood full in it, against my will, and contrary to my vow,—till I shrank back fearing, almost desponding; hesitating to venture even a passing association with our great poet before the face of the public.[1]

This is what Elizabeth Barrett wrote in her 'Preface' to *Poems* (1844) with *A Drama of Exile* (based on the story of Adam and Eve) as the lead poem for the first volume. What she implies in this 'Preface' is suggestive: that she has somehow sought to distance herself from Milton, but could not avoid his influence, so that her work is subsequently susceptible to Miltonic resonances. Her statement is perhaps more revelatory of her own anxieties than of her own poetic practice: she makes a deliberate break away from Milton in her treatment of Prometheus in a manner similar to Shelley. This is one of the commonalities of the two poets that the following analysis will investigate, arguing that, in fact, it is not Milton, but, rather, Shelley whose influence Elizabeth Barrett sought to keep at bay but could not. Apart from the overt Christianity in Elizabeth Barrett's

---

1 See *Works of EBB* 2: 567–71 (567–68).

poetry, her ideas come uncannily close to those of Shelley. Elizabeth Barrett's revision of Shelley is not as simple as her Christianisation of the Romantic poet is often thought to be.[2] After all, Shelley understood Christianity well and even assimilated its fundamental ideas into his work without couching them in explicitly religious terms. However, it seems to be the case that Elizabeth Barrett was not willing to acknowledge Shelley, precisely because of his religious position, but was willing to take a lot of his ideas. The fact that she did not idolise Shelley in the way that Browning did has left their relationship comparatively unexplored when compared to the critical writings on Browning and Shelley; however, this does not license one to continue ignoring such similarities that exist between them and the possible influence Shelley had on Elizabeth Barrett.

Elizabeth Barrett, who was six years older than Browning, was exposed to, and possibly influenced by, Romanticism even more than Browning: in the year she privately published her first major effort, *The Battle of Marathon* (1820), the second-generation Romantics, namely Byron and Shelley, were not only still alive but in the midst of their active literary careers.[3] Indeed, when she lamented over Byron's premature death in 1824, she was already 18 years old. It is natural, therefore, to situate her among the Romantics as Marjorie Stone does in her book on Elizabeth Barrett.[4] Although the relationship between Elizabeth Barrett's early texts and those of the Romantic poets has been noted, no extensive research has been carried out to date on Shelley and Elizabeth Barrett. This chapter is an attempt at doing just that. I shall begin by examining her early texts, such as *The Battle of Marathon* (1820), *The Seraphim* (1838) and her English translation of Aeschylus's *Prometheus Bound* (1833). My argument will mainly focus on the prefaces rather than the poems themselves, as they contain elements that are comparable

2 Elizabeth Barrett was called 'Christian Shelley without Shelley's art'; see 'English Poetry and Poets of the Present Day', *The Knickerbocker* (June 1845), pp. 534–42 (540).

3 Byron had published *Childe Harold's Pilgrimage* in 1812 and 1818, and was engaged in his composition of *Don Juan* (1819–24); Shelley had published three of his major poems, *The Revolt of Islam* (1818), *The Cenci* (1819) and *Prometheus Unbound* (1820).

4 Marjorie Stone, *Elizabeth Barrett Browning* (New York: St. Martin's Press, 1995), p. 10.

to Shelley's prefaces of poems such as *The Revolt of Islam* (1818) and *Prometheus Unbound* (1820). In addition to exploring Barrett's links to Shelley, I shall also be looking at the texts of Mary Shelley for purposes of comparison, as the Shelleys were both engaged in concerns such as how to keep liberty alive in an age of reactionary forces.

The first reference to Shelley is when Elizabeth Barrett compares Anacreon's ode to Shelley' poem (which has not been conclusively identified) in a letter of 1828 addressed to her mentor and tutor of Greek, Hugh Stuart Boyd.[5] There are several references to Shelley in her diary entry of 1831:[6] she mentions *Queen Mab* (1813) as 'not in my opinion, written in the highest vein of poetry; & it is dull & heavy' (p. 180); she refers to *Adonais* (1821) as being 'perfectly exquisite', a work whose author 'walks in Bion's footsteps' and is 'one of Θεοιπσρεδροι [Those sitting near the gods]' (pp. 180–81). She read *The Defence of Poetry* in *Essays, Letters from Abroad, Translations and Fragments* given to her by her father in 1840.[7] Although there is evidence to suggest that Elizabeth Barrett was familiar with Shelley's works from an early period, they are still patchy, thus making it more difficult to establish a solid case for Shelley's influence on the young poet than it is for his concomitant influence on Browning. Given her voracious appetite for poetry, however, it is highly unlikely that she did not read most of the major works of somebody as celebrated, if somewhat notorious, as Shelley. After all, critics were quick to point out the similarities that exist between the poetry of Shelley and that of Elizabeth Barrett.[8] *The Metropolitan Magazine* had this to say about Elizabeth Barrett's *Seraphim, and Other Poems*:

5 The editors of *The Brownings' Correspondence* surmise that the poem in question was 'Love's Philosophy', published in *The Indicator* on 22 December 1819 (2: 159).

6 See *The Barretts at Hope End: The Early Diary of Elizabeth Barrett Browning*, ed. Elizabeth Berridge (London: John Murray, 1974).

7 Elizabeth Barrett's letter to Septimus Moulton-Barrett dated 6 February 1840 (a conjecture by the editors): 'Tell him [Papa] too what I forgot to tell, that I have finished Shelley's volume [*Letters from Abroad*]' (*Brownings' Correspondence* 4: 233).

8 Elizabeth Barrett's poem entitled *The Seraphim* (1838) attracted such a comparison in *The Metropolitan Magazine* 22.88 (August 1838), pp. 97–101, and in *The Literary Gazette* (1 December 1838), pp. 759–60.

> At our first glance at this extraordinary little book, we were
> singularly struck with the originality, ideality, earnestness, and
> masterly power of expression and execution; and a more careful
> examination has deepened this first impression, and awakened in
> us a great respect for the fair author's uncommon learning. [...]
> The style and manner resulting from this combination remind us
> more of Shelley than of any other recent English writer. (p. 97)

The Literary Gazette also mentions Shelley: '[h]er poetry is of a very
high order, and, in numerous instances, will bear comparison with
the best of Shelley' (p. 759). Taking my cue from these early reviewers,
I would like to highlight the similarities that exist between the early
texts of Elizabeth Barrett and some of the major poems of Shelley.

The Battle of Marathon is, as the title suggests, a poem that deals
with the military victory of Greece over Persia in 490 BC. This poem
has hitherto been discussed in the context of the nineteenth-century
Greek independence movement, and therefore has been associated
with Byron, who fought in that war.[9] Although Shelley's *Hellas*
(1822) has been mentioned as another example of Romantic interest
in Greece in relation to Elizabeth Barrett's poem,[10] his earlier work,
entitled firstly *Laon and Cythna* (1817) and later revised as *The
Revolt of Islam* (1818), has gone largely unnoticed as a text that bears
comparison to *The Battle of Marathon*. This may be due to the fact
that *The Revolt of Islam* deals with an imaginary setting and that it
does not concern Greece and Turkey directly; however, it is clear that
the imaginary Golden City (where the revolution takes place) and the
rulers of that city are loosely based on the liberal Western forces and
Ottoman Empire. In this context, *The Battle* shares as much with *The
Revolt* as it does with *Hellas*.[11]

9 See Simon Avery and Rebecca Stott, *Elizabeth Barrett Browning* (Harlow:
   Longman, 2003), p. 47.
10 Avery and Stott, *Elizabeth Barrett Browning*, p. 47.
11 There is evidence of Elizabeth Barrett's familiarity with the poem: 'Read some
   passages from Shelley's Revolt of Islam before I was up. He is a great poet;
   but we acknowledge him to be a great poet as we acknowledge Spenser to be
   so, & do not love him for it. He resembles Spenser in one thing, & one thing
   only, that his poetry is too immaterial for our sympathies to enclasp it firmly.
   It reverses the lot of human plants: its roots are in the air, not earth!—But as I
   read him on, I may reverse this opinion.' See her diary entry of 26 August 1831
   in *The Barretts at Hope End*, p. 149. In a letter dated 16 April 1838 (a conjecture

What marks the prefaces to both *The Battle* and *The Revolt* is the poets' appeal to 'liberty' as a concept vital to a democratic society. While Shelley's exhortation is more directly targeted at a post-Revolutionary England that had become reactionary (precisely because of the French Revolution), Elizabeth Barrett's is more general (although given the political milieu of the time and the Barretts' interest in contemporary political events, as Simon Avery notes, it is likely that she had in mind immediate domestic incidents such as the Peterloo Massacre).[12] Elizabeth Barrett writes:

> Who can be indifferent, who can preserve his tranquility, when he hears of one little city rising undaunted, and daring her innumerable enemies, in defence of her freedom—of a handful of men overthrowing the invaders, who sought to molest their rights and to destroy their liberties? Who can hear unmoved of such an example of heroic virtue, or patriotic spirits, which seems to be crying from the ruins of Athens for honour and immortality? The heart, which cannot be fired by such a recital, must be cold as the icy waters of the Pole, and must be devoid at once of manly feeling and patriotic virtue; for what is it that can awaken the high feelings which sometimes lie dormant in the soul of man, if it be not liberty?[13]

Elizabeth Barrett is direct in her appeal for liberty by conjuring up emotions that are associated with ancient Greece and its ideals. This evocation of ancient Greece is then associated with the England of the Magna Carta, the intention of which was to protect the liberty of the English people. By such associations, the reader is solicited to (re)member the significance of liberty in an age that has subdued it.

Shelley does something similar in *The Revolt of Islam* by discerning the traces of 'liberty' among the people. He couches this discernment as 'an experiment', thereby applying a more systematic

---

by the editors) to Mary Russell Mitford, Elizabeth Barrett refers to 'your charmèd words', which possibly resonates with 'thy charmed voice' in Shelley's *Revolt of Islam* (4. 28. 1559); see *Brownings' Correspondence* 4: 28.

12 See Avery and Stott, *Elizabeth Barrett Browning*, pp. 52–54.

13 *Works of EBB* 4: 17–18. All citations from *The Battle of Marathon* are from *Works of EBB*, Vol. 4.

approach to the generation and subsequent blossoming of the spirit of liberty in a reactionary age:

> It is an experiment on the temper of the public mind, as to how far a thirst for a happier condition of moral and political society survives, among the enlightened and refined, the tempests which have shaken the age in which we live. I have sought to enlist the harmony of metrical language, the ethereal combinations of the fancy, the rapid and subtle transitions of human passion, all those elements which essentially compose a Poem, in the cause of a liberal and comprehensive morality; and in the view of kindling within the bosoms of my readers, a virtuous enthusiasm for those doctrines of liberty and justice, that faith and hope in something good, which neither violence nor misrepresentation, nor prejudice, can ever totally extinguish among mankind.[14]

As Shelley writes, he proffers poetry to his readers as being a means to 'awaken the feelings' of 'true virtue' and 'liberty'. Elizabeth Barrett likewise claims 'that Poetry is the parent of liberty, and of all the fine arts'.[15] Their appeal to their readers for such a politicised emotional response and their utilisation of poetry to such ends thus bind them together as being in pursuit of near-identical aims, and furthermore firmly situate them among those writers of the Romantic period who sought to disseminate liberty among people in order to realise it within and beyond England. It was not Shelley alone, of course, but Byron also who wrote poetry on behalf of liberty's cause; however, Shelley is by far the most systematic and thorough of poets to deal with this topic in the post-Napoleonic era. Although Wordsworth and Coleridge expressed their revolutionary sentiments in their poetry in the 1790s,[16] they were seen to have turned their backs on liberalism by the time Elizabeth Barrett came

---

14 *Poems of Shelley* 2: 32. All citations from *The Revolt of Islam*, unless otherwise indicated, are from *Laon and Cythna*. For the publication history behind *The Revolt* as well as for the text itself, see *Poems of Shelley*, Vol. 2.

15 *Works of EBB* 4: 19.

16 See their poems on the French Revolution: most notably, Wordsworth's reflection on the event in *The Prelude* (1805) and Coleridge's *France: An Ode* (1798), which outlines his feelings about the Revolution, from initial support to eventual disillusionment.

to write poetry, and what she takes from Wordsworth is the ballad form as an appropriate technical solution for the expression of human emotions.[17] It is therefore reasonable to claim that Elizabeth Barrett's political sentiments have much more in common with Shelley than with the other Romantic poets.[18]

It is Barrett's belief that poetry is crucial to the emergence and development of a democratic society, an idea shared by the Shelleys, with the most notable example of its articulation being Shelley's *Defence of Poetry* (1821). For instance, Barrett writes of Homer as being the ultimate force behind enlightenment and liberal thought in ancient Greece:

> It is worthy of remark, that when Poetry first burst from the mists of ignorance—when first she shone a bright star illumining the then narrow understanding of the Greeks—from that period when HOMER, the sublime Poet of antiquity, awoke the first notes of poetic inspiration to the praise of valour, honour, patriotism, and, best of all, to a sense of the high attributes of the Deity, though darkly and mysteriously revealed; then it was, not till then, that the seed of every virtue, of every great quality, which had so long lain dormant in the souls of the Greeks, burst into the germ [...]. Then it was that Greece began to give those immortal examples of exalted feeling, and of patriotic virtue, which have since astonished the world; then it was that the unenlightened soul of the savage rose above the degradation which assimilated him to the brute creation, and discovered the first rays of social independence, and of limited freedom; not the freedom of barbarism, but that of a state enlightened by a wise jurisdiction, and restrained by civil laws. (*Works of EBB* 4: 16)

According to Elizabeth Barrett, the virtues that are associated with ancient Greece came to life precisely *because* of Homer and not the

---

17 See Stone, *Elizabeth Barrett Browning* for the influence of Wordsworth and Coleridge on Elizabeth Barrett's ballads (pp. 105–07) and also for her revision of their ballads (pp. 107–14).

18 Stone writes: 'In her later career, however, Barrett Browning was inclined to be more radically polemical than Wordsworth in appropriating the ballad for political purposes, following Shelley's example more than Wordsworth's' (*Elizabeth Barrett Browning*, pp. 106–07).

other way around. In other words, Homer's poetry instigated the civilising effect of the Greeks. As Greece was perceived as being the father of democracy in the West, it is particularly pertinent that poetry was attributed as the originator of it.

In *Valperga*, Mary Shelley talks of Dante in similar terms:

> The other nations of Europe were yet immersed in barbarism, when Italy, where the light of civilization had never been wholly eclipsed, began to emerge from the darkness of the ruin of the Western Empire, and to catch from the East the returning rays of literature and science. At the beginning of the fourteenth century Dante had already given a permanent form to the language which was the offspring of this revolution; he was personally engaged in those political struggles, in which the elements of the good and evil that have since assumed a more permanent form / were contending; his disappointment and exile gave him leisure to meditate, and produced his *Divina Comedia*.[19]

Although, strictly speaking, Dante was not a member of the Guelphs who upheld liberty, nonetheless he was considered a *de facto* descendant of the movement, such was the force of his dramatisation of the 'struggle' that, as expressed through the voice of *Valperga*'s heroine Euthanasia, characterises liberty:

> Florence was free, and Dante was a Florentine; none but a freeman could have poured forth the / poetry and eloquence to which I listened: what though he were banished from his native city, and had espoused a party that seemed to support tyranny; the essence of freedom is that clash and struggle which awaken the energies of our nature, and that operation of the elements of our mind, which as it were gives us the force and power that hinder us from degenerating, as they say all things earthly do when not regenerated by change.[20]

Despite the fact that Dante was a Ghibelline, his poetry embodies 'the essence of freedom', the forces of which were germinating at the

---

19 *N&SW of Mary Shelley* 3: 7. All citations from *Valperga* are from *N&SW of Mary Shelley*, Vol. 3.
20 *N&SW of Mary Shelley* 3: 81–82.

time in the city-states of Italy. This is part of a liberal tradition—a convention that was constructed in seeing the Western democracy originate in ancient Greece, being carried on in medieval Italy and further into modern England, France and America—that the Shelleys address repeatedly in their writings.[21] Although Elizabeth Barrett does not fully develop such a notion at this point (or rather, such an idea remains quiescent), she does go on to embrace this tradition later in her career when she writes on the subject of Italian independence.

What separates *The Battle* from *The Revolt*, however, is the means by which liberty triumphs (although we should be mindful that, in *The Revolt*, such a triumph is temporary in any case). In *The Battle*, it is the valour and high spiritedness of the commanders that lead to their victory; in *The Revolt*, however, it is a peaceful revolution that relies more on the ideals, such as 'love' and 'truth', as communicated by the protagonists, that brings about the dismantling of tyranny, if only for a limited time. When the rulers are reinstated with the aid of reactionary powers, Cythna communicates to Laon that their idealism will not die even if they should face death:

> 'The good and mighty of departed ages
> Are in their graves, the innocent and free
> Heroes, and Poets, and prevailing Sages,
> Who leave the vesture of their majesty
> To adorn and clothe this naked world;—and we
> Are like to them—such perish, but they leave
> All hope, or love, or truth, or liberty,
> Whose forms their mighty spirits could conceive
> To be a rule and law to ages that survive. (9: 3712–20)

As an embodiment and enforcer of 'hope', 'love', 'truth' and 'liberty', their endeavours will not be in vain even if the individuals themselves

---

21 As Jennifer Wallace points out, '[t]he notion of Greece as an ideal example touching with flames is especially prevalent in the study of the hellenism of previous centuries' and 'the assumption is still that the interest in Greece during Romantic and Victorian periods was far less questioning and far more adulatory than it is today'; see *Shelley and Greece: Rethinking Romantic Hellenism* (London: Macmillan, 1997), p. 2. In contrast, modern understanding of ancient Greek society regards its democracy as being limited by class and gender.

fall to the ground. In other words, their legacy will remain alive long after they themselves are dead and can no longer exert influence. This knowledge derives from the fact that many like them in the past had left behind such legacies upon the basis of which later generations acted. Such is the reassurance which Cythna communicates to Laon. Shelley was to rework this idea into his famous 'Ode to the West Wind' (1820) included in his collection of poems with *Prometheus Unbound*. What lies at the heart of *The Revolt*—from brute force to knowledge (by this I mean the civilising and democratising force dependent on intellect rather than valour)—is exactly what Elizabeth Barrett was to engage with in her major poem, *The Seraphim* (1838).

In discussing *The Seraphim*, a poem on the crucifixion of Christ as viewed by two seraphim, we should realise that Barrett's translation of Aeschylus's *Prometheus Bound* (undertaken five years earlier) holds significance as she compares Aeschylus's Prometheus with Christ in the 'Preface'. This comparison was by no means a new attempt (in seeing them suffering on behalf of humanity);[22] however, the way she developed *Prometheus Bound* into *The Seraphim* deserves attention for the ways that are reminiscent of Shelley's reworking of the Prometheus figure in *Prometheus Unbound* (1820), as noted by Marjorie Stone.[23]

Before we examine the two poems in tandem, a brief personal and social background to Elizabeth Barrett's act of translating Aeschylus's play may prove useful. Women in the nineteenth century, unlike privileged men who received (public) schooling, did not have access to a formal education, let alone training in the classics (until female students were officially admitted to colleges towards the end of the century). Highly motivated women who were interested in Greek, for example, had to resort to private means or self-teaching for language acquisition. Elizabeth Barrett too showed early interest in Greek, which was developed and enforced through private tutelage offered by a Hugh Stuart Boyd. Elizabeth Barrett was one of the first in a line of female translators who were to gain publicity through their translation works in the nineteenth century. Thus, although Elizabeth Barrett's translation did become a model which others followed and emulated to some extent, she was not a singular figure in this field. What

---

22 See Linda M. Lewis, *The Promethean Politics of Milton, Blake, and Shelley* (Columbia: University of Missouri Press, 1992), pp. 25–26.

23 Stone, *Elizabeth Barrett Browning*, p. 54.

characterised the female translators (with a range of variety of course) was the meticulousness and attentiveness to the original language, which gained public praise as well as recognition by reviewers and the like. When Elizabeth Barrett showed no qualms in dashing her criticism targeted at Shelley's inaccurate translation of the Greek texts, it is precisely this realm of linguistic competence (not as a philologist, however) that female translators came to inhabit and take pride in.

Another aspect is how the act of translating the Greek original, in this case, Aeschylus's *Prometheus Bound*, fed into gender politics. Yopie Prins argues in *Ladies' Greek* that it was not simply subversive empowerment (associated with Promethean politics) with its liberating and mastering force that was equally enjoyed by female translators, as pointed out by other critics, but also the state of 'subjection'—how they too were 'bound' to the text as translators and as women—that they inscribed into their translated texts.[24] This was no exception for Elizabeth Barrett: she too, as I shall be demonstrating below, emphasised the 'suffering' of Prometheus that became the prominent feature of her first attempt at translating the Greek play. Her second endeavour at translating the very same play in 1850 is altogether a different kind of text that reflects her courtship with Robert Browning (based on a textual exchange mediated by Aeschylus's play). As their courtship correspondence shows, their frequent reference to the Andromeda myth adds a different dimension to the play that reinforces Elizabeth Barrett's initial state of being bound and her subsequent release. As the 1850 translation falls outside the scope of my main argument, I shall not be referring to it further beyond the fact that its inscription of liberation (owing much to Browning's collaborative contribution) was underpinned by Elizabeth Barrett's intentional move away from literal translation.

Let us return to examining Elizabeth Barrett's first translation of *Prometheus Bound* in relation to the Shelleys' literary output that hinges on a similar thematic dramatisation before taking a look at Shelley's *Prometheus Unbound*. In the 'Preface', Elizabeth Barrett argues that, had Aeschylus known of Christ,

He would have turned from such to the rent rocks and darkened sun—rent and darkened by a sympathy thrilling through nature

---

24 Yopie Prins, *Ladies' Greek: Victorian Translations of Tragedy* (Princeton: Princeton University Press, 2017), p. 59.

but leaving man's heart untouched—to the multitudes, whose victim was their Saviour—to the Victim, whose sustaining thought beneath and unexampled agony, was not the Titanic 'I can revenge,' but the celestial 'I can forgive!'[25]

The epistemic transition from 'revenge' to 'forgiveness'[26] is one that lies at the heart of Shelley's major texts, namely *The Revolt of Islam*, *The Cenci* (1819) and *Prometheus Unbound*, and Mary Shelley's early novels such as *Frankenstein* (1818) and *Valperga*. In the 'Preface' to *The Revolt of Islam*, Shelley reassures the reader that '[t]here is no quarter given to Revenge or Envy, or Prejudice. Love is celebrated everywhere as the sole law which should govern the moral world.'[27] The protagonists do not resort to revenge even in their state of captivity and knowledge of their impending deaths. As the above quotation indicates, they maintain high-mindedness throughout their lives. In *The Cenci*, Shelley reminds readers in the 'Preface' that '[r]evenge, retaliation, atonement, are pernicious mistakes'[28] by creating a heroine who tragically becomes a victim of such passion, thereby bringing about her own death. The virtuous heroine, Beatrice, in *The Cenci* becomes subjected to her father's malicious conduct towards her. After being sexually assaulted by her father, which is only hinted at in the text, Beatrice seeks revenge with her brother and mother who likewise had been maltreated by the Count. Their plot to kill the Count is discovered after his murder and Beatrice is sentenced to death. Shelley goes on to explain that, if the actual Beatrice had avoided revenge, 'she would have been wiser and better' and that

It is in the restless and anatomizing casuistry with which men seek the justification of Beatrice, yet feel that she has done what

---

25 *Works of EBB* 4: 289. All citations from the 'Preface' to *Prometheus Bound* and the 'Preface' to *The Seraphim* are from *Works of EBB*, Vol. 4.

26 For the second translation of *Prometheus Bound* (1850), Elizabeth Barrett 'attempted a less literal and more poetic version which emphasized the hero's Christ-like self-sacrifice and suffering'; see Isobel Hurst, *Victorian Women Writers and the Classics: The Feminine Homer* (Oxford: Oxford University Press, 2006), p. 102.

27 *Poems of Shelley* 2: 47.

28 *Poems of Shelley* 2: 730. All citations from *The Cenci* are from *Poems of Shelley*, Vol. 2.

needs justification; it is in the superstitious horror with which they contemplate alike her wrongs and their revenge; that the dramatic character of what she did and suffered, consists.[29]

In other words, it is only with the aid of 'casuistry' (problematic precisely because of its pejorative connotations) that readers can excuse Beatrice. Shelley applies this word again—'pernicious casuistry'—to describe how readers 'weigh his faults with his wrongs', referring to Satan—another figure who became prey to revenge—in his preface to *Prometheus Unbound*.[30] However different Beatrice and Satan are in their degree of virtue or moral excellence, the fact that they both become victims of the impulse to vengeance makes them guilty parties. Shelley depicted *The Cenci* as the 'sad reality' denoting people's inclination to revenge given the circumstances to which Beatrice was placed. *The Cenci* is a reminder, therefore, of the danger of such vengeful passion as a response to such atrocity.

If *The Cenci* is about the 'sad reality' of how things are, then *Prometheus Unbound* is about how things ought to be. Prometheus, under the cruel treatment of Jupiter, does not give in to 'revenge' but is able to embrace 'love' and thereby release himself from the 'mind-forged manacles'. This is the central message of the play. As Shelley notes, he makes a point of changing the meaning of deliverance of Prometheus from Aeschylus's play: from a reconcil-iation between the 'Champion' and the 'Oppressor of mankind' to one of Prometheus's internal transformation from 'revenge' to 'love'. At the beginning of the drama, when Prometheus is bound to the precipice in the Indian Caucasus, his words of 'revenge' are repeated by the phantom of Jupiter:

> I curse thee! let a sufferer's curse
> Clasp thee, his torturer, like remorse,
> Till thine Infinity shall be
> A robe of envenomed agony,
> And thine Omnipotence a crown of pain
> To cling like burning gold round thy dissolving brain.
>
> (I. 286–91)

29 *Poems of Shelley* 2: 731.
30 *Poems of Shelley* 2: 472. All citations from *Prometheus Unbound* are from *Poems of Shelley*, Vol. 2.

Prometheus's turning point comes when he is able to forgive his oppressor:

> I pity thee. What ruin
> Will hunt thee undefended through wide Heaven!
> How will thy soul, cloven to its depth with terror,
> Gape like a Hell within! I speak in grief
> Not exultation, for I hate no more
> As then, ere misery made me wise. (1. 53–58)

In resisting the Furies that torture him, Prometheus then comes under the influence of the Spirits that remind him of his true nature:

> How fair these air-born shapes! And yet I feel
> Most vain all hope but love; and thou art far,
> Asia! who, when my being overflowed,
> Wert like a golden chalice to bright wine
> Which else had sunk into the thirsty dust.

* * *

> I would fain
> Be what it is my destiny to be,
> The saviour and the strength of suffering man,
> Or sink into the original gulph of things...
> There is no agony, and no solace left;
> Earth can console, Heaven can torment no more.
> (1. 807–11, 815–20)

Prometheus's rejection and abandonment of vengeful passion for forgiveness and love, with the aid of Asia and Panthea, eventually brings Jupiter's reign to the point of collapse. More significantly, however, it releases him from the 'self-forged manacles' created by hatred and revenge against Jupiter.

Mary Shelley likewise wrote about the danger of vengeful passion that ought to be replaced by love and forbearance in *Frankenstein* and *Valperga*. The creature in the first novel seeks revenge owing to the maltreatments he receives from his creator and other human beings. By killing off Victor's friends and family one by one, he seeks to bring misery onto his creator as a punishment for his wretched life. This course of action, of course, does not lead to the fulfilment of the creature's wish to become happy, but only leads him further astray into the depth of despair. In *Valperga*, her next novel, Mary Shelley dramatises the political development surrounding a Shelleyan character, Euthanasia, whose creed is love and peace. Unlike the formulaic happy ending of a historical novel written by, say, Walter Scott, Mary Shelley deliberately concludes the novel with the tragic death of the heroine. By juxtaposing the peace-loving Euthanasia with the historical hero, Castruccio Castracani, whose political and military aggression, fuelled by revenge, led to her exile and death, Mary Shelley invites the reader to lament the sad reality of how idealism fails in the face of brute force. If Shelley was more optimistic in his depiction of idealism, Mary Shelley had an acute sense of reality that did not always accord with such idealism.

Elizabeth Barrett, in *The Seraphim*, comes uncannily close to these Shelleyan formulations, especially those of *Prometheus Unbound*—the supreme expression of Shelley's idealism. Firstly, the perspective of both texts is from above: in *Prometheus Unbound*, Prometheus's subjection to torture followed by his delivery is mediated through the spirits rather than from human voices; in *The Seraphim*, Christ's suffering is observed by the two seraphim in order 'to glance at it, as dilated in seraphic eyes, and darkened and deepened by the near association with blessedness and Heaven'.[31] Elizabeth Barrett continues to question the way the suffering of Christ has been depicted in the past: 'Are we not too apt to measure the depth of the Saviour's humiliation from the common estate of man, instead of from His own peculiar and primæval one?' (p. 291). Secondly, Prometheus and Christ are uncompromising in their will to sacrifice themselves completely for the sake of humankind. As the above quotation from *Prometheus Unbound* demonstrates, Shelley's Prometheus is a saviour as well as a fire-bearer to humankind. In other words, it is not simply knowledge that Prometheus provides to humans but also their spiritual salvation. The endings of these two works differ if somewhat superficially, with Prometheus's yielding himself to higher principles such as 'Love' and 'Truth', whereas Christ yields himself to God by uttering the last word of 'FATHER! MY SPIRIT TO THINE HANDS IS GIVEN.' There is scope to

---

31 *Works of EBB* 1: 290–91. All citations from *The Seraphim* are from *Works of EBB*, Vol. 1.

argue that these endings are not that different, once one concedes that Shelleyan 'Love' and 'Truth' can be subsumed under Christian ideas. The transition from Aeschylus's Prometheus to Christ in *The Seraphim* is in line with the Shelleys' ideas of peaceful resistance towards tyranny in an age of wrath and vengeance. Whether its political aspect had been registered in Elizabeth Barrett's thinking remains questionable, but her attempt at appealing to Christ as the model of love and sacrifice binds her to the Shelleys, who likewise created figures to the same effect.

As intimated at the outset of this chapter, in Elizabeth Barrett's preface to her translation of Aeschylus's *Prometheus Bound*, her depiction of the difference between Satan and Prometheus becomes even closer to that of Shelley in his own preface to *Prometheus Unbound*. Shelley writes:

> The only imaginary being resembling in any degree Prometheus, is Satan; and Prometheus is, in my judgement, a more poetical character than Satan, because, in addition to courage, and majesty, and firm and patient opposition to omnipotent force, he is susceptible of being described as exempt from the taints of ambition, envy, revenge, and a desire for personal aggrandizement, which in the Hero of Paradise Lost, interfere with the interest. The character of Satan engenders in the mind a pernicious casuistry which leads us to weigh his faults with his wrongs, and to excuse the former because the latter exceed all measure. In the minds of those who consider that magnificent fiction with a religious feeling, it engenders something worse. But Prometheus is, as it were, the type of the highest perfection of moral and intellectual nature, impelled by the purest and the truest motives to the best and noblest ends.[32]

Elizabeth Barrett writes equally of the difference:

> [T]he Satan of Milton and the Prometheus of Aeschylus stand upon ground as unequal, as do the sublime of sin and the sublime of virtue. Satan suffered from his ambition; Prometheus from his humanity: Satan for himself; Prometheus for mankind: Satan dared perils which he had not weighed; Prometheus devoted

---

32 *Poems of Shelley* 2: 472–73.

himself to sorrows which he had foreknown. 'Better to rule in hell,' said Satan; 'Better to serve this rock,' said Prometheus. But in his hell, Satan yearned to associate [with] man; while Prometheus preferred a solitary agony: nay, he even permitted his zeal and tenderness for the peace of others, to abstract him from that agony's intenseness.[33]

Shelley and Elizabeth Barrett are in agreement with the following: that Satan is ambitious as well as self-aggrandising, whereas Prometheus is not; to excuse Satan for his faults is a mistake. This similarity is striking when their reworking of Satan and Prometheus, as inherited from Milton, is taken into account. Milton saw them almost as overlapping characters: both were 'thieving and fraudulent [...] who brought upon mankind untold suffering'.[34] This had been largely due to the confusion 'between the iconography and the tortures of Prometheus and Tityus', which further led to the association of Prometheus with 'the less favorable traits of the Titan generation'.[35] In other words,

> When critics identify the tragic hero of Aeschylus's *Prometheus Bound* as the single Prometheus archetype for Milton's Satan, they overlook the rich subtleties of Milton's text and the provocative suggestiveness of a figure at once Satan, Prometheus, Tityus, and generic Titan.[36]

From this rich array of associations, Shelley sought to extricate the qualities that were specific to Prometheus and further stood in opposition to Satan. This disentanglement of characters is then passed down to Elizabeth Barrett, so that she, likewise, dissociates her Prometheus from Satan, in his likeness to Christ.

What separates their views on Satan, however, is religion. Whereas Elizabeth Barrett sees Satan as a sinner, Shelley avoids labelling him in religious terms only, noting that '[i]n the minds of those who consider that magnificent fiction with a religious feeling, it engenders something worse'. This is exactly what Elizabeth Barrett does

---

33 *Works of EBB* 4: 181.
34 See Lewis, *Promethean Politics*, p. 55.
35 Lewis, *Promethean Politics*, pp. 74–76.
36 Lewis, *Promethean Politics*, p. 76.

whether the consequences are 'worse' as Shelley states: her interpretation of Satan as a sinner further results in the fact that he does not know what he does (unlike Prometheus who does); that he prefers Hell over Heaven; and that he incriminates humankind. Elizabeth Barrett's religious take on Satan downplays the heroic aspect of Satan, which Shelley is willing to grant.

What can be inferred from Elizabeth Barrett's early works is that she was firmly entrenched in the Romantic tradition, especially of the liberal ideas of the second-generation Romantics. Although her poems have been mainly read alongside the work of Byron and Keats, Shelley's influence is thrown into relief when one looks at their texts in tandem. Elizabeth Barrett's high praise of Keats, and idolatrous feelings for Byron, do not necessarily make them the strongest of poetic influences. Also, her objection to Shelley's atheism is not a good enough reason to avoid seeking his presence in her works. In truth, Shelley comes closest of all the other Romantic poets in terms of matching Barrett's political aspirations and of how such aspirations were intertwined with her poetic practice.

Romanticism at Stake: 'A Vision of Poets'

It was Shelley that high, & yet too low, elemental poet, who froze in cold glory between Heaven & earth, neither dealing with man's heart, beneath, nor aspiring to communion with supernal Humanity, the heart of the God-Man. Therefore his poetry glitters & is cold—and it is only by momentary stirrings that we can discern the power of sweet human love & deep pathos which was in him & shd have been in it.[37]

This is Elizabeth Barrett commenting on Shelley in full for the first time. There are a number of things implicit in the above quotation: Shelley is idealistic ('high'), but not idealistic enough, because he lacks religiosity owing to his atheism ('too low'); he suffers in limbo from not embracing Christianity and by demonstrating a lack of empathy with his fellow men. What is interesting is the choice of words Elizabeth Barrett uses to describe Shelley and his

---

37 See the letter dated 14 June 1841 from Elizabaeth Barrett to Mary Russell Mitford in *Brownings' Correspondence* 5: 57–61 (60).

poetry: he 'froze in cold glory' while his poetry 'glitters'. These images deserve attention as they are not common Victorian modes of expression. The image of 'a nightingale, who sits in darkness and sings to cheer its own solitude with sweet sounds'[38] is a familiar enough trope in the Victorian period, but these are not. Barrett's image, in fact, seems to be not unrelated to her description of Shelley in her poem 'A Vision of Poets': 'in his white ideal, / All statue-blind' (ll. 406–07).[39] So not only is Shelley's poetry 'cold', but it is 'white' in colour. This choice of words then becomes reminiscent of the depiction of Shelley's own 'white light' that blinds everything, including people and nature, in his last (unfinished) poem, 'The Triumph of Life': 'And a cold glare, intenser than the noon / But icy cold, obscured with [blinding] light / The Sun as he the stars' (ll. 77–79).[40] We might argue, then, that Elizabeth Barrett had 'The Triumph' in mind as Shelley's final pronouncement not only upon life in general but also upon the relationship between art and life, as, indeed, many critics of Shelley were prone to do. Harold Bloom puts it thus:

> The unwilling dross that cannot be tortured into spirit, the hardened element that will not wish its own redemption, becomes increasingly the feared antagonist in Shelley's poetry, until at last it wins over Imagination the triumph of life and closes Shelley's poetic career in the welter of a watery chaos.[41]

'Love' and 'Imagination', which played such a great role in Shelley's early philosophy, are eclipsed by the hard reality that resists change even in the face of such agents. As a final, yet incomplete, text, it has invited an interpretation that has now become a critical commonplace, whereby Shelley is deemed to have ended his poetical

---

38 From *A Defence of Poetry* quoted from *Shelley's Poetry and Prose*, selected and ed. Donald H. Reiman and Neil Fraistat, 2nd edn (New York: Norton, 2002), p. 486.

39 Browning found this expression to be 'perfect'; see *Brownings' Correspondence* 11:15.

40 Mary Shelley inserted 'blinding' in the blank; see *Shelley's Poetry and Prose*, ed. Reiman and Powers, p. 457.

41 See for example Harold Bloom in *The Visionary Company: A Reading of English Romantic Poetry* (Ithaca: Cornell University Press, 1971), p. 323.

career on a particularly pessimistic note, with such pessimism then being seen as the final encapsulation of his thoughts and ideas. In the same way that Shelley's condescending attitude towards the people, through his deployment of the speaker-narrator, attracted Browning's criticism (see Chapter Five), Elizabeth Barrett here claims, in similar terms, that Shelley does not treat human emotions in sufficient depth. In other words, his condescending view of the people, depicted as simple and ignorant, robs him of his understanding of the human heart. In 'The Triumph', the speaker-narrator is caught between the ignorant masses who are run over by the Car of Life and the world leaders who are chained to it. In other words, there is no room for spiritual salvation for the speaker-narrator, who is at once alienated by the spectacle and devoid of empathy for his fellow beings. The cold light of the chariot in 'The Triumph' becomes for Barrett, we might infer, a synonym for Shelley the poet himself.

Let us trace the trajectory by which she reached this opinion. As early as 1831, she wrote:

> Read some passages from Shelley's Revolt of Islam before I was up. He is a great poet; but we acknowledge him to be a great poet as we acknowledge Spenser to be so, & do not love him for it. He resembles Spenser in one thing, & one thing only, that his poetry is too immaterial for our sympathies to enclasp it firmly. It reverses the lot of human plants: its roots are in the air, not earth!—But as I read him on, I may reverse this opinion.[42]

Elizabeth Barrett's critique of The Revolt as being 'too immaterial' (i.e. otherworldly) in its subject matter and depiction seems justified if we consider the nature of the poem, which is 'an experiment on the temper of the public mind, as to how far a thirst for a happier condition of moral and political society survives, among the enlightened and refined'.[43] It is an idealistic and metaphysical rendering ('its roots are

---

42 See her diary entry of 26 August 1831 in The Barretts at Hope End, p. 149.

43 Preface to Laon and Cythna in Poems of Shelley 2: 32. Shelley made alterations between Laon and Cythna and The Revolt of Islam in the nature of the relationship between the two main characters (from sibling to 'friend or lover'), and removed any remarks that might 'outrage religious sensibilities and constitute grounds for prosecution' (pp. 16–17).

in the air') rather than expressive of human emotions *per se* ('in the ground'). This view is consistent, then, with the general Victorian idea of Shelley 'as a man of angelic goodness, beauty, and unworldliness, his poetry, like its creator, pure and ethereal'.[44] In order to bridge the critique above of *The Revolt of Islam* with the opinion quoted at the beginning—that not only was Shelley idealistic, but he was lacking in religiosity, thereby falling short of ultimate idealism as well as humanism—we need a text that might thus give rise to these later claims that Barrett was to make about Shelley's poetry. For this, 'The Triumph' provides that link between her initial impression and her rather hardened view on Shelley.

It is perhaps enlightening to look at what Browning had to say on the matter in relation to Elizabeth Barrett's view on Shelley. That Shelley did not engage in the human heart, but rather in idealism and philosophical ideology, partly accords with Browning's understanding of Shelley's poetry; however, he was able to discern another side of Shelley who could also express the worldly, 'the doings of men' as he stated in his 'Essay on Shelley'. This bifurcation into earthly and heavenly poetic themes is couched as 'objective' and 'subjective' by Browning as we have seen in previous chapters. According to Browning, Elizabeth Barrett shares with Shelley the quality of a 'subjective' poet and that the latter is not suffering in limbo, as Elizabeth Barrett made him out to be, because he took his idealism for what it was (a secular formation) rather than for what it was not (a religious one).[45] It is suggestive that Robert Browning associates the poetry of Elizabeth Barrett with that of Shelley by using the same simile: to Elizabeth Barrett, he writes, 'you speak out, you—I only make men and women speak—give you truth broken into prismatic hues'.[46] Similarly, Browning refers

---

44 Julian North, *The Domestication of Genius: Biography and the Romantic Poet* (Oxford: Oxford University Press, 2009), p. 101.

45 Despite Browning's acceptance and even exaltation of Shelleyan idealism, there is evidence to suggest that Shelley would have eventually been led to Christianity: 'I shall say what I think,—had Shelley lived he would have finally ranged himself with the Christians'; 'Essay on Shelley', in *Browning: Selected Poems*, ed. John Woolford, Daniel Karlin and Joseph Phelan (Harlow: Pearson Education, 2010), p. 871.

46 See the letter dated 13 January 1845 (the second letter), which Robert Browning addresses to Elizabeth Barrett in *Brownings' Correspondence* 10: 21–23 (22).

to 'its own self-sufficing central light' in talking about Shelley's poetical faculty.[47] In other words, both Shelley and Elizabeth Barrett communicate the 'white light' that becomes 'broken into prismatic hues' by poets of Browning's type.

In fact, we find this imagery in Shelley's poem itself entitled *Adonais* (1821), an elegy Shelley wrote for Keats upon the wake of his premature death:

> The One remains, the many change and pass;
> Heaven's light forever shines, Earth's shadows fly;
> Life, like a dome of many-coloured glass,
> Stains the white radiance of Eternity,
> Until Death tramples it to fragments. (ll. 460–64)

According to Shelley, individuals who all originate in the 'white' light become refracted into 'many-coloured' entities, which return to the 'white' light at their death. While 'white' light is meant to signify eternity, the 'many-coloured glass' stands for earthly lives. Browning utilises this imagery when he develops his notion of the 'subjective' and 'objective' poets respectively. In the 'Essay on Shelley', Browning singles out Shelley as an example of a 'subjective poet' (radiating the 'white light' that communicates eternity) while designating himself as an 'objective poet' (concerned with earthly existence in different colours). The lyrical vision that characterises Shelley's poetry is also discerned by Browning in Elizabeth Barrett's poetry. While he agrees with Elizabeth Barrett's depiction of Shelley in 'A Vision of Poets', his *interpretation* of that depiction differed from Barrett's: whereas she saw Shelley in the 'white' light of 'The Triumph', Browning meant it to designate a lyrical profusion that emanates from his being in a way that is akin to the 'white' light in *Adonais*.

In order to examine further this similarity that Browning discerned, let us turn next to Elizabeth Barrett's 'A Vision of Poets' and Shelley's 'The Triumph of Life'. This particular comparison has never been undertaken in the past, with criticism hitherto focusing mainly on Keats's influence on Elizabeth Barrett. While Keats's *Hyperion* in 'A Vision of Poets' is undoubtedly present,[48] the poem

---

47 'Essay on Shelley', p. 865.
48 Stone writes in *Elizabeth Barrett Browning*: '"A Vision of Poets" is her most Keatsian poem. But the work it most strikingly resembles is not Keats'

also addresses a problem that is central to 'The Triumph of Life': the role of poets in history, as Barrett seeks to re-write Shelley's attempt at depicting history. In this connection, Shelley's *Defence of Poetry* will become relevant as an antithesis to 'The Triumph'.

Although the subject matter of these two poems may seem considerably different, there are enough thematic and structural similarities for us to read the latter as a *de facto* re-writing and completion of the former. Both poems are written in a form that evokes the medieval dream-poetry and specifically Dante's *Divina Commedia*.[49] In the 'Vision', the poet wanders through a forest in a similar manner to Dante in the Inferno:

> And thus he rose disquieted
> With sweet rhymes ringing through his head,
> And in the forest wandered (ll. 4–6)

> In the midway of this our mortal life,
> I found me in a gloomy wood, astray
> Gone from the path direct (Hell 1. 1–3)[50]

The speaker-narrator in 'The Triumph' is at 'the steep / Of a green Apennine' (ll. 25–26) when he finds himself awake for the entire night. Sure enough, there is also a guide in both of these poems, just as there is in *La Divina Commedia*—Virgil and Beatrice— who interprets for the main character the visions they encounter together. In 'A Vision of Poets', the lady guides the poet to drink from each pool that they come to, and explains what he would learn in doing so, until they come to a church where he witnesses the presence of the dead poets. He is then told the answers to the questions posed by the lady at the outset. In 'The Triumph of Life', Rousseau tells the speaker-narrator of the nature of the pageant they witness as being representative of 'Life' (l. 180), and urges him 'from

Hyperion fragment, which Barrett read in 1831, or *Endymion* which she echoes in "A Vision of Poets" itself, but *The Fall of Hyperion*, a work that Barrett probably did not know since it was not yet published in 1844' (p. 85).

49 The difference being that 'The Triumph' is composed in *terza rima* whereas the 'Vision' is in octosyllabic triplets.

50 Dante Alighieri, *The Divine Comedy*, trans. Henry Francis Cary (London: The Colonial Press, 1901), p. 1.

spectator turn / Actor or victim in this wretchedness' (ll. 305–06). Both poems employ the dream vision and allegorical quest integral to the dream-poem in general.

The *Trionfi* by the Italian poet Petrarch is also a textual presence in the poems. Deploying the categories 'Love', 'Death', 'Chastity', 'Fame', 'Time' and 'Eternity', which are given hierarchical positioning according to their fixed values, Petrarch sought to delineate a soul's progress from earthly passion to a fulfilment in God. Elizabeth Barrett's poem recalls just such a structural development—from the poet's enlightenment concerning the world's 'use', 'love' and 'cruelty' to a rite of passage to becoming a true poet—which leads to the final triumph of God as figured by the introduction of the child at the end of the poem. Shelley's 'Triumph', on the other hand, barely adheres to such epistemic hierarchy and refuses to align itself with a Christian worldview by embracing scepticism at best. Even when Rousseau recounts how Dante was transformed by Love, it is a localised experience that does not affect others beyond himself:

> from the lowest depths of Hell
> Through every Paradise and through all glory
> Love led serene, and who returned to tell
>
> 'In words of hate and awe the wondrous story
> How all things are transfigured, except Love;
> For deaf as is a sea which wrath makes hoary
>
> 'The world can hear not the sweet notes that move
> The sphere whose light is melody to lovers (ll. 472–79)

Unlike the *Trionfi*, there is no conviction on Shelley's part that 'Love' is triumphant; it is an isolated case in 'The Triumph' that is only 'wondrous' as a tale. Shelley's re-writing of the *Trionfi* is deliberate in its challenge to the traditional worldview that ultimately God reigns.

Furthermore, there are specific sections of the individual poems which, when taken together, can be seen to resonate with each other. For instance, both poems open with the main character remaining awake during the night. In Elizabeth Barrett's 'Vision', the text reads:

A poet could not sleep aright,
For his soul kept up too much light,
Under his eyelids for the night. (ll. 1–3)

Whereas, in 'The Triumph', we are told:

But I, whom thoughts which must remain untold
Had kept as wakeful as the stars that gem
The cone of night (ll. 21–23)

In other words, the deep concern of each about their respective poetic identities, which makes them stay awake all night, precipitates such a vision. The poet in the 'Vision' holds the view that poets 'are scorned / By men they sing for, till inurned' (ll. 59–60). Although the anxieties of the speaker-narrator who remains awake in 'The Triumph' are not directly expressed, if the fate of poets in the vision that he sees is taken into consideration, it becomes clear that their absence in history is a major source of concern to Shelley.

In both poems, the act of drinking upon the request of a female figure produces a certain kind of knowledge. The poet in the 'Vision' 'swooned backward to a dream / Wherein he lay 'twixt gloom and gleam / With Death and Life at each extreme' (ll. 190–93), and in 'The Triumph'

suddenly my [his] brain became as sand
'Where the first wave had more than half erased
The track of deer on desert Labrador,
Whilst the fierce wolf from which they fled amazed
'Leaves his stamp visibly upon the shore
(ll. 405–09)

For the poet in the 'Vision', drinking becomes an initiation process for becoming a true poet, whereas, in 'The Triumph', it turns Rousseau's mind into a *tabula rasa*. Although there is a difference between the two in the degree of knowledge produced, the act of drinking leads them both to an insight otherwise unavailable to them.

Suffering is regarded as a necessary component to knowledge in both poems: in the 'Vision' we are told that 'Knowledge by suffering entereth' (l. 929). This accords with the Keatsian view that a true poet must suffer, as his poets do in the *Hyperion* poems.

In 'The Triumph', Rousseau has 'suffered what I [he] wrote, or viler pain!' (l. 279). As the gloss to this section suggests, Rousseau, unlike the true poets, has actually acted out the passions before writing them and therefore transmits them, as 'ill-considered actions do'.[51] Rather than being exemplary, Rousseau's case is presented as one that requires scrutiny for his shortcomings. Therefore, although both the poet and Rousseau suffer, the nature of their suffering varies significantly, which leads to the conclusion that the poet in the 'Vision' is led to God whereas Rousseau in 'The Triumph' is abandoned in misery. This is not to suggest, however, that Shelley succumbed to criticism waged at Rousseau's immorality and furthermore, by implication, to his own; rather, he is interested in why the French Revolution failed (we must take into account how Rousseau was perceived to be the parent of the revolutionary movement in the 19th century). In other words, to scrutinise the character of Rousseau will lead us to an insight into his flaws, which were reflected in his writings and, as a consequence, in the actions influenced or generated by those writings.

If we read the 'Vision' as a reworked continuation of 'The Triumph', then two central revisions can be discerned. Firstly, the 'Vision' manifests a Christian faith that counters the scepticism of 'The Triumph', which accords with Barrett's view of Shelley.[52] As I have already stated, the 'Vision' utilises the hierarchical development, as Petrarch does in the *Trionfi*, that ends in God's grace. Unlike Rousseau's conclusion that people either act or suffer in wretchedness without any purpose, the lady in the 'Vision' leads the poet to a conviction that 'Thou, Poet-God, are great and good!' (l. 816).

The second significant change is the status Elizabeth Barrett's text accords to poets. Whereas the poets are entirely absent from the pageant-vision in 'The Triumph', they take centre stage in the 'Vision'. In 'The Triumph', Shelley ends up showing how poets and philosophers, despite his early belief in them as the 'unacknowledged legislators of the world', actually play a minor role in history, and

---

51 See *Shelley's Poetry and Prose*, ed. Reiman and Powers, p. 463.

52 In a letter dated [6] December 1843 to Richard Hengist Horne, she writes: 'You know Shelley in the midst of the grand signatures of God, wrote at Chamonoui. "Atheist". Poor Shelley!—He lied against himself as against the Creator!—.' See *Brownings' Correspondence* 8: 75–78 (76).

that the best endeavours of the poets and philosophers are wasted. This attitude is exactly what comes under scrutiny in the 'Vision'. Elizabeth Barrett, who had read Shelley's *Defence of Poetry* with much admiration (a topic addressed in more detail later), seeks to salvage poetry as the means to bettering society by focusing on poets alone in her 'Vision'. Barrett framed her poem about the role of the poets in society within a poetic structure that Shelley had deployed some 22 years previously to denote his disappointment and disillusionment with the role of poets in society.

Lastly, I would like to focus on the narrative framework of the 'Vision'. For this, I shall first look at Shelley's *Alastor* and Elizabeth Barrett's 'The Poet's Vow'. The protagonist of *Alastor*, a poet, is the prototype of one who suffers from a futile visionary quest because of his severance from any human ties. The poet who seeks an ideal vision that corresponds with his own image, instead of finding this in real human relationships, faces an early death owing to a lack of communion with his fellow beings, as Shelley himself declared in the 'Preface': 'The Poet's self-centred seclusion was avenged by the furies of an irresistible passion pursuing him to speedy ruin.'[53] There is an Arab maiden who appears in the poem who 'brought him food' (l. 129), but even her love for him—'Enamoured, yet not daring for deep awe / To speak her love' (ll. 133–34)—is not reciprocated, thereby leaving the poet to wander further into the wilderness of nature. 'The Poet's Vow' similarly dramatises a poet who disavows humanity as an act of atonement for human sin, while Rosalind, who loves him like the Arab maiden loves the *Alastor*-poet, is left to die of unrequited love for the poet. When her dead body is carried to the poet's abode, he realises his loss and neglect, and grieves over having spurned her love. Both poems evoke Wordsworth—*Alastor*, through the Wordsworthian poet who lives in seclusion from human society, and 'The Poet's Vow' in its invocation of Wordsworth through a quote from his 'Lines Left upon a Seat in a Yew-Tree' (1798) at the outset. Whether Shelley's allusion to Wordsworth had registered with Elizabeth Barrett remains open to debate, but it is intriguing that she should quote from Wordsworth in a poem that thematises a poet who, like the *Alastor*-poet, is led to his spiritual ruin because of his neglect of his fellow beings. However, whereas the Arab maiden

---

53 *Shelley's Poetry and Prose*, selected and ed. Donald H. Reiman and Sharon B. Powers (New York: Norton, 1977), p. 69.

is simply forgotten and replaced by the visionary ideal of the poet, in 'The Poet's Vow', the female is given a voice and enacts a response to the poet who abandons her. Like the Lady of Shalott, Rosalind orders her dead body to be carried to the poet's hall with a 'scroll' written by herself. The poet is forced to face the consequences of his own actions by reading her last words. This is a radical gesture to the otherwise male-centred vision of the Romantic poem.

What Elizabeth Barrett does in the 'Vision' seems to be in line with her gendered re-writing of *Alastor* in 'The Poet's Vow': she inscribes a female voice in the conclusion of the poem. The female narrator follows the steps of the poet to find his son, who recites what he had been told by the poet himself. Whether one interprets this framing of the Romantic vision experienced by a male poet as one of self-alienation as Marjorie Stone does, or one of self-empowerment, as Stephanie L. Johnson does, is open to debate:

> If 'A Vision of Poets' dramatically illustrates how a woman poet can be marginalized by a male canonical tradition, it also reveals that meaning can 'be something that happens on the margins', as theorists of narrative framing point out.[54]

> Barrett Browning uses the imagery of the Jewish and Christian apocalyptic mode, which is founded in a belief in the necessary end of human history, to envision instead the end of a gendered history and its replacement by a differently gendered history; in her order of events, prophecy follows an end of history rather than the other way around, and her prophetic voice indicates the future prosperity of the matrilineal poetic line as detached from the patrilineal.[55]

These two contrasting interpretations of the 'Vision' and its framework are partly due to their different respective positionings of the 'Vision' in Elizabeth Barrett's oeuvre. Whereas Stone interprets Elizabeth Barrett's poetic voice in the 'Vision' as a developmental stage towards the culminating art of *Aurora Leigh*, Johnson sees the

54 Stone, *Elizabeth Barrett Browning*, p. 92.
55 Stephanie L. Johnson, 'Aurora Leigh's Radical Youth: Derridean "Parergon" and the Narrative Frame in "A Vision of Poets"', *Victorian Poetry* 44.4 (winter 2006): 425–44 (429).

'Vision' as the radical gesture of departure from the 'patrilineal' to 'the matrilineal poetic line', which becomes downplayed in *Aurora Leigh*. There is little doubt, however, that Elizabeth Barrett sought to inscribe her own gender in an otherwise patrilineal tradition.

In addition to the gendered apotheosis of inscribing the female voice into what otherwise remains a masculine tradition, I would like to suggest that this female voice is a masking device for Barrett's ambitious endeavour to join that club of poets. To compare the 'Vision' to *Aurora Leigh* naturally raises the question of her gender and its positioning in the male poetic tradition; however, to see it in the context of Elizabeth Barrett's more mature political poems—namely *Casa Guidi Windows* (as I shall argue below)—is to regard her poetic framing in a different way. As I have already stated, Elizabeth Barrett is reinstating the significance of poets in society along the lines of Shelley's argument in the *Defence*, and her bold assertion is masked by her inscription of the female as a way of exercising power without transgressing the gendered demarcations of poetic subjects. As the next section will develop more fully, Elizabeth Barrett's strategic device for exercising power is to make her gender explicit, thereby creating a rift between herself and the male poetic tradition, while at the same time endorsing political messages through the mediated masculine voice. It is successful because, superficially, there is no threat of her infringing upon the masculine poetical subject, but, at the same time, she exploits her difference for her own end by creating a more mediated masculine voice that seeks to work towards that end. As much as there is in Elizabeth Barrett a will to re-write the patrilineal poetic tradition, there is also a desire to join that tradition by exercising power as a poet in relation to society at large.

Appropriating Radical Aesthetics: *Casa Guidi Windows*

I shall now focus on Elizabeth Barrett's political poem *Casa Guidi Windows* (1851), simply because the political aspect of her poetry is one that is arguably most in need of examination in relation to Shelley.[56] Even though her poetry has been compared to that

56 Most past criticism of *Casa Guidi Windows* tended to focus on Elizabeth Barrett's reworking of the image of Italy 'as a beautiful but wronged victim

of Wordsworth, whom Elizabeth Barrett worshipped and whose poetry she sought to emulate, her later political ballads, as noted by Marjorie Stone, were 'inclined to be more radically polemical than Wordsworth in appropriating the ballad for political purposes, following Shelley's example more than Wordsworth's'.[57] Elizabeth Barrett had more in common with Shelley when it came to radical politics; this was the case not only with the ballads, but also with her major political effort, *Casa Guidi Windows*.

Although it is difficult to pin down which editions Elizabeth Barrett used when familiarising herself with Shelley's poetry, it can be inferred that she had read, and indeed familiarised herself with, most of his major poems, and a few of the more obscure ones, by the time she wrote *Casa Guidi Windows*.[58] For instance, she quotes from Shelley's poems even before her correspondence with Browning in 1845—*Prometheus Unbound*, 'Song' ('Rarely, rarely, comest thou', 1821), *The Revolt of Islam*, 'Epipsychidion', 'Julian and Maddalo', 'Ode to the West Wind', 'The Two Spirits', 'Music', 'To a Skylark'.[59] We know for a fact that she owned Shelley's *Essays, Letters from Abroad, Translations and Fragments*, edited by Mary Shelley and published in 1840. Barrett's copy, with markings and marginalia, is held in the library collection at Princeton University.[60] As I argue below, Elizabeth Barrett's engagement with the *Essays* was a

of history', which she saw as being counterproductive for the regeneration of Italy. See, for example, Joe Phelan, 'Elizabeth Barrett Browning's *Casa Guidi Windows*, Arthur Hugh Clough's *Amours de Voyage*, and the Italian National Uprisings of 1847–9', *Journal of Anglo-Italian Studies* 3 (1993): 137–52 (139–40). Leigh Coral Harris mentions the significance of Barratt's British identity in formulating her politics on Italy, although her argument mainly focuses on Milton. See 'From Mythos to Logos: Political Aesthetics and Liminal Poetics in Elizabeth Barrett Browning's *Casa Guidi Windows*', *Victorian Literature and Culture* 28.1 (2000): 109–31.

57 Stone, *Elizabeth Barrett Browning*, pp. 106–07.

58 Browning lent her a copy of the *Posthumous Poems* (1824) in 1845, in which Elizabeth Barrett read 'Marianne's Dream' for the first time, thereby ruling out all editions that contain it as having been in her possession. See Elizabeth Barrett's letter to Browning postmarked 19 September 1845 in *Brownings' Correspondence* 10: 91.

59 See letters dated 16 April 1838, 15 February 1841, 8 November 1841, 16 March 1842, 3 November 1842, 2 September 1843, 8 January 1844, 21 February 1844.

60 Held at the Rare Books and Special Collection, South East (RB) EX 3928.333.

sustained one, even to the extent that it shaped her own subsequent poetical practice.[61]

Italy was not a unified country during Shelley or Barrett Browning's time.[62] After the Treaty of Vienna (concluded in 1815), the French influence had been replaced by that of Austria, whose reactionary policies reversed the liberalism indulged by Napoleon. It was indeed the French Revolution and the Napoleonic Empire that had inspired the idea of a unified Italy. The significance of this for the texts I wish to discuss lies in the provision, through historical circumstance, of a pan-European movement towards liberalism. In Europe, 1820 and 1821 were critical years for such activities: within Italy, Naples, Sicily and Piedmont were affected, and a revolution in Spain (which is relevant to Shelley's 'Ode to Liberty') occurred in January 1820, by which the military restored the 1812 constitution, thereby restricting royal power. The insurrections, however, were quickly suppressed by the foreign powers—France in the case of Spain and Austria with Italy. The next wave of revolutions came in 1830–32; they started in France and spread to Parma, Modena and the Papal States. Again, the Austrian army subdued the insurrections. The third significant revolution in Italy came in 1848 in Palermo, and called for a Sicilian constitution. When the king asked for Metternich, the chancellor of the Austrian Empire, to intervene and was declined, he was forced to grant the constitution in January. This further led to the grand duke of Tuscany and the king of Sardinia promising a constitution in the following month. The Civic Guard, which the grand duke had allowed to form, implying his granting of citizenship, is the celebratory background for Part I of Casa Guidi Windows. The Civic Guard 'had been infiltrated by lower middle-class recruits, with the result that it became less reliable as a repressive tool'[63] and Tuscany became too radical for the grand duke, who eventually fled

---

61 David G. Riede writes: 'Barrett's Poems of 1844 [are] rightly viewed as a turning point in her career, a shift from the perspective of the meek Christian "poetess" to that of the outspoken romantic prophet-bard.' 'Elizabeth Barrett's Poetry of Exile: Difficulties of a Female Christian Romanticism', Victorians Institute Journal (2000): 91–112 (110).

62 The following sketch is based on Derek Beales and Eugenio F. Biagini, The Risorgimento and the Unification of Italy (London: Longman, 2002).

63 Beales and Biagini, The Risorgimento, p. 95.

in February 1849 only to be escorted back two months later with the aid of Austrian troops. The victory of the Austrian power over the Italian forces at the Battle of Novara in March 1849 restored the reactionary governments throughout Italy and led further to the Austrian occupation of Tuscany.

The repetitive manner in which the insurrections occurred throughout Europe makes them part of a process rather than isolated incidents, and it is within this context that Barrett's texts can be fruitfully situated. Although *Casa Guidi Windows* is basically a series of Barrett's impressions from the period, and immediate aftermath, of Florence's short-lived liberal movement, it is grounded in a liberal tradition associated with Italian artists who further inspired liberty in other European countries and in the New World:

> Help, lands of Europe! for, if Austria fight,
> The drums will bar your slumber. Had ye curled
> The laurel for your thousand artists' brows,
> If these Italian hands had planted none?
> Can any sit down idle in the house,
> Nor hear appeals from Buonarroti's stone
> And Raffael's canvas, rousing and to rouse?
> Where's Poussin's master? Gallic Avignon
> Bred Laura, and Vaucluse's fount has stirred
> The heart of France too strongly, as it lets
> Its little stream out [...]

>   that she should not gird
> Her loins with Charlemagne's sword when foes beset
> The country of her Petrarch. Spain may well
> Be minded how from Italy she caught,
> To mingle with her tinkling Moorish bell,
> A fuller cadence and a subtler thought.
> And even the New World, the receptacle
> Of freemen, may send glad men, as it ought,
> To greet Vespuccio Amerigo's door.
> While England claims, by trump of poetry,
> Verona, Venice, the Ravenna-shore,
> And dearer holds John Milton's Fiesole
> Than Langland's Malvern with the stars in flower.
>
>   (1. 1104–28)

Elizabeth Barrett reminds the reader how other Western countries—from France to Spain and 'even the New World', not to mention England—are indebted to Italy for their own development of political and artistic sentiment. It is precisely because of the rich cultural and political heritage of Italy that Europe has thrived and continues to do so: 'let us give / The blessing of our souls [...] To this great cause of southern men, who strive / In God's name for man's rights, and shall not fail' (1. 1197–98, 1201–02). Although Byron has been mentioned by critics as having laid the foundation for *Casa Guidi Windows*, with his *Childe Harold's Pilgrimage* (1812–18),[64] Shelley likewise contributed to it by his coherent set of politically inspired aesthetic practices.

Of all the major poems Shelley wrote on the uprising of the people, 'Ode to Liberty' (1820) stands out as one of the most direct expressions of the celebratory mood that is most akin to Part I of *Casa Guidi Windows*. The opening stanzas to *Casa Guidi Windows* and 'Ode to Liberty', however, make a stark contrast: while Shelley's 'Ode' is overlaid with allusions to Pindar, Plato, Horace and Milton, to name but a few, Barrett Browning takes her cue from 'a little child' singing 'O bella liberatà, O bella!' In a gesture similar to the one in 'A Vision of Poets', her poetic voice is mediated through a child rather than rendered directly, and the child figure symbolises the future as opposed to the past. In the 'Ode', Shelley himself acts as the mediator to the voice of 'Liberty':

> A glorious people vibrated again
> The lightning of the nations: Liberty
> From heart to heart, from tower to tower, o'er Spain,
> Scattering contagions fire into the sky,
> Gleamed. My soul spurned the chains of its dismay,
> And, in the rapid plumes of song,
> Clothed itself, sublime and strong;
> As a young eagle soars, the morning clouds among,
> Hovering in verse o'er its accustomed prey;
> Till from its station in the heaven of fame
> The Spirit's whirlwind rapt it, and the ray
> Of the remotest sphere of living flame

---

64 See Dorothy Mermin, *Elizabeth Barrett Browning: The Origins of a New Poetry* (Chicago: University of Chicago Press, 1989), p. 167; Avery and Stott, *Elizabeth Barrett Browning*, p. 162.

Which paves the void was from behind it flung,
A foam from a ship's swiftness, when there came
A voice out of the deep: I will record the same. (ll. 1–15)[65]

Elizabeth Barrett, on the other hand, hears it in the voice of a child:

I heard last night a little child go singing
'Neath Casa Guidi windows, by the church,
O bella liberatà, O bella! stringing
The same words still on notes he went in search
So high for, you concluded the upspringing
Of such a nimble bird to sky from perch
Must leave the whole bush in a tremble green,
And that the heart of Italy must bear,
While such a voice had leave to rise serene
'Twixt church and palace of a Florence street!
A little child, too, who not long had been
By mother's finger steadied on his feet,
And still O bella liberatà he sang. (1. 1–13)[66]

Barrett's strategic device of making use of a child's singing has been noted by critics, but not in comparison to Shelley.[67] Shelley's abstract rendering of 'Liberty' as a 'force' to be felt, heard and seen is given a human voice in *Casa Guidi Windows*. This is in line with Barrett's depiction of Shelley as being 'high' and divorced from humanity, a position from which she wished to distance herself. By giving 'Liberty' a child's voice, she succeeded not only in humanising it, but also in rendering it as something belonging to the future.

Elizabeth Barrett was given a copy of Shelley's *Essays, Letters from Abroad, Translations and Fragments* by her father upon its publication in 1840. What she singles out in a letter addressed to Septimus Moulton-Barrett written soon after her receiving it was that she had problems with Shelley's translations from the Greek:

65 All references to Shelley's poetry unless noted otherwise are from *Poems of Shelley*, Vol. 3.
66 All citations of *Casa Guidi Windows* are from *Works of EBB*, Vol. 2.
67 Mermin, *Elizabeth Barrett Browning*, pp. 172–73; Avery and Stott, *Elizabeth Barrett Browning*, pp. 162–63.

I have fallen out too with Shelley about his translations from Plato. The general impression was, & my particular impression certainly was that he 'ate Greek drank Greek'—whereas it almost appears to me now that he starved upon it. At any rate he knew little or nothing of Plato—& the translations so extolled in the preface, are only wonderful from their extreme incorrectness. I am wondering if any of the Critics par excellence will take notice of this.[68]

She had found 37 errors and 'also complained of his failure to render the sense of a Greek pun'; '[t]he tenor of her comments shows her real feeling for, and grasp of, the Greek language'.[69] To accentuate her superiority in her knowledge of Greek was to privilege her linguistic skills over Shelley's. This illustrates how Elizabeth Barrett was not afraid to criticise Shelley and that she was prepared to stand her ground when it came to translation. What this vignette fails to convey, however, is how much she was engaged in Shelley's ideas, which she did not acknowledge openly. She was quick to mention, however, that, 'if it were not for the here & there defilement of his atrocious opinions', it 'would have very deeply delighted me'.[70] Again, Shelley's religious views were sharply censured by Elizabeth Barrett, who crossed out most of the sections that had anything to do with these issues.

James Thorpe has done a great service by reproducing most of Elizabeth Barrett's marginalia in her own copy of the *Letters*.[71] What we can deduce from those comments is that she was not willing to take on Shelley's ideas wholesale, and that she had an opinion of her own, especially when it came to religious matters. This said, however, she did mark up much more of what she had agreed with, and *Casa Guidi Windows* can now be re-read as effectively engaging in a dialogue with Shelley's text.[72] For instance, Elizabeth Barrett

68 See letter dated 6 February 1840, *Brownings' Correspondence* 4: 233–36 (233).
69 *Brownings' Correspondence* 4: 236.
70 *Brownings' Correspondence* 4: 233.
71 'Elizabeth Barrett's Commentary on Shelley: Some Marginalia', *Modern Language Note* 66 (1951): 455–58.
72 Of all the essays and fragments, in *A Defence of Poetry*, three sections are marked (///), seven pages are marked (/) and five pages of text are crossed out; 'On Love', three pages are marked (/); 'The Coliseum', four pages are marked

refers to 'Dante's Florence' in the opening stanza of Part II as she addresses 'Tuscany' and 'Florence':

> O Tuscany,
> O Dante's Florence, is the type too plain?
> Didst thou, too, only sing of liberty,
> As little children take up a high strain
> With unintentioned voices, and break off
> To sleep upon their mother's knees again? (2. 7–12)

Shelley makes a similar comment in the *Defence* when he writes that Dante was 'the Lucifer of that starry flock which in the thirteenth century shone forth from republican Italy, as from a heaven, into the darkness of benighted world'.[73] Interestingly, both writers take it for granted that Dante was connected to liberty and republicanism although, strictly speaking, he was not a Guelph (an upholder of republicanism). The explanation to this is given in Mary Shelley's *Valperga*, in which she elaborates on the connection between Dante and liberty: 'he was personally engaged in those political struggles, in which the elements of the good and evil that have since assumed a more permanent form were contending.'[74] In other words, it was not his own allegiance to the party as such that mattered; rather his own individual 'struggles' led to his association with the cry for liberty. The fact that Elizabeth Barrett marked up Shelley's account of Dante proves that it left an impression on her and that it arguably led her to depict him in a similar manner to the Shelleys.[75]

Another passage Elizabeth Barrett marked was Shelley's ideas on the nature of utility. As Shelley's essay was meant as a rebuttal against Peacock's treatise on utility, his central argument in the *Defence*

(/); 'On the Punishment of Death', four pages are marked (/) and a section is crossed out; 'On Life', two pages are marked (/); 'On a Future State', three pages are marked (/) and three pages are crossed out.

73 All citations are from *Essays, Letters from Abroad, Translations and Fragments*, ed. Mary Shelley, 2 vols. (London: Moxon, 1840), 1: 40.

74 *N&SW of Mary Shelley* 3: 7.

75 Esther H. Schor writes: '[h]er [Elizabeth Barrett's] Dante owes a great debt to Shelley's Defence of Poetry'; 'Poetics of Politics: Barrett Browning's *Casa Guidi Windows*', *Tulsa Studies in Women's Literature* 17.2 (autumn 1998): 305–24 (316).

was to prove that poets and artists at large held greater utility than economists or political scientists: 'The production and assurance of pleasure in this highest sense is true utility. Those who produce and preserve this pleasure are poets or poetical philosophers.'[76] Furthermore, Elizabeth Barrett marked up the section that called for 'imagination' instead of 'calculation': in an age that is overloaded with 'facts and calculating processes', '[w]e want the creative faculty to imagine that which we know'.[77] We find this articulated in *Casa Guidi Windows*:

> And yet we must
> Beware, and mark the natural kiths and kins
> Of circumstance and office, and distrust
> [...]
> The poet who neglects pure truth to prove
> Statistic fact (1. 887–89, 891–92)

The 'poet' who 'neglects pure truth' and who instead 'prove[s]'' statistic fact' goes against Shelley's definition of a poem as 'the very image of life expressed in its eternal truth'.[78] They should, according to Shelley, be deemed lesser than the true poet who exercises imagination:

We have more moral, political and historical wisdom, than we know how to reduce into practice; we have more scientific and oeconomical knowledge than can be accommodated to the just distribution of the produce which it multiplies. [...] We want the creative faculty to imagine that which we know; we want the generous impulse to act that which we imagine; we want the poetry of life: our calculations have outrun conception; we have eaten more than we can digest. The cultivation of those sciences which have enlarged the limits of the empire of man over the external world, has, for want of the poetical faculty, proportionally circumscribed those of the internal world; and man, having enslaved the elements, remains himself a slave.[79]

---

76 *Essays, Letters from Abroad*, 1: 43–44.
77 *Essays, Letters from Abroad*, 1: 45.
78 *Essays, Letters from Abroad*, 1: 485.
79 *Essays, Letters from Abroad*, 1: 502–03.

Shelley's reservations concerning the general importance placed on 'the external world' are echoed by Elizabeth Barrett.

Perhaps the most influential of Shelley's ideas in *Casa Guidi Windows* manifests itself in Elizabeth Barrett's reference to artists in the poem: Giotto, Michelangelo, Boccaccio, Dante, Petrarch, Rafael, Cimabue, Margheritone, Fiesole, Cellini, Brunelleschi and Pellico, to name a few examples. In an overtly political poem, to mention artists in this context is to make an explicit link between art and politics. For example, Michelangelo's 'Night and Day / And Dawn and Twilight' (1. 73–74) are mentioned as examples of how the artist had disapproved of the retrogressive politics in Florence and had hoped for the return of liberty:

> Michel's Night and Day
> And Dawn and Twilight wait in marble scorn,
> Like dogs upon a dunghill, couched on clay
> From whence the Medicean stamp's outworn,
> The final putting off of all such sway
> By all such hands, and freeing of the unborn
> In Florence and the great world outside Florence. (1. 73–79)

The message that is encoded in his work continues to inspire the present generation and as such ensure the continued value of such works of art. It is worth noting that, to the question 'what is Italy?', the answer given in the poem mainly consists of artists '[w]hose strong hearts beat through stone, or charged again / The paints with fire of souls electrical, / Or broke up heaven for music' (1. 182–84). Although the ordinary Italians, '[t]hese oil-eaters, with large, live, mobile mouths / Agape for maccaroni' (1. 200–01), do not manifest strong promise for political action, the Italian past, in the form of its surviving art, '[s]till argue[s] "evermore"' for the rejuvenation of Italy: 'her graves implore / Her future to be strong and not afraid; / Her very statues send their looks before' (1. 214–16). Elizabeth Barrett stresses the importance of the artists of the past for inspiring the present: 'Could I sing this song, / If my dead masters had not taken heed / To help the heavens and earth to make me strong' (1. 432–34).

It is not simply the long tradition of artists inspiring other artists that Elizabeth Barrett dwells on, but the fact that artists can be active agents of societal change. As societies evolve, 'we shall have thinkers in the place / Of fighters' (1. 727–28), implying that 'knowledge would replace 'force'. While the past was characterised by people conquering each other through brute force, people who know what is best for society will govern the present and the future. Elizabeth Barrett's argument thus comes close to Shelley's conception of the poet who will act on the basis of disinterested virtue, namely 'truth':

> The poet shall look grander in the face
> Than even of old [...]
>   seeing he shall treat
> The deeds of souls heroic toward the true—
> The oracles of life (1. 731–36)

This idea comes close to Shelley's conclusion in the *Defence*:

> Poets are the hierophants of an unapprehended inspiration; the mirrors of the gigantic shadows which futurity casts on the present; words which express what they understand not; the trumpets which sing to battle and feel not what they inspire; the influence which is moved not, but moves. Poets are the unacknowledged legislators of the world.[80]

If Elizabeth Barrett's idea of a leader was more Carlylean in the sense that she was calling for a political leader of some kind—'Pope, prince, or peasant!' (1. 1047)—she still held on to the notion that 'poets' in the most general sense of the word were ones who guided people towards 'truth'. Unlike Shelley, who sought to influence the public with his writings, Elizabeth Barrett's gesture falls short of such explicitness; nevertheless, her will to enact such political movement is discernible, especially if one is attentive to her reaction to, and development of, Shelley's ideas as I shall argue below.

Elizabeth Barrett's commitment to Whig politics, as she traces the history of Italy, accords with Shelley's depiction of 'Liberty' as something that had been passed down from one age to the next. Although Barrett is more interested in delineating a tradition of artists, she basically implies that Italy inherited 'liberty' from the Greeks and pre-empted (in the figure of Savonarola) the liberalisation of the Church later to be developed further by the German

80 *Essays, Letters from Abroad*, 1: 57.

Protestant reformers, thereby asserting a Protestant influence on the tradition of liberty.[81] They both subscribe to the same Whig discourse of history. It is also the case, however, that both of them were becoming increasingly sceptical of the progressive narrative of that history.

As Simon Avery argues, *Casa Guidi Windows* 'marks a new relationship of history with EBB [Elizabeth Barrett Browning]'. Previously subscribing to the Whig view of history, Elizabeth Barrett had placed her faith in progress and civilisation, which would bring about the gradual perfection of society; however, she came to see history in a problematic and complex way that would require an active agency to bring about such change. Avery writes:

> [W]hile there is still a sense of progressive history working throughout the poem—the images of renewal and change are particularly dominant towards its close—the majority of the poem emphasizes the need to escape from the weight of history if transformative political action is to be achieved. In this work, then, history's power is repositioned by the call for a new political Risorgimento.[82]

This notion finds a correlative in Shelley's 'Lines Written among the Euganean Hills' (1818), in which he writes of Venice:

> if Freedom should awake
> In her omnipotence, and shake
> From the Celtic Anarch's hold
> All the keys of dungeons cold,
> Where a hundred cities lie
> Chained like thee, ingloriously,
> Thou and all thy sister band
> Might adorn this sunny land,
> Twining memories of old time
> With new virtues more sublime;

81 See lines 424–25 in Part I for reference to Greece; lines 256–57, 270 for Savonarola as Martin Luther's predecessor.
82 Simon Avery, 'Mapping Political History: Elizabeth Barrett Browning and Nineteenth-Century Historiography', *Victorian Review* 33.2 (autumn 2007): 17–33 (30).

If not, perish thou and they,—
Clouds which stain truth's rising day
By her sun consumed away,
Earth can spare ye: while like flowers,
In the waste of years and hours,
From your dust new nations spring
With more kindly blossoming. (ll. 150–66)[83]

In this poem, the Italian city-states are dramatised as being at a crossroads: either liberating themselves from the Austrian rule ('the Celtic Anarch's hold') and thereby regaining their past glory, or dying in captivity so as to give birth to other 'new nations'. For the former, Shelley depicts here the possible force of 'Liberty' as an agent that would unfetter the 'chains' of history in which Italy had been held captive. While Shelley did not envision a clear agent (other than 'Liberty') to bring about the Risorgimento, Elizabeth Barrett was inclined towards the notion of a Carlylean leader:[84]

Whatever man (last peasant or first pope
Seeking to free his country!) shall appear,
Teach, lead, strike fire into the masses, fill
These empty bladders with fine air, insphere
These wills into a unity of will,
And make of Italy a nation—dear
And blessed be that man! (1. 835–41)

Her hopes in the pope (although qualified by her scepticism)[85] and the grand duke of Tuscany are played out in Part I of the poem. As both of these figures eventually proved to be disappointing, she came to resort to Shelley's political metaphor of a seasonal renewal in Part II of her poem.

The idea that with spring comes rejuvenation has a long history in Shelley's oeuvre. Shelley worked through his ideas mainly in 'Ode to the West Wind' (1820) and *Laon and Cythna* (1817)—later revised as

83 *Poems of Shelley*, Vol. 2.
84 For Carlyle's ideas on a strong leader, see *On Heroes, Hero-Worship and the Heroic in History* (London: James Fraser, 1841).
85 See line 1131 in Part I: 'But only the ninth Pius after eight', suggesting that he would be the same as his predecessors.

The Revolt of Islam (1818)—and it is in these two poems that we can find Shelley grappling with notions of history, as Elizabeth Barrett was to do in *Casa Guidi Windows*. To rehearse the historical and political background to the Shelley poems, *Laon and Cythna* was written in the wake of reactionary forces in England and in Europe after the failure of the French Revolution; 'Ode to the West Wind' was composed in the aftermath of the Peterloo Massacre that had taken place in Manchester the previous year. In other words, both of these poems were conceived at a time of liberal setback, as was the case with Part II of *Casa Guidi Windows*.

The famous, epigrammatic line 'If Winter comes, can Spring be far behind?' (l. 70) has a proleptic echo in the following lines from *Laon and Cythna*:

> 'The blasts of autumn drive the wingèd seeds
> Over the earth,—next come the snows, and rain,
> And frosts, and storms, which dreary winter leads
> Out of his Scythian cave, a savage train;
> Behold! Spring sweeps over the world again,
> Shedding soft dews from her etherial wings;
> Flowers on the mountains, fruits over the plain,
> And music on the waves and woods she flings,
> And love on all that lives, and calm on lifeless things.
>
> (9. 21)

***

> 'This is the winter of the world;—and here
> We die, even as the winds of Autumn fade,
> Expiring in the frore and foggy air.—
> Behold! Spring comes, though we must pass, who made
> The promise of its birth,—even as the shade
> Which from our death, as from a mountain, flings
> The future, a broad sunrise; thus arrayed
> As with the plumes of overshadowing wings,
> From its dark gulf of chains, Earth like an eagle springs.
>
> (9. 25)

***

'The good and mighty of departed ages
Are in their graves, the innocent and free,
Heroes, and Poets, and prevailing Sages,
Who leave the vesture of their majesty
To adorn and clothe this naked world;—and we
Are like to them—such perish, but they leave
All hope, or love, or truth, or liberty,
Whose forms their mighty spirits could conceive
To be a rule and law to ages that survive.

(9. 28)

In an attempt to overthrow the reactionary forces that put them in captivity, the heroine Cythna tells the hero Laon that their efforts will not be in vain. Elizabeth Barrett emulates these last lines in *Casa Guidi Windows*, where she sheds the weight of the past in order for her to act in the present. In essence, however, the significance of the legacy of the present as it is passed down to future generations remains the same as that depicted by Shelley in *Laon and Cythna*:

We will not henceforth be oblivious
Of our own lives, because ye [the Dead] lived before,
Nor of our acts, because ye acted well.
We thank you that ye first unlatched the door,
But will not make it inaccessible
By thankings on the threshold any more.
We hurry onward to extinguish hell
With our fresh souls, our younger hope, and God's
Maturity of purpose. Soon shall we
Die also! and, that then our periods
Of life may round themselves to memory,
As smoothly as on our graves the burial-sods,
We now must look to it to excel as ye,
And bear our age as far, unlimited
By the last mind-mark! so, to be invoked
By future generations, as their Dead. (1. 234–49)

In short, the weight of the past should not prevent the present generation from acting; if anything, they should act to advance 'the last mind-mark' so that the future generation can act upon that advancement also. Although the language is more subdued than

Shelley's, it nevertheless expresses the significance of action (even when in failure) over inaction. This mental progress (from 'the last mind-mark') outweighs in importance material progress, which Elizabeth Barrett was to criticise in the very same poem.

In her reference to the Great Exhibition of 1851, she first depicts the material wonders of the world that were displayed there, only to question their worth:

> O Magi of the east and of the west,
> Your incense, gold, and myrrh are excellent!—
> What gifts for Christ, then, bring ye with the rest?
> Your hands have worked well. Is your courage spent
> In handwork only? Have you nothing best,
> Which generous souls may perfect and present,
> And He shall thank the givers for? no light
> Of teaching, liberal nations, for the poor,
> Who sit in darkness when it is not night? (2. 628–36)

As the exhibits are compared to the gifts brought to Christ, Elizabeth Barrett questions the spiritual aspect that is wanting in the overall material emphasis of the Fair. In her pleading for the 'poor', which 'liberal nations' ought to enlighten, her critique of English expansionism grows to a climax: in the following lines the list of her pleading extends to groups of people such as children, women and American slaves who are exploited for the prosperity of a nation.

The mental progress made by the younger generations, which Elizabeth Barrett dramatises in the poem, is further brought home in her own poetry by her use of a Shelleyan metaphor used in the 'Ode to the West Wind'. Shelley comes up with a trope for the 'Wind'— what James Chandler calls 'the spirit of the age'[86]—to '[d]rive my dead thoughts over the universe / Like withered leaves to quicken a new birth!' (ll. 63–64). In other words, the seasonal rejuvenation that is dramatised in the 'Ode' is not simply that of vegetative renewal but a spiritual and political one as well. Furthermore, it is brought about not by a passive process, but by an interactive one between the 'Wind' and Shelley's poetry: the spirit of the age (the 'Wind') acts

---

86 James K. Chandler, *England in 1819: The Politics of Literary Culture and the Case of Romantic Historicism* (Chicago: Chicago University Press, 1998), pp. 553–54.

upon Shelley's writing, and his writing in return shapes the spirit of the age. We find the same metaphor of seasonal renewal exploited by Barrett towards the end of Part II of her poem:

> These Dead be seeds of life, and shall encumber
> The sad heart of the land, until it loose
> The clammy clods and let out the spring-growth
> In beatific green through every bruise. (2. 663–66)

This is the first reference to such seasonal regeneration that will bring a new life. The lives sacrificed for the liberal cause remain dormant as the dead leaves wait for the renewal of life. It is particularly poignant that, at this juncture, Barrett Browning cites Anita Garibaldi (the wife of the famous leader of the Risorgimento) as having lost her life in fighting while pregnant with a child. Barrett Browning's meandering account, which lists individuals who in one way or another contributed to the cause of liberty (including those who turned out to be false), ends with her hope in poets:

> Poets are soothsayers still, like those of old
> Who studied flights of doves,—and creatures young
> And tender, mighty meanings, may unfold. (2. 739–41)

In the lines that follow shortly after the above, Barrett Browning reverts to the seasonal cycle, in her address to her own son, 'Pen':

> Now shake the glittering nimbus of thy hair,
> And be God's witness that the elemental
> New springs of life are gushing everywhere
> To cleanse the water-courses, and prevent all
> Concrete obstructions which infest the air!
> That earth's alive, and gentle or ungentle
> Motions within her, signify but growth!—
> The ground swells greenest o'er the laboring moles.
> (2. 760–67)

While noting that she is nominally addressing her son, 'Pen', we can nonetheless see clearly that she is evoking the very same metaphor as the one deployed in Shelley's 'Ode'. My aim is to challenge some of the orthodox ways in which the last section of the poem has been read, that is, as Barrett Browning's political compromise that privileges the private (couched in traditional imagery of mother and child) over the public. In my opinion, to settle on such resolution does not do full justice to the text. In order to explicate what I mean by this, I shall first of all engage briefly with the idea of a radical aesthetic, introduced and convincingly argued by Isobel Armstrong in a book of that very same title.

Barrett Browning's deliberate deployment of the aesthetic, that is, of the affect associated with the unity of the mother and child at the end, is something that requires our cautious attention, especially given the overtly political nature of the poem. As Terry Eagleton identified Kant's aesthetic in this very icon (of mother and child), the association of the aesthetic and the feminine has been one of long-lasting practice.[87] What Armstrong proposes to do in *The Radical Aesthetic* is to salvage the aesthetic from bourgeois conservatism (with which it so often becomes conveniently coupled) by asking: 'Can the aesthetic be reclaimed for radical thought?'[88] In order to do this, she first examines Derrida's reading of Kant, followed by de Man's reading of Hegel, concluding that one needs 'to theorize an aesthetic free from an autotelic view of the subject and from the rage of the ego to possess the world through symbol by rejecting alterity'.[89] For this, she goes on to single out 'play' as a concept that holds the potential to elide neat resolution of binaries (i.e. the all too familiar subject/object or masculine reason/feminine affect) that lie at the heart of Western thinking (Kant and Hegel being no exception). Focusing on affect (by far the strongest association with the aesthetic with which we are concerned here) opens up a way in which one may think of affect as constituting knowledge and knowledge as constituting affect. Armstrong advocates regarding the aesthetic in its hybridity, citing Gillian Rose's work as a case in point. Rose's insistence on the 'middle' arises from her attempt at 'trying out or working through of opposite solutions while suspending closure by returning to the middle'.[90] In her refusal to eject what resists assimilation (as in Kant) on the one hand, or to collapse opposition for the sake of unity (in

---

87 Isobel Armstrong, *The Radical Aesthetic* (Oxford: Blackwell, 2000), p. 29.
88 Armstrong, *The Radical Aesthetic*, p. 28.
89 Armstrong, *The Radical Aesthetic*, p. 56.
90 Armstrong, *The Radical Aesthetic*, p. 64.

Hegel) on the other, the 'middle'—of the residue that does not quite get used up— provides that very potential of a different kind of discourse Armstrong is longing for. Furthermore, if it is the 'middle' that comes to hold significance as the locus of meaning, it is to be located not in the subject, but in the artwork itself: she substitutes the text for the subject as 'what thinks' in her examination of mediation. What all this leads to is a shift in how artwork is seen: from a special kind of creativity divorced from experience to lived experience in the form of mediation (not of the subject but of 'what thinks') that imparts thinking and knowledge. Armstrong finds the 'middle' in the mediation process particularly promising for the kind of potential it holds 'to know, to misknow, and yet to grow'.[91] Armstrong is quick to add that, although it is not exclusively women who occupy that space, it tends to be women precisely because of their place in culture.

With Armstrong's argument in mind, let us return to the ending of *Casa Guidi Windows*. There is a subtle manoeuvre discernable in the last stanza, where Barrett Browning addresses her son, as I intimated earlier. What appears to be indeed a cliché closure that deploys the affect, the feminine, turns out to be otherwise: it becomes apparent that she is in fact utilising the affect towards different ends from what we would normally expect it to do. Whereas the section on the seasonal cycle requires Shelley's 'Ode to the West Wind' to enact the kind of reading it invites, Barrett Browning spells out more clearly in the lines that follow:

> The blank interstices
> Men take for ruins, He will build into
> With pillared marbles rare, or knit across
> With generous arches, till the fane's complete. (2. 776–79)

Barrett Browning is here referring to the works of God that will fill in the void left by men; however, the gender switch to 'He' reminds us that God too is a man rather than a woman. In other words, Barrett Browning performs the traditional role assigned to women as a mother, whereas she leaves creativity of a political and spiritual/philosophical kind to men. If Barrett Browning is valorising the

---

91 Gillian Rose, *The Broken Middle: Out of Our Ancient Society* (Oxford: Blackwell, 1992), p. 246.

aesthetic through the emphasis of motherhood, it works towards different ends, so that it is not just affect associated with the mother/ child icon that becomes the focus of our attention, but rather the gendered fissure created by such an aesthetic gesture that compels us to feel and think what she cannot articulate openly in the way Shelley is able to do in his text: surely this is one kind of radical aesthetic Armstrong is inviting us to see and appreciate. Underlying her hope entrusted in Pen, it is possible to read her text as the bearer of political aspirations to be disseminated among her readers, rather than signifying her giving up taking political action or finding a Carlylean hero. In truth, this last gesture conceals Elizabeth Barrett's more ambitious aim for her poetry to do the same as what Shelley's 'Ode' had hoped to do: to inspire and disseminate liberal thinking among the people.[92]

---

92 Jean Hoffmann Lewis argues for the tension between the feminine poetic voice and the patriarchal tradition in which she is writing. See 'Casa Guidi Windows: Elizabeth Barrett Browning's Aesthetic Struggle', Victorians Institute Journal (1998): 159–76.

Coda

My original project began with Shelley, looking at his art, philosophy and politics as they became inscribed in his texts. For this very reason, I found much to appreciate in the works of Mary Shelley and Browning (Shelley's best readers and admirers) as part of a consideration of the full impact and ramifications of Shelley's influence. Taking such an approach is not intended to deny that their works hold interest and value in themselves. On the contrary, both Mary Shelley and Browning are fully acknowledged canonical writers who deserve critical attention as much as Shelley does. However, it is also true that taking my specific approach has led me to areas that I would never have been able to identify or explore otherwise. It has inspired me to go beyond the individual (author or text) to trace thematic threads that cross various boundaries. Consequently, it has enabled me to make discoveries within the texts that would otherwise have remained undisclosed.

Incorporating Elizabeth Barrett into the aforementioned group of writers has opened up new vistas in my thinking about 'coupling', 'coterie' and 'community', which bear relevance to a given text if we accept the notion that texts are products of a specific social network as much as they are of their socio-political milieu. Each chapter is a reminder of how writers create, not in a vacuum, but always in response to, in reaction against or even as a way of challenging existing texts. In a ceaseless dialogue that takes place on different levels—amongst contemporaries or with past writers—texts have a way of generating proliferating meanings that will never be exhausted. Therefore, my own treatment of the four writers only opens future possibilities for further enquiry.

I have been particularly interested in exploring the writers' political engagement and identification with the cause of liberty, whether articulated through direct or mediated expression. I have tried to demonstrate how the Brownings valorise their thoughts and ideas through their re-imagining of the Shelleys' texts. 'Historical consciousness' is a vital concept here. If Romantic historicism denotes an idea that situates itself in time with the full understanding of its difference from other spaces and temporalities, accompanied by an awareness of its own position in this ongoing process, then we can say that both the Shelleys were participants in this kind of historicist enactment. And so were the Brownings, who appropriated Romantic historicism as they reassessed and at times displaced it with their own Victorian historical consciousness. Therefore, it is not a simple question of the influence of aesthetics or ideas that one needs to examine when considering the texts of the Shelleys and the Brownings; rather, it is one of historical consciousness, which becomes transferred (at the point of re-imagining), and later partially displaced, as the later writers assert their own historicity. For example, Mary Shelley's creative reconstruction of medieval Italy imagined through her own specificity of time and place (i.e. post-Napoleonic Europe) becomes transposed onto Browning's text: the connection Mary Shelley made in her novel between the past and present serves to strengthen Browning's re-imagining of the past for the sake of the present. Yet Mary Shelley's historical situatedness is displaced as Browning instates his own. In a manner similar to that of circles expanding outwards as they overlap, each age and society becomes transposed onto another with traces of the previous circles remaining—medieval Italy onto Romantic Europe, onto Victorian England and so on.

It is to be hoped that my examination of the intertextual relationship between the Shelleys and the Brownings will be the beginning of further investigations into the works of these four writers. For example, the impact of Shelley's feminism on Elizabeth Barrett, or Mary Shelley's overall influence on Elizabeth Barrett, or the Brownings' dialogic understanding of the Shelleys are just a few potential topics one might pursue. It is high time we revisited the Shelley–Browning constellation with a mind to defamiliarising this extraordinary network of relationships.

Bibliography

Primary sources

Browning, Elizabeth Barrett. *The Barretts at Hope End: The Early Diary of Elizabeth Barrett Browning*. Edited by Elizabeth Berridge. London: John Murray, 1974.

—. *Casa Guidi Windows*. Edited by Julia Markus. Barre, MA: Imprint Society, 1977.

—. *The Works of Elizabeth Barrett Browning*. General editor, Sandra Donaldson. 5 volumes. London: Pickering & Chatto, 2010.

Browning, Robert. *Browning: Selected Poems*. Edited by John Woolford, Daniel Karlin and Joseph Phelan. Harlow: Pearson Education, 2010.

—. *Browning's Major Poetry*. Edited by Ian Jack. Oxford: Clarendon Press, 1973.

—. *Letters of Robert Browning Collected by Thomas J. Wise*. Edited by Thurman L. Hood. New Haven: Yale University Press, 1933.

—. *The Poems of Browning*. Edited by John Woolford, Daniel Karlin and J. P. Phelan. Harlow: Longman, 1991–.

—. *The Poetical Works of Robert Browning*. Volume 1. Edited by Ian Jack and Margaret Smith. Oxford: Clarendon Press, 1983.

—. *Prince Hohenstiel-Schwangau, Saviour of Society*. London: Smith, Elder, 1871.

—. *The Ring and the Book*. Edited by Richard D. Altick and Thomas J. Collins. Peterborough, ON: Broadview Press, 2001.

—. *Robert Browning and Julia Wedgwood: A Broken Friendship as Revealed in Their Letters*. Edited by R. Curle. London: John Murray and Jonathan Cape, 1937.

—. *Robert Browning: The Poems*. Edited by John Pettigrew and supplemented and completed by Thomas J. Collins. 2 volumes. New Haven: Yale UP, 1981.

Browning, Robert and Elizabeth Barrett Browning. *The Browning Collections: A Reconstruction with Other Memorabilia*. Compiled by Phillip Kelley and Betty A. Coley. Winfield, KS: Wedgestone Press, 1984.

—. *The Brownings' Correspondence*. Edited by Philip Kelley, Ronald Hudson and Scott Lewis. Winfield, KS: Wedgestone Press, 1984–.

Burke, Edmund. *A Philosophical Enquiry into the Sublime and Beautiful*. London: Routledge, 2008.

—. *The Writings and Speeches of Edmund Burke*. Edited by T. O. McLoughlin, James T. Boulton and William B. Todd. Oxford: Clarendon Press, 1997.

Carlyle, Thomas. *On Heroes, Hero-Worship and the Heroic in History*. London: James Fraser, 1841.

Dante Alighieri. *The Divine Comedy*. Translated by Henry Francis Cary. London: The Colonial Press, 1901.

Domett, Alfred. *Diary of Alfred Domett*. Edited by E. A. Horsman. London: Oxford University Press, 1953.

Godwin, William. *Things As They Are, or The Adventures of Caleb Williams*. Edited by Maurice Hindle. Harmondsworth: Penguin, 1988.

Machiavelli, Niccolò. *Life of Castruccio Castracani*. Translated by Andrew Brown. London: Hesperus Press, 2003.

Shelley, Mary. *Frankenstein, or The Modern Prometheus: 1818 Text*. Edited by Marilyn Butler. Oxford: Oxford University Press, 1993.

—. *Frankenstein, or The Modern Prometheus: The 1818 Text*. Edited by James Rieger. Chicago: University of Chicago Press, 1974.

—. *The Letters of Mary Wollstonecraft Shelley*. Edited by Betty T. Bennett. Baltimore: Johns Hopkins University Press, 1980.

—. *The Novels and Selected Works of Mary Shelley*. General editor, Nora Crook with Pamela Clemit. 8 volumes. London: William Picker, 1996.

—. *The Westminster Review* 11.12. 1829–30. 127–40. [Review of Simond and Best]

Shelley, Percy Bysshe. *The Complete Works of Percy Bysshe Shelley*. Edited by Roger Ingpen and Walter E. Peck. 10 volumes. New York: Gordian Press, 1965.

—. *Essays, Letters from Abroad, Translations and Fragments*. Edited by Mary Shelley. 2 volumes. London: Edward Moxon, 1840.

—. *The Letters of Percy Bysshe Shelley*. Edited by Frederick L. Jones. Oxford: Oxford University Press, 1964.

—. 'Lines Written in the Bay of Lerici'. Edited by Richard Garnett. *Macmillan's Magazine* 6. June 1862. 122–23.

—. *Peter Bell the Third and The Triumph of Life: Bodleian Shelley MS. Shelley adds. c. 5, folios 50–69, and Bodleian Shelley MS. Shelley adds. c. 4, folios 18–58*. Edited by Donald H. Reiman. New York: Garland, 1986.

—. *Poems and Prose*. Edited by Timothy Webb. London: J. M. Dent, 1995.

—. *The Poems of Shelley*. Edited by Geoffrey Matthews, Kelvin Everest, Jack Donovan, Michael Rossington, Cian Duffy and Ralph Pite. London: Longman, 1989–.

—. *The Poetical Works*. 3 volumes. London: 1867.

—. *Shelley's Poetry and Prose*. Selected and edited by Donald H. Reiman and Sharon B. Powers. 1st edn. New York: Norton, 1977.

—. *Shelley's Poetry and Prose*. Selected and edited by Donald H. Reiman and Neil Fraistat. 2nd edn. New York: Norton, 2002.

—. 'A Statue of Minerva'. *Athenaeum* 256. 22 September 1832. 617.

Wordsworth, William. *Lyrical Ballads*. Edited by Michael Mason. London: Longman, 1992.

Secondary sources

Alaya, Flavia. 'The Ring, the Rescue, & the Risorgimento: Reunifying the Brownings' Italy'. *Browning Institute Studies* 6. 1978. 1–41.

Armstrong, Isobel. *The Radical Aesthetic*. Oxford: Blackwell, 2000.

—. *Victorian Poetry: Poetry, Poetics and Politics*. London: Routledge, 1993.

—, ed. *Writers and Their Background: Robert Browning*. Athens: Ohio University Press, 1975.

Avery, Simon. 'Mapping Political History: Elizabeth Barrett Browning and Nineteenth-Century Historiography'. *Victorian Review* 33.2. Autumn 2007. 17–33.

Avery, Simon and Rebecca Stott. *Elizabeth Barrett Browning*. Harlow: Longman, 2003.

Barthes, Roland. *Image-Music-Text*. Translated by Stephen Heath. London: Fontana, 1977.

Beales, Derek and Eugenio F. Biagini. *The Risorgimento and the Unification of Italy*. London: Longman, 2002.

Belchem, John. *'Orator' Hunt: Henry Hunt and English Working-Class Radicalism*. Oxford: Clarendon Press, 1985.

Bloom, Harold. *The Anatomy of Influence: Literature as a Way of Life*. New Haven: Yale University Press, 2011.

—. *The Anxiety of Influence: A Theory of Poetry*. New York: Oxford University Press, 1973.

—. 'Browning: Good Moments and Ruined Quests'. In *Poetry and Repression*. New Haven: Yale University Press, 1976. 175–204.

—. *A Map of Misreading*. Oxford: Oxford University Press, 1975.

—. *Poetry and Repression*. New Haven: Yale University Press, 1976.

—. *Ringers in the Tower*. Chicago: University of Chicago Press, 1971.

—. *The Visionary Company: A Reading of English Romantic Poetry*. Ithaca: Cornell University Press, 1971.

Brand, C. P. *Italy and the English Romantics: The Italianate Fashion in Early Nineteenth-Century England*. Cambridge: Cambridge University Press, 1957.

Bullen, J. B. *The Pre-Raphaelite Body: Fear and Desire in Painting, Poetry, and Criticism.* Oxford: Clarendon Press, 1998.

Calabresi, Guido. *Ideals, Beliefs, Attitudes, and the Law: Private Law Perspective on a Public Law Problem.* Syracuse: Syracuse University Press, 1985.

Carlson, Julie A. *England's First Family of Writers: Mary Wollstonecraft, William Godwin, Mary Shelley.* Baltimore: Johns Hopkins University Press, 2007.

Chadwick, John W. *The Christian Register.* 19 January 1888. 37.

Chandler, James K. *England in 1819: The Politics of Literary Culture and the Case of Romantic Historicism.* Chicago: Chicago University Press, 1998.

—. *Wordsworth's Second Nature: A Study of the Poetry and Politics.* Chicago: University of Chicago Press, 1984.

Chapman, Alison. *Networking the Nation: British and American Women's Poetry and Italy 1840–1870.* Oxford: Oxford University Press, 2015.

Chapman, Alison and Jane Stabler, eds. *Unfolding the South: Nineteenth-Century British Women Writers and Artists in Italy.* Manchester: Manchester University Press, 2003.

Collins, Thomas J. *Robert Browning's Moral-Aesthetic Theory 1833–1855.* Lincoln: University of Nebraska Press, 1967.

—. 'Shelley and God in Browning's *Pauline*: Unresolved Problems'. *Victorian Poetry* 3. 1965. 151–60.

Corbeau-Parsons, Caroline. *Prometheus in the Nineteenth Century: From Myth to Symbol.* Oxford: Legenda Books, 2013.

Cox, Jeffrey. *Poetry and Politics in the Cockney School: Keats, Shelley, Hunt and Their Circle.* Cambridge: Cambridge University Press, 2004.

Cressman, Edmund D. 'Classical Poems of Robert Browning'. *The Classical Journal* 23.3. December 1927. 198–207.

Cronin, Richard. *Romantic Victorians: English Literature 1824–1840.* Basingstoke: Palgrave, 2002.

Cundiff, Paul. *Robert Browning: A Shelley Promethean.* St Petersburg, FL: Valkyrie Press, 1977.

—. 'Robert Browning: "Our Human Speech"'. *Victorian Newsletter* 15. Spring 1959. 1–9.

Dejordin, Ian. *Dulwich Picture Gallery, London.* London: Scala, 2009.

Delaura, David J. 'The Context of Browning's Painter Poems: Aesthetics, Polemics, Histories'. *PMLA* 95.3. May 1980. 367–88.

DeVane, William Clyde, Jr. *A Browning Handbook.* New York: Appleton-Century-Crofts, 1955.

—. *Browning's Parleyings: The Autobiography of a Mind.* New Haven: Yale University Press, 1927.

Donaldson, Sandra, ed. *Critical Essays on Elizabeth Barrett Browning.* New York: G. K. Hall, 1999.

'English Poetry and Poets of the Present Day'. *The Knickerbocker*. June 1845. 534–42.

Fermanis, Porscha. 'Anatomising the "Case": Shelley's *The Cenci*, Browning's *The Ring and the Book*, and the Origins of the Dramatic Monologue'. In *Legacies of Romanticism: Literature, Culture, Aesthetics*. Edited by Carmen Casaliggi and Paul March-Russell. New York: Routledge, 2012. 37–50.

Finn, Mary E. 'In the House (of Cards) that Rome Built: Shelley's *The Cenci* and Browning's *The Ring and the Book*'. In *Influence and Resistance in Nineteenth-Century English Poetry*. Edited by G. Kim Blank and Margot K. Louis. New York: St. Martin's Press, 1993. 188–202.

Fulford, Tim. *Romantic Poetry and Literary Coteries: The Dialect of the Tribe*. New York: Palgrave Macmillan, 2015.

Gest, John Marshall. *The Old Yellow Book: Source of Browning's The Ring and the Book*. Boston: Chipman Law, 1925.

Gilbert, Katherine Anne. 'The Politics of Character: The Lawyers and Pompilia in Robert Browning's *The Ring and the Book* (1868–69)'. *Victorian Poetry* 49.3. Autumn 2011. 317–45.

Griffin, William Hall and H. C. Minchin. *The Life of Robert Browning, with Notices from His Writings, His Family and His Friends*. London: Methuen, 1938.

Hackett, Susan and John Ferns. 'A Portrait of the Artist as a Young Monk: The Degree of Irony in Browning's "Fra Lippo Lippi"'. *Studies in Browning and His Circle* 4.2. Autumn 1976. 105–18.

Hamilton, Paul. *Historicism*. 2nd edn. London: Routledge, 2003.

Harris, Leigh Coral. 'From Mythos to Logos: Political Aesthetics and Liminal Poetics in Elizabeth Barrett Browning's *Casa Guidi Windows*'. *Victorian Literature and Culture* 28.1. 2000. 109–31.

Harrison, Anthony H. *Victorian Poets and Romantic Poems: Intertexuality and Ideology*. Charlottesville: University Press of Virginia, 1990.

Hawlin, Stefan. 'Browning, Shelley, and "On Worming Dogs"'. *Essays in Criticism* 40.2. April 1990. 136–55.

Honan, Park. *Browning's Characters: A Study in Poetic Technique*. New Haven: Yale University Press, 1961.

Hurst, Isobel. *Victorian Women Writers and the Classics: The Feminine Homer*. Oxford: Oxford University Press, 2006.

Johnson, Stephanie L. 'Aurora Leigh's Radical Youth: Derridean "Parergon" and the Narrative Frame in "A Vision of Poets"'. *Victorian Poetry* 44.4. Winter 2006. 425–44.

Jonsen, Albert R. and Stephen Toulmin. *The Abuse of Casuistry: A History of Moral Reasoning*. Berkeley: University of California Press, 1988.

Karlin, Daniel. *The Courtship of Robert Browning and Elizabeth Barrett*. Oxford: Clarendon Press, 1985.

—. *Robert Browning and Elizabeth Barrett: The Courtship Correspondence 1845–1846*. Oxford: Oxford University Press, 1989.

Kasmer, Lisa. *Novel Histories: British Women Writing History, 1760–1830*. Madison: Fairleigh Dickinson University Press, 2012.

Keenan, Richard C. 'Shelley's Influence on the Poetry of Robert Browning'. Unpublished PhD thesis. Temple University, 1974.

Kelly, Gary. *The English Jacobin Novel*. Oxford: Clarendon Press, 1976.

Kent, C. B. Roylance. *The English Radicals: An Historical Sketch*. New York: Burt Franklin, 1971.

Kristeva, Julia. *Desire in Language: A Semiotic Approach to Literature and Art*. Edited by Leon S. Roudiez and translated by Thomas Gora et al. New York: Columbia University Press, 1980.

—. 'Women's Time'. *Signs* 7.1. Autumn 1981. 13–35.

Kurobane, Shigeko. '"Scorpion Ringed with Fire" and "A Rose for the Breast of God": *The Cenci* and *The Ring and the Book*'. *Studies in Browning and His Circle* 24. June 2001. 68–77.

Langbaum, Robert. *The Poetry of Experience: The Dramatic Monologue in Modern Literary Tradition*. New York: Norton, 1957.

Laporte, Charles. '"Sacred Legendary Artists": Anna Jameson and Barrett Browning in the Hagiography of Pompilia'. *Victorian Poetry* 39.4. Winter 2001. 551–72.

Levine, George and U. C. Knoepflmacher, eds. *Endurance of Frankenstein: Essays on Mary Shelley's Novel*. Berkeley: University of California Press, 1979.

Lewis, Jean Hoffman. '*Casa Guidi Windows*: Elizabeth Barrett Browning's Aesthetic Struggle'. *Victorians Institute Journal*. 1998. 159–76.

Lewis, Linda M. *The Promethean Politics of Milton, Blake, and Shelley*. Columbia: University of Missouri Press, 1992.

The Literary Gazette. 1 December 1838. 759–60. [Review of EBB's poetry]

Lockhart, John Gibson. *Blackwood's Edinburgh Magazine* 13.74. March 1823. 283–93. [A review of *Valperga*]

London Literary Gazette & Journal of Belles Lettres, Arts, Sciences, Etc. 19 November 1831. 740–42. [A review of *Frankenstein*]

Martens, Britta. *Browning, Victorian Poetics and the Romantic Legacy: Challenging the Personal Voice*. Farnham: Ashgate, 2011.

Maynard, John. *Browning's Youth*. Cambridge, MA: Harvard University Press, 1977.

McCue, Maureen. *British Romanticism and the Reception of Italian Old Master Art, 1793–1840*. Farnham: Ashgate, 2014.

McCusker, Jane A. 'Browning's "Aristophanes' Apology" and Matthew Arnold'. *The Modern Language Review* 79.4. October 1984. 783–96.

McGann, Jerome J., ed. *Historical Studies and Literary Criticism*. Madison: University of Wisconsin Press, 1985.

Mellor, Anne K. *Mary Shelley: Her Life, Her Fiction, Her Monsters*. New York: Routledge, 1988.

Mercer, Anna. *The Collaborative Literary Relationship of Percy Bysshe Shelley and Mary Wollstonecraft Shelley*. London: Routledge, 2020.

Meredith, Michael. 'Flight from Arezzo: Fact and Fictions in *The Ring and the Book*'. *Studies in Browning and His Circle* 25. 2003. 101–16.

Mermin, Dorothy. *Elizabeth Barrett Browning: The Origins of a New Poetry*. Chicago: University of Chicago Press, 1989.

The Metropolitan Magazine 22.88. August 1838. 97–101. [Review of EBB's poetry]

Miller, Betty. *Robert Browning: A Portrait*. New York: Charles Scribner's Sons, 1952.

Miller, Nancy K. *Subject to Change: Reading Feminist Writing*. New York: Columbia University Press, 1988.

Murray, E. B. 'Shelley's Contribution to Mary's Frankenstein'. *Keats-Shelley Memorial Bulletin* 29. 1978. 50–68.

Myerson, George. 'Paracelsus: The Science of the Text'. *Browning Society Notes* 15.2 & 3. Winter/spring 1985–86. 20–47.

Newlyn, Lucy. *Coleridge, Wordsworth and the Language of Allusion*. Oxford: Oxford University Press, 1986.

Norman, Sylvia. *Flight of the Skylark: The Development of Shelley's Reputation*. London: Marx Reinhardt, 1954.

North, Julian. *The Domestication of Genius: Biography and the Romantic Poet*. Oxford: Oxford University Press, 2009.

Orr, Mrs. Sutherland. *Life and Letters of Robert Browning*. London: Mith, Elder & Co., 1891.

Phelan, Joe. 'Elizabeth Barrett Browning's *Casa Guidi Windows*, Arthur Hugh Clough's *Amours de Voyage*, and the Italian National Uprisings of 1847–9'. *Journal of Anglo-Italian Studies* 3. 1993. 137–52.

Pollock, Griselda. *Differing the Canon: Feminist Desire and the Writing of Art Histories*. New York and London: Routledge, 1999.

Poovey, Mary. *The Proper Lady and the Woman Writer: Ideology as Style in the Works of Mary Wollstonecraft, Mary Shelley, and Jane Austen*. Chicago: Chicago University Press, 1984.

Poston, Lawrence, III. 'Browning Rearranges Browning'. *Studies in Browning and His Circle* 2.1. Spring 1974. 39–54.

Pottle, Frederick. *Shelley and Browning: A Myth and Some Facts*. 1923. Hamden, CT: Anchor Books, 1965.

Prins, Yopie. *Ladies' Greek: Victorian Translations of Tragedy*. Princeton: Princeton University Press, 2017.

Radford, Andrew and Mark Sandy, eds. *Romantic Echoes in the Victorian Era*. Aldershot: Ashgate, 2008.

Raymond, William O. *The Infinite Moment and Other Essays in Robert Browning*. Toronto: University of Toronto Press, 1950.

—. *The Infinite Moment and Other Essays in Robert Browning*. 2nd edn. Toronto: University of Toronto Press, 1965.

Reiman, Donald H., Michael C. Jaye and Betty T. Bennett. *The Evidence of the Imagination: Studies of Interactions between Life and Art in English Romantic Literature*. New York: New York University Press, 1978.

Riede, David G. 'Elizabeth Barrett's Poetry of Exile: Difficulties of a Female Christian Romanticism'. *Victorians Institute Journal*. 2000. 91–112.

Rio, Alexis-François. *The Poetry of Christian Art*. Translated from the French. London: T. Bosworth, 1854.

Rose, Gillian. *The Broken Middle: Out of Our Ancient Society*. Oxford: Blackwell, 1992.

Russell, J. Stephen. *The English Dream Vision: Anatomy of a Form*. Columbus: Ohio State University Press, 1988.

Ryals, Clyde de L. 'Browning's "Fifine at the Fair": Some Further Sources and Influences'. *English Language Notes* 7.1. September 1969. 46–51.

Schlegel, August Wilhelm von. *Lectures on Dramatic Art and Literature*. Translated by John Black. London: Baldwin, Cradock and Joy, 1815.

Schor, Esther H. 'Poetics of Politics: Barrett Browning's *Casa Guidi Windows*'. *Tulsa Studies in Women's Literature* 17.2. Autumn 1998. 305–24.

Sismondi, J. C. L. Simonde de. *Histoire des républiques italiennes du moyen âge*. 16 volumes. Zurich: Henri Gessner, 1807–18.

Southwell, Samuel B. *Quest for Eros: Browning and 'Fifine'*. Lexington: University of Kentucky Press, 2014.

Stabler, Jane. *The Artistry of Exile: Romantic and Victorian Writers in Italy*. Oxford: Oxford University Press, 2013.

Stone, Marjorie. *Elizabeth Barrett Browning*. New York: St. Martin's Press, 1995.

Stone, Marjorie and Judith Thompson, eds. *Literary Couplings: Writing Couples, Collaborations, and the Construction of Authorship*. Madison: University of Wisconsin Press, 2006.

Struve, Laura. '"This Is No Way to Tell a Story": Robert Browning's Attack on the Law in *The Ring and the Book*'. *Law and Literature* 20.3. Autumn 2008. 423–43.

The Sunbeam. 13 October 1838. 295. [Review of EBB's poetry]

Suzuki, Rieko. 'Browning on Romanticism: "Fra Lippo Lippi" and Leigh Hunt'. *Keats-Shelley Review* 27.1. April 2013. 31–38.

—. *Negotiating History: From Romanticism to Victorianism*. Tokyo: Waseda University Press, 2012.

—. 'Shelley's "The Triumph of Life": A Resistance to History and the Art of Forgetting'. In *The Influence and Anxiety of the British Romantics*. Edited by Sharon Ruston. Lampeter: Edwin Mellon, 1999. 89–107.

Swinburne, Algernon. 'Notes on the Text of Shelley'. *The Fortnightly Review*. 1 May 1869. 539–61.

—. *Saturday Review* 27.3. April 1869. 460–61.

Thorpe, James. 'Elizabeth Barrett's Commentary on Shelley: Some Marginalia'. *Modern Language Note* 66. 1951. 455–58.

Tucker, Herbert F. *Browning's Beginnings: The Art of Disclosure*. Minneapolis: University of Minnesota Press, 1980.

Vargo, Lisa. 'Close Your Eyes and Think of Shelley: Versioning Mary Shelley's Triumph of Life'. In *Evaluating Shelley*. Edited by Timothy Clark and Jerold E. Hogle. Edinburgh: Edinburgh University Press, 1996. 215–24.

Vasari, Giorgio. *The Life of Giovanni Angelico da Fiesole*. Translated by Giovanni Aubrey Bezzi. Chiswick: C. Whittingham, 1850.

—. *Le Vite de' più eccellenti architetti, pittori et sculptori italiani da Cimabue insino a' tempi nostri, Rezeption*. Florence: Lorenzo Torrentino, 1550.

Waley, Daniel. *The Italian City-Republics*. New York: McGraw-Hill, 1969.

Wallace, Jennifer. *Shelley and Greece: Rethinking Romantic Hellenism*. London: Macmillan, 1997.

Walling, William. *Mary Shelley*. New York: Twayne, 1972.

Webb, Timothy, ed. *English Romantic Hellenism 1700–1824*. Manchester: Manchester University Press, 1982.

Whitla, William. 'Browning and the Ashburton Affair'. *The Browning Society Notes* 2. July 1972. 12–41.

Woolford, John. 'Browning Rethinks Romanticism'. *Essays in Criticism* 43.3. 1993. 211–27.

—. *Browning the Revisionary*. Basingstoke: Macmillan, 1988.

—. '"Life—That's Venice!" Browning's Romanticism in *Fifine at the Fair*'. In *Browning e venezia*. Florence: Leo S. Olschki, 1991. 233–49.

Woolford, John and Daniel Karlin. *Robert Browning*. London: Longman, 1996.

Index